SCOTTISH
BURGH & COUNTY
HERALDRY

Scottish Burgh and County Heraldry

by

R. M. URQUHART

Gale Research Company   The Book Tower   Detroit, Michigan 48226

[1973]

Printed in Great Britain

FOR
CHRIS AND CAROL

CONTENTS

PART III

THE ARMS OF THE BURGHS AND COUNTY COUNCILS
(arranged under Counties)

AUTHOR'S NOTE

A long-standing interest in the heraldry associated with the Burghs and Counties of Scotland has often made me feel that something more should be written about it. There has been nothing of a major nature since the turn of the century when the late Lord Bute's two books on Burgh Arms and Mr. Porteous' book on Town Council Seals were published and since then one hundred and forty-six Burghs and twenty-five County Councils have matriculated their arms.

The heraldic achievements of the several Burghs and County Councils are generally well known, at least by sight, to local residents and they have been introduced to a much wider public by their display in guide-books and at municipal and county boundaries. There must be many who would like to know more about them. The forthcoming Reform of Local Government in Scotland makes the present a very appropriate time to make a record of these things, especially as local knowledge about them varies in amount and quality and local memories are apt to be all too short.

I therefore set out, with the help of the Lyon Office case files, by correspondence with Town Clerks and County Clerks, by reference to local histories and local newspapers of the relevant periods, and by private enquiries, to examine and put together the story behind each coat of arms. This proved a greater task than I had anticipated, particularly as the Lyon Office records before 1850 are scanty and some of the correspondence with the Burghs in 1929–31 has not been preserved there. Before going very far, I discovered that the story of Scottish Burgh and County Heraldry is in itself a rather fascinating aspect of our national social history and is well worthy of the telling. This I have endeavoured to do in the first two parts of my book, the individual coats of arms being dealt with in the third, and largest, part. The whole work is intended to provide a record of some features of Scottish tradition which, in my view, should not be allowed to be forgotten; I hope that this record will interest not only Scots but also all those to whom civic custom and heraldry have appeal.

I would like to pay a very special tribute to Miss Mary Gordon, Herald Painter to the Court of the Lord Lyon, who did all the drawings for me with such admirable skill, care and patience and who gave me much assistance in other ways.

My most grateful thanks are due to Mr. Malcolm Innes of Edingight, Lyon Clerk and Marchmont Herald, who has so freely allowed me access to the relevant case files and other material in the Lyon Office and who has given me much help and advice; to the late Sir Thomas Innes of Learney, Lord Lyon King of Arms 1945–69, for his interest in my work and his personal kindnesses to me; to Colonel H. A. B. Lawson, Rothesay Herald, Lyon Clerk 1929–65, whose personal recollections of his period of office have been invaluable; and to all the members of the Lyon Office staff who have invariably been so kind and helpful on my visits there.

I am also much indebted to the many Town Clerks, County Clerks, and their staffs, who have been so very helpful in furnishing information, often by searching back in old records and often by allowing me to search for myself when I called at their offices, frequently without notice; to the Secretary of the Convention of Royal Burghs of Scotland and the Edinburgh City Archivist for allowing me access to the Convention Minutes; to the late Professor G. S. Pryde for his book *The Burghs of Scotland* which provided ready-made most of the information I required about the constitutional history of the Burghs, particularly the Royal Burghs; to Mr. William Borland, S.S.C., former Town Clerk of Edinburgh, for much of the information about the Princes Street banners mentioned on page 20; to Mr. W. A. Thorburn, Keeper of the Scottish United Services Museum, for advice on military insignia; to Mr. A. S. Burn of the Geography Department of the University of Southampton, and his staff, for the preparation of the map showing the Burghs and Counties; and to the many other people who have given me help and information.

I would thank the University of Glasgow for permission to use material from *The Burghs of Scotland* by G. S. Pryde (Oxford, 1965); the Convention of Royal Burghs of Scotland for permission to use material from their Minutes of 1903, 1905, 1929, 1930; the Editor of *The Scotsman*, the Editor of *The Glasgow Herald*, and the Executors of the late Sir Thomas Innes of Learney for permission to quote from the article mentioned on pages 15–16 and to print the letter which appears on pages 16–18; the Lyon Clerk for permission to quote from the letter to the Town Clerk of Kirkintilloch mentioned on page 20; and the Historical Association for permission to use the quotation which appears on pages 33–34 from *Central and Local Government in Scotland since 1707* by G. S. Pryde (London, 1960).

For all the help and kindness I have received from the staffs of the British Museum Newspaper Library, the National Library of Scotland, the Scottish Record Office, and the University Library at Southampton, I am indeed grateful. I should also like to thank Miss Wendy Spashett who typed (more than once) the manuscript so expertly and who helped me so efficiently in other ways. And, finally, my most grateful thanks are due to my wife for all her help, forbearance and encouragement, without which this book would probably never have been completed.

Southampton
1973

PART I

Burgh Heraldry
in
Scotland

1.   The Scottish Burgh System

The Convention of Royal Burghs of Scotland, which in 1972 included all the two hundred and one effective Burghs, divides its members into Royal Burghs (sixty-eight), Parliamentary Burghs (fourteen), and Police Burghs (one hundred and nineteen), but there is now little administrative difference between them.

The *Royal Burghs* are towns which were granted their burghal privileges direct from the Crown. Originally, a Royal Burgh was "the king's Burgh; it was on the king's land, its burgesses were the king's men, its rents were the king's rents, it was subject to the jurisdiction of the king's officers".[1a] For centuries, the Royal Burghs possessed considerable and exclusive trading privileges, formed "the burgess estate" in Parliament, and until 1879 the entire membership of the Convention of Royal Burghs. At least fifteen of these Burghs date from the reign of King David I (1124–1153) and only twelve have been created since 1600. Of the latter, only one was a *de novo* erection, as seven were pre-Reformation ecclesiastical Burghs (four of which had for some time been accepted by Parliament and Convention as *de facto* Royal Burghs) and four were former Burghs of Barony. No Royal Burghs have been created since the 1707 Treaty of Union, though one, Auchterarder, which had lost its privileges somewhere around 1600, was reinstated in 1951.

The *Parliamentary Burghs* were, with one exception, created as such under the Reform Acts of 1832 and 1867–68 in order to enlarge the Burgh franchise which had, before 1832, been confined to the Royal Burghs. They are mostly large towns in the central industrial belt, and, of those which still survive as separate municipalities, eleven were created under the 1832 Reform Act,† two under the 1867–68 Act, the fourteenth being made a Burgh by Private Act in 1885. Five of the Parliamentary Burghs were already Burghs of Regality and eight Burghs of Barony (including one lapsed Royal Burgh‡). Under the Parliamentary Burghs Act of 1833, these non-Royal Burghs were granted powers very similar to those possessed by their Royal counterparts. They were admitted to the Convention in 1879.

The *Police Burghs* derive their authority from the General Police Acts, the short title for a series of legislation (including one or two Local Acts) passed between 1833 and 1889, and from the Burgh Police (Scotland) Act, 1892. Of the former the more important are the Acts of 1833, 1847, 1850 (known as Lock's Act) and 1862 (known as Lindsay's Act) which, in stages, allowed the inhabitants of Royal (and Parliamentary) Burghs, of Burghs of Barony, and of "populous places" (finally defined in Lindsay's Act (1862) as those with over 700 inhabitants) to adopt a "police system"—

† Thirteen Parliamentary Burghs were created under the 1832 Act but two, Leith and Portobello, are now part of Edinburgh.

‡ Cromarty, which ceased to be a Royal Burgh in 1672.

hence the name "Police Burgh". The police system, which covered such things as the watching, cleaning, lighting and other general amenities of the Burgh, could be adopted in whole or in part and was to be administered by elected magistrates and councillors who had powers to levy rates for the general upkeep of Burgh services. As the century went on, it became possible for the smaller Burghs to leave the provision of a police force to the County authorities, but, on the other hand, additional duties were laid on the Town Councils in the fields of public health and housing, some of which were later transferred to the new County Councils in 1890. The definitive position of the Police Burghs was set out in the consolidating Burgh Police (Scotland) Act, 1892, and further changes of importance were included in the Town Councils (Scotland) Act, 1900. They were admitted to the Convention in 1895.

Many of the places which became Police Burghs were Burghs of Barony—one or two were Burghs of Regality—and several of them already had Town Councils of a kind. But it should be noted that "it was not the existing burgh which became the police burgh, it was the residents therein who initiated the new local authority (with much wider powers than the old), so that a system of dual administration could come into being—one town maintaining, at the inhabitants' choice, two separate burghs".[1b] In the majority of cases, the baronial Burgh was either immediately, or over the years, replaced by the Police Burgh, but in some towns it was not, and there are several instances where two systems of local government continued side by side in the same town right up to 1892.[†]

Since Burghs of Barony and Burghs of Regality will be mentioned frequently later in the book, it may be helpful if I include a brief note about them.

Under the feudal system which developed in Scotland, some of the great nobles held their lands as "regalities", and within these regalities they were able to exercise, without Royal interference, heritable jurisdictions and many of the powers of the Crown. Other landowners held their estates as "baronies", with lesser powers. Within his fief, a landholder could be granted a charter by the Sovereign for the erection of a burgh: hence the terms "Burgh of Regality" and "Burgh of Barony". The more prosperous of these non-Royal Burghs were frequently in conflict with the Royal Burghs, particularly over trading privileges.

The pre-Reformation ecclesiastical Burghs were Burghs either of Regality or of Barony erected in favour of a bishop, abbot or other Church dignitary; as mentioned above, some became Royal Burghs, while others were re-erected under lay Superiors.

Regalities, as such, disappeared when certain heritable jurisdictions were abolished in 1747; the latest Burgh of Regality dates from 1707.[‡] The last of the Burghs of Barony, Ardrossan, was created in 1846 but they survived as legal entities until the passing of the Burgh Police (Scotland) Act, 1892, although by then most of the active ones had become Police Burghs.

The use of the title "City" in Scotland also needs a word of explanation. *The Municipal Year Book, 1972,* gives the Scottish Cities as Edinburgh, Perth, Dundee,

† Notable examples are Thurso, Fraserburgh, Leslie and Kirkintilloch.
‡ This was Dudhope in Angus which has not survived. Dollar (1702) is the most recent Burgh of Regality which is an effective Burgh.

Aberdeen, Glasgow and Elgin, but the title "City" is also used officially by the ancient Capital, Dunfermline, and by Brechin and Kirkwall, both pre-Reformation episcopal sees; in the other old cathedral towns, which are Burghs, the title is commonly used unofficially in Dunblane and St. Andrews, but not to any significant extent in Dornoch, Fortrose and Whithorn.

Since the passing of the Local Government (Scotland) Act, 1929, the Burghs have been divided for constitutional purposes into (i) *the four Counties of Cities* (Edinburgh, Dundee, Aberdeen and Glasgow) which enjoy the same powers as the County Councils; (ii) *Large Burghs* (normally those with a population of 20,000 or more) which exercise similar powers except in education and, recently, police; and (iii) *Small Burghs* which have considerably lesser powers.† In 1972, there were twenty-one Large Burghs and one hundred and seventy-six Small Burghs; of the latter, eighteen, of which nine were Royal Burghs, had a population of less than 1,000.

2.   Burgh Heraldry before 1672

There is not a great deal of evidence of Burghs using coats of arms before 1672, although it is known that the science of heraldry was well established in Scotland by the fourteenth century. Yet neither the famous 1542 armorial manuscript of Sir David Lindsay of the Mount (Lord Lyon King of Arms, 1530–1555) nor any other well-known Scottish armorial of the same period has any mention of Burgh arms. There is, however, clear evidence that Aberdeen had some heraldic problems to sort out with the Lord Lyon in 1637[2] and it seems more than likely that the Lyon Registers, which were either destroyed by fire about 1670 or were otherwise lost during the Cromwellian Wars, contained some entries relating to the Burghs. In this connection, it is of interest to note that during a visitation of Glasgow by Heralds in 1668, action was taken against "delinquent citizens", but not against the Town Council, and this might have been because the City's arms had been recorded.[3]

In the absence of the Lyon Registers, we must turn to the evidence which can be found from the official Burgh seals, and here we are fortunate in being able to consult Bain's Calendar of Documents relating to Scotland (1887), the Catalogues of Henry Laing (1850 and 1866) and J. H. Stevenson and Marguerite Wood (1940) as well as Birch's British Museum Catalogue (1895).

The earliest extant collection of Burgh seals is attached to the Acts of Homage to Edward I (1296) and comprises those of Perth, Edinburgh*, Roxburgh*, Jedburgh,

† Under the Act, twenty Burghs were declared to be Large Burghs, including Arbroath, whose population was then just under 20,000, but excluding Buckhaven and Methil, whose population was just over that figure. Since then, East Kilbride has been added to the Large Burghs, but six, all with a population of over 20,000, have remained Small Burghs.

Haddington, Peebles*, Linlithgow, Montrose, Inverkeithing, Stirling and Aberdeen*;
in those cases marked * the seals have been lost but of the others, those of Haddington,
Linlithgow, Montrose, Inverkeithing and Stirling show devices which, though not in
every case heraldic, have come to be used as the basis of the Burgh arms.[4] Another
interesting collection comes from the Bond for the Ransom of King David II (1357)
which was attested by Dunbar,† Perth*, Aberdeen, Dundee, Inverkeithing, Crail,
Cupar, St. Andrews, Montrose, Stirling*, Linlithgow, Haddington, Dumbarton,
Rutherglen, Lanark, Dumfries and Peebles*; in those cases marked * the seals have
been lost, but the seals of Dunbar, Inverkeithing, Crail, St. Andrews, Montrose,
Linlithgow, Haddington, Dumbarton, Rutherglen and Lanark show devices, some
heraldic, some non-heraldic, which later developed into the coats of arms of these
Burghs.[5]

At this point it is convenient to refer to the use by many of the Royal Burghs in these
early days of double-sided seals, i.e. with one device on the obverse and a different
one on the reverse. One of the devices was normally, although not invariably, a
secular subject, while the other was a religious one, usually referring to the patron
saint of the town. For example, Crail's seal had a night fishing scene on the obverse
and the Virgin and Child on the reverse; Inverkeithing's had St. Peter on the
obverse and a ship with a mast-head cross on the reverse; Rutherglen's a ship with
sailors on the obverse and the Virgin and Child on the reverse; but Inverness had the
Saviour on the Cross on the obverse and the Virgin and Child on the reverse.[6]

From this practice, it became customary to regard it as possible for Burghs to
have two sets of armorial bearings, secular and sacred, the former being what we
would now call a coat of arms and the latter usually a representation of the patron
saint of the Burgh. In the annual civic processions, it was the practice to carry both
the municipal arms and banner and a different and sacred flag which was hung from
a cross bar. A very interesting relic of the custom is found in the two coats of arms
which were matriculated in the seventeenth century by Aberdeen, Kirkcaldy, Linlithgow and Montrose, and, of course, this old tradition explains, at least in part, the
many appearances of saints in Burgh arms, some of which, e.g. Banff and Dumfries,
indicate that the sacred bearings have outlasted the secular ones.[7]

Reverting to our search for heraldic seals, we find other early examples in the
cases of Aberdeen (1430)—A castle within the Royal tressure with lion supporters
and the motto "Bon Accord", and (1440)—Three towers within the Royal tressure;
of Perth (1378)—An eagle bearing the Agnus Dei within the Royal tressure. The
earliest representation of Edinburgh's arms on a shield is dated 1496 but the castle
device (somewhat different from that used later) appears on a document dated
c. 1350. Ayr's castle with its accompanying symbols of John the Baptist can be traced
back to the thirteenth century, Auchterarder's falcon to the fourteenth century,
Dundee's pot of lilies to 1416, Dingwall's sun and stars to 1438–39, Peebles' three
salmon to 1473, while Brechin's "Three piles conjoined in base" appears on a small
shield at the base of a seal of fifteenth-century date. In Rothesay's case there is a

† Stevenson and Wood preferred to regard this seal as probably that of Dunbar rather than that of Edinburgh
as Bain had done.

fifteenth-century impression showing a castle and a lymphad on the obverse and the Stewart fess chequy on the reverse. The Royal arms appear on an early seal of Dumfries and on fifteenth-century impressions of the seals of Cupar and Selkirk and on an even earlier one (possibly thirteenth-century) of Roxburgh where it hangs from a rose tree. From Berwick-upon-Tweed come examples of a shield bearing the arms of England strapped to a tree (1292) and of another showing a bear chained to a tree within the Royal tressure (1330). In all these cases the matrices of the seals are probably older, sometimes much older, than the impressions which have survived.[8]

There are, of course, many other examples of pre-seventeenth-century seal impressions and a number of them display a patron saint or some other religious symbol, or a device which is not heraldic. I have purposely confined myself in my comments to early examples of seals which are clearly heraldic. From this, it can reasonably be asserted that there was certainly a use of heraldry in the Royal Burghs before 1672. The fact that a section of Volume I of the 1672 Lyon Register was set aside for the arms of the Royal Burghs also indicates that there was a heraldic tradition in many of them, even if, as will appear subsequently, few of them were greatly concerned at the need to comply with the law and matriculate the arms they were using.

3.   The Act of 1672 and its Immediate Effect

From time to time, the Scottish Parliament has shown considerable interest in heraldic matters, both as regards seals and armorial bearings. We read of several old Scots laws requiring and regulating the use of seals by every free-holder—for example, an Act of King Robert III in 1400 said that "every baron or person holding of the King shall have a seal of his own for the King's service".[9] The jurisdiction of the Lord Lyon King of Arms over armorial bearings was well established by the middle of the sixteenth century and was confirmed by Act 1592, c. 125; fol. edit. c. 29 (Jac. VI): "Concerning the Office of Lyon King-of-Arms and his Brother Heralds" and the subsequent Act 1672, c. 21; fol. edit. c. 47 (Car. II): "Concerning the Privileges of the Office of Lyon King-at-Arms". In addition to repeating the provisions of the earlier Act, the Act of 1672 provided for the introduction of the Public Register of All Arms and Bearings (commonly referred to as the Lyon Register), and all those making use of "arms or signs armorial" were required to matriculate them in the new Register. Penalties were laid down for imposition in cases of use of unmatriculated, and therefore illegal, arms.

In 1673, in response to an approach by Lord Lyon Erskine, the Convention of Royal Burghs passed the following enactment:

The Convention considdering the contents of a missive direct to them be the lord lyon anent the matriculating of the arms of the royall burrows and of his lordshipps kynd expression to them therein whereof they are verrie sensible, and furder conceaveing that it is most convenient for avoyding of future truble, and that it tends much to the securities and preservation in all tyme coming of the particular coatts of arms of eatch severall burgh that the arms of the whole burrows of the kingdome be registrat and matriculat in the said lord lyons books, to the effect extract may be given furth thereof, therefor the Convention ordains the haill burrows of this kingdome to take furth extracts of thair respective coatts of arms out of the said lord lyons books, and that betuixt and the next generall convention as they will be ansuerable to the censure of the said convention.[10]

This certainly confirms the view, expressed above, that there was a heraldic tradition in the Burghs before 1672.

In 1676, the Convention considered the matter again and enacted as follows:

The Convention revives ane former act made at the generall conventione holden at Perth ordaining the haill royall burrows to matriculate their coatts of arms in the lord lyons books, and appoynts such of the burghs as have not as yet taken extracts of thair coatts of arms furth of his books to doe the same with all convenient diligence.[11]

Despite these expressions of good intentions, by 1694 only sixteen Burghs had matriculated, namely:

Perth, Kirkcaldy, Dumbarton, Tain, Queensferry, Stranraer	c. 1673†
Linlithgow, Dundee, Pittenweem, Ayr, Banff	1673
Aberdeen	1674
Renfrew	1676
Elgin	1678
Jedburgh	1680
Montrose	1694

Jedburgh's registration followed some pressure from the Lyon Office; the Burgh was instructed to discontinue the use of a coat of arms bearing a unicorn which it had been using since 1650; the Town Council Minutes state that "since the unicorn is part of the King's arms, the Town cannot warrantably assume or make use of same".[12]

It appears from Minutes of the Town Council of Edinburgh in March and May 1710 that the City agreed to matriculate, but no action seems to have been taken.[13] There is also an indication that the Town Council of Inverness may have decided to matriculate in 1680, but this decision does not appear to have been recorded in the Council Registers, and there is no trace of any resultant action.[14]

In 1728, Lord Lyon Brodie sent the Convention a Memorial "concerning the matriculating in his Books such as bear Arms or signs armorial" which mentioned

† No dates are shown in the Lyon Register in these cases.

that only fifteen Burghs (the sixteen above, less Elgin whose matriculation in 1678 was not recorded but was later proved in 1888—see page 12 below) and referred very gently to the possibility of legal action. The Convention remitted the matter to its Annual Committee but no action seems to have followed.

4. The Edinburgh Case and Afterwards

In 1732 the Town Council of Edinburgh reported to the Convention (Minute dated 13 December 1732) that an action was pending against them by the Lord Lyon for not matriculating the City's coat of arms.[15] Edinburgh asked the Convention to make it a test case as they had obtained legal advice "that the town would not be bound in law to matriculat". The Convention agreed and approved expenditure of £20 sterling in support of the action. But, apart from two entries in the Town Treasurer's Accounts (one for legal fees in December 1732 and one for copying fees in July 1733), there is no record of what happened next, and the case seems to have fallen through. In 1771 there appears to have been an attempt to revive it when the Lord Lyon and the Town Council exchanged conflicting legal opinions (see page 10 below) and in the following year Lyon Depute Boswell required the Town Council to matriculate the City's arms. Soon afterwards, however, the matter resolved itself in a surprising way; a Town Council Minute of 23 November 1774 mentions the delivery to the Council of a Certificate of Matriculation of "the Ensigns Armorial or Coat of Arms of the good town of Edinburgh", signed by Lord Lyon Brodie and bearing date 21 April 1732. This Certificate had been found among the papers of the late William Dewar, W.S., an Edinburgh lawyer who must have been acting for the Council. Why its existence had not been recorded in the Lyon Office and was not known to the Town Council cannot now be explained. Suffice it to say that Lyon Depute Boswell accepted the Certificate and agreed to record the matriculation without fee. With the Council's agreement this was done on 23 November 1774, the same date as the above-mentioned Minute.

The Edinburgh case is not, however, just an interesting story of early eighteenth-century muddle; it appears to have had a significant influence on the Convention's decision in 1732 to refuse a Memorial from Lord Lyon Brodie insisting that all the Burghs should matriculate their arms. This marks a radical change in attitude by the Convention. From then on the view began to prevail, supported from time to time by legal opinion, that the Royal Burghs had possessed the privilege of using seals and armorial bearings from a remote period which far outdated the Acts of 1592 and 1672, from which the Lord Lyon derived his jurisdiction, and that since neither of these Acts specifically mentioned the Burghs, they did not apply to them.

And so the argument about Burgh arms continued. In 1771 Lord Lyon Hooke Campbell obtained a legal opinion from the Dean of the Faculty of Advocates, the

Solicitor-General and Mr. James Boswell (the biographer of Dr. Samuel Johnson) which favoured his views and, on their advice, he issued an "Advertisement or Requisition" on 22 June 1771 calling on "all persons whether Nobility, Gentry, Towns or Bodies Corporate, bearing arms any manner or way which are recorded in terms of the Act . . . to give in or send to the Lyon Office an account of such Arms and of the title whereby they claim to wear the same". The Lord Lyon, as mentioned above, sent this opinion to the Town Council of Edinburgh, which immediately obtained a contrary one and decided that they did not need to matriculate their arms. The Edinburgh case, as we have seen, settled itself on the discovery of the 1732 Certificate of Matriculation, but the Convention did not alter its views and, when, in 1786, it decided to obtain a seal for its own use, it refused to recognise that the Lord Lyon had any rights in the matter. The seal (an armorial one) was not obtained until 1821 but no ensigns armorial were then matriculated by the Convention nor have been subsequently.

After 1774, the matter, as far as the Burghs were concerned, seems to have rested there for nearly a century. Out of sixty-four places left for the arms of the Royal Burghs in Volume I of the Lyon Register, forty-eight remained unfilled, and the only Burgh to record arms between 1732 and 1849 was Musselburgh (1771), as a Burgh of Regality. But this does not necessarily indicate the complete state of affairs, as allowance must not only be made for several Burghs whose seals were non-armorial, e.g. Whithorn, Nairn, Cullen, Lauder, Kintore, Inverbervie, but also for certain other factors concerned with the Lyon Court itself.

In the first place, it is only too clear that for the first one hundred and fifty years after 1672, the Lyon Office was not one of the most efficient of Government Departments. The Office of Lord Lyon was largely executed through Lyons Depute; there were actually two of these from 1677 to 1687, an arrangement which can only have invited trouble. Then several of the Lyons Depute were Edinburgh lawyers who carried out their duties from and jealously retained their heraldic records in their professional offices. We know from the 1800 Parliamentary Return submitted by the Lyon Office that "several volumes of the proceedings of the Lyon Court are lost or missing from the Office and it is believed are irrecoverable".[16] There is also evidence, e.g. Edinburgh and Elgin, and the cases of Scott of Harden and the Bank of Scotland, that entries in the Lyon Register were not always kept up to date.[17]

Against this background, a matter of special interest is the existence of a manuscript, mostly in the handwriting of James Cumming, Herald Painter, who was Lyon Clerk Depute from 1770 to 1773, and one of the first Secretaries of the Society of Antiquaries of Scotland. This manuscript was made available to Lord Bute by the Lyon Office, but it cannot now be traced in the library there. From Lord Bute's comments on it[18] and such other reasonable conclusions as can be drawn, it would seem that the document may have listed the coats of arms of forty-three or forty-four Burghs, including the sixteen which had been matriculated and entered in the Lyon Register. The Cumming MS. is not considered by present-day experts to have had any authority behind it, and some of the blazons it gives can be faulted; nevertheless, it describes pretty accurately the devices on Burgh seals (in unmatriculated cases) and the Burgh arms which had been matriculated and it was produced by an official of the Lyon Office. It is just possible that some of the entries in it were awaiting transfer to the Register. The document appears to have been the source of the list of Scottish Royal Burgh arms which is included in Joseph Edmundson's *A Complete Body of Heraldry* (1780) where the blazons of the arms of forty-three Royal Burghs are listed (along with the names of the other twenty-three) and described as "such as are matriculated in the Registers of the Lyon Office". A similar list is given in Thomas Robson's *The British Herald* (1830).

Burke's *General Armory* (1842) gives only the blazon of Aberdeen but in the revised edition of 1884, in which Lord Lyon Burnett is thanked for his help, we find the blazons of eighteen out of the nineteen Burghs whose matriculations had been entered in the Lyon Register and four others.† All this is more than a little confusing and makes one wonder if there had not been at some stage a degree of confusion in the Lyon Office itself.

5. A Nineteenth-century Revival of Interest

In the second half of the nineteenth century, there was a reawakening of interest in Burgh heraldry in Scotland. In 1866, Andrew Macgeorge published *An Inquiry as to the Armorial Insignia of the City of Glasgow* and in 1888, John Cruickshank *The Armorial Ensigns of the Royal Burgh of Aberdeen*. In his Catalogues of Seals (1850 and 1866), Henry Laing gave many instances of old Burgh seals, and in 1896, James Urquhart presented a paper to the Society of Antiquaries of Scotland entitled *Preliminary Notice of the Seals of the Royal Burghs of Scotland* mainly about a collection of drawings and impressions of these seals by C. S. Davidson; in this he gave much information about the law relating to armorial bearings in Scotland.[19]

More important still were two books of which John, 3rd Marquess of Bute (1847–1900), was the principal author. In *The Arms of the Royal and Parliamentary Burghs of Scotland* (1897), he collaborated with J. R. N. MacPhail and H. W. Lonsdale and in *The Arms of the Baronial and Police Burghs of Scotland* (1903) with J. H. Stevenson (then Unicorn Pursuivant and later Marchmont Herald) and H. W. Lonsdale. Lord Bute and his fellow authors were most careful to point out that, in the vast majority of cases, arms had not been matriculated and they went on to suggest a suitable coat of arms for each of these Burghs, generally based on the device on the Burgh seal. These books are scholarly and full of antiquarian and ecclesiological interest and, in not a few cases, accurately forecast arms which were later granted to individual Burghs. A copy of the relevant volume was presented to each Burgh and in course of time the two

† The exception is Montrose; the unmatriculated arms are those of Arbroath, Dunbar, Dysart (now part of Kirkcaldy) and Kilrenny.

books acquired, particularly in local government circles, an authority far beyond anything their authors would have wished to claim.

Finally, in 1906, Alexander Porteous published his book on *The Town Council Seals of Scotland*, a definitive work which, if not intended to be of heraldic significance, is invaluable in helping us to understand the coats of arms granted to various Burghs twenty or so years later.

There are also articles in publications of the time such as *Notes and Queries*, *Scottish Notes and Queries* and *Proceedings of the Society of Antiquaries of Scotland* which evince an interest in civic heraldry north of the Border. The Heraldic Exhibition in Edinburgh in 1891, in which many examples of Burgh seals were on show,[20] must also have helped. In 1899, the Convention of Royal Burghs invited Lord Lyon Balfour Paul to give the principal toast, "The Burghs of Scotland", at their Annual Dinner and in his speech "he spoke at some length on the armorial bearings of the Burghs".[21]

In another field, we find that in his celebrated Historical Mural Paintings added to the entrance hall of the Scottish National Portrait Gallery in 1900, the artist, William Hole, included the coats of arms of Edinburgh, Glasgow, Linlithgow, Jedburgh, Aberdeen, Stirling, Perth, Dundee, Inverness and Kirkwall, together with unmatriculated coats for St. Andrews & Dunfermline, and ensigned each with a mural coronet, just as Lord Bute had done in his book on the Royal and Parliamentary Burghs. It also had become fashionable to collect heraldic porcelain—small pieces of china bearing civic arms (mostly unmatriculated) and examples of these can readily be found in antique shops today.

Against this background, it is not surprising that between 1849 and 1903 fifteen Burghs recorded arms as shown below:

Royal Burghs
Stirling (1849), Glasgow (1866), Kirkwall (1886), Rutherglen (1889), Peebles (1894), Dingwall (1897), Arbroath (1900), Inverness (1900).

Parliamentary Burghs
Portobello (1886), Hamilton (1886), Leith (1889), Oban (1901).

Police Burghs
Lerwick (1882), Govan (1884), Alloa (1902).

(Note: Portobello and Leith are now merged with Edinburgh, and Govan with Glasgow.)

In addition in 1888 Elgin, as previously mentioned, was able to prove that it had matriculated in 1678 but that no entry had been made in the Register.

As far as can be traced, none of these Burghs was pressed by the Lyon Office; each seems to have taken the initiative itself for one reason or other. I have not been able to find out much about Stirling's case as it is not referred to in the Town Council Minutes of the time; Glasgow registered its arms following the publication of Macgeorge's book referred to above; Kirkwall wanted arms to mark its quatercentenary; Rutherglen matriculated mainly because of the interest shown by its Town Clerk, and Peebles because local feeling was aroused by letters to the local newspaper from A. C. Fox-Davies (author of *The Book of Public Arms*) questioning the Burgh's right to bear its ancient arms. Dingwall's arms were recorded because a local philanthropist wished to display them on a small building he was presenting to the town: those of Arbroath to commemorate the tercentenary of the Burgh Charter, and those of Inverness because of the interest of a local antiquarian.[22]

Turning to the Parliamentary Burghs, Portobello recorded its arms so that they could be displayed at the 1886 Edinburgh International Exhibition; Hamilton wished to purchase a Provost's Chain-of-Office and other civic insignia; Leith so that a banner bearing its arms could be flown in the British Section of the 1889 Paris Exhibition, and Oban because the Town Council wanted a new and armorial seal.[22]

As to the Police Burghs, Lerwick and Govan seem to have recorded arms so that they could use armorial seals and display their arms on public buildings, and Alloa's coat of arms was provided on the initiative of the Superior of the Burgh, the Earl of Mar and Kellie.[22]

It is, however, strange that there were not more cases of Burghs seeking grants of arms since the Burgh Police (Scotland) Act, 1892, required every Town Council to have a Common Seal and it is only too clear from Porteous' book that many of the seals which were adopted were definitely of an armorial character. In some of these cases, the seals showed (with his permission) the arms of the Burgh's Superior, and in others, heraldic devices relating to the Burgh's historical associations, devices which were designed either locally or by the seal engravers, of whom Mr. D. Cunningham of Glasgow was a notable example. From all this, some interesting "coats of arms" emerged, not all of them bad, if irregular, heraldry, and we shall hear more about them as we go through to 1929. But the Lyon Office does not seem to have been very much involved, as an examination of its letter books from 1886 to 1906 has disclosed that, apart from the eleven Burghs which recorded arms during that period, only four Burghs, Dumfries, Bathgate, Dunblane and Ellon, consulted the Lyon Office about their seals, and only three, Kirkcaldy (already armigerous), Dunoon (unofficially) and Motherwell, about coats of arms.

6.   The Lyon and the Convention, 1903

The year 1903 brought some interesting developments.[23] On 20 May, the Assessor for the Burgh of Partick (Partick is now merged with Glasgow) informed the Convention of Royal Burghs that Lord Lyon Balfour Paul had objected to the use of an unmatriculated coat of arms on the Provost's lamp, etc., as an infringement of the law and had indicated that Partick ought to matriculate arms. This led to the setting up of a sub-committee to consider "The Matriculation of the Arms of Burghs" with a membership of the Assessors for Partick, Dornoch, Linlithgow, Peebles and Inner-leithen. A majority Report by the first three, which recited all the arguments used in the early eighteenth century, recommended that the question of the matriculation of Burgh arms be allowed to rest; a minority Report, which is a scholarly document, was submitted by the other two members and recommended that the Royal Burghs with existing coats of arms should matriculate these arms, and that Burghs presently without coats of arms and wishing to have them, should apply for Grants of arms; it added that there was no need to obtain a Grant of arms for a device on a seal which was not of a heraldic nature.

The two Reports are both lengthy and full of interest; they include much of the historical information I have used above in Sections 3 and 4. They show that Lord Lyon Balfour Paul was given every opportunity to state his point of view. In a letter dated 22 February 1904, commenting on a Memorandum prepared by the Agent of the Convention, and which became the basis of the majority Report, he made it clear "that in the event of any formal resolution being come to by the Convention to the effect that Burghs are not affected by the provisions of the Act of 1672, and are there-fore at liberty to invent Arms for themselves, I shall take proceedings against any Burgh using unauthorised Arms for the recovery of the Statutory Penalties".

In 1905, the Convention resolved that both Reports, which had been printed and circulated, be received and that no further action be taken. The Assessor for Peebles (Mr. William Buchan) referred to the views taken by the Colleges of Heralds in London and Dublin, which were in support of the minority Report, but he acquiesced in the motion which was carried unanimously.[24]

So the Lord Lyon was left to take such action as he saw fit.

7.   Developments, 1906–1928

In 1906, the Parliamentary Burgh of Falkirk petitioned for arms, as the Town Council wished to have a more appropriate and more impressive civic device than the Highland warrior on the Burgh seal. The following year, after some correspondence, proceedings were instituted against Dunfermline for presenting an unmatriculated coat of arms for display at the Royal Caledonian Schools at Bushey in Hertfordshire; the Town Council, which had shown some resistance, decided in 1909 to settle for matriculation of its arms. In 1912, Paisley and St. Andrews were asked and agreed, apparently quite readily, to record their arms so that they could be displayed on the restored roof of Glasgow Cathedral; the matter had come to Lord Lyon Balfour Paul's notice through the Office of Works which was carrying out the repairs; Paisley had previously considered and shelved the matter of matriculation four years earlier.[25]

Between 1918 and 1926, there were only six matriculations. Armadale and Annan (both 1918) were due to local interest and initiative, while Prestwick (1921) came up over the local War Memorial. Kirkcudbright (1921) arose because the Town Council's wish, to place its arms on the Town gallery of the parish church, had come to the notice of Lord Lyon Balfour Paul. Greenock (1923) was the result of representations made by Lord Lyon Balfour Paul in 1918 over the Burgh's illegal use of arms. Rothesay (1925) followed a suggestion to the Provost by Mr. F. J. Grant, Rothesay Herald and Lyon Clerk (later Lord Lyon Grant), while on a private visit to the Burgh.[25] During the same period, the Lyon Office received enquiries about possible grants of arms from Dysart (now part of Kirkcaldy) and from Airdrie in 1921 and from Irvine in 1924.

In 1927, the question of the registration of County Council arms was raised because of the proposal to place many of them on the Scottish National War Memorial at Edinburgh Castle (see page 36 below), and, at the suggestion of Lord Lyon Swinton, Inveraray and Haddington recorded their arms in that year so that they could appear with those of other Burghs on the Memorial. Irvine, which as mentioned above had made enquiries in 1924, also decided to matriculate in the same year, apparently in intelligent anticipation of what the years 1929–30 were to bring.[25]

8.   The Lyon and the Burghs, 1929–1939

On 11 February 1929 there appeared in the *Aberdeen Press and Journal* a photograph of a replica of the emblem on the Provost's Chain-of-Office† which had been presented to Ex-Provost Donald Munro of Banchory to mark his long and distinguished service to the Burgh. The photograph of the emblem, entitled "The Banchory Badge", attracted the attention of Mr. Thomas Innes of Learney, in Aberdeenshire, then Carrick Pursuivant in the Court of the Lord Lyon, and later to become Lord Lyon Innes. In an article in the *Aberdeen Weekly Journal* of 28 February 1929, he pointed out that the emblem, while it included some unobjectionable features like a figure of St. Ternan, the patron saint of the Burgh, and some thistles, also included three family coats of arms, Burnett of Leys, Burnett impaled with Ramsay of Dalhousie, and Davidson of Balgay, none of which the Burgh had any legal right to use. He straightaway took up the matter with the Town Council which, on 11 March 1929, decided to change the Burgh seal by replacing the existing device, which consisted of the three coats of arms shown on the emblem, with a figure of St. Ternan, but temporised about the future use of the emblem. Almost simultaneously, Mr. Innes raised similar objections over the use of armorial seals by other Aberdeenshire Burghs, and within a short time the Town Councils of Ballater and Old Meldrum had decided to conform to the law by adopting non-armorial seals.[26]

On 2 April 1929, Mr. Innes contributed an article on "Scots Burgh Arms" to

† The Chain-of-Office was purchased in 1910 from a bequest left for that purpose by a well-known Banchory merchant, Mr. James Hunter. The emblem remains unaltered.

both *The Scotsman* and *The Glasgow Herald*. The article was singularly well timed, as the Convention of Burghs was meeting on the two days following, and it drew attention to the fact that seventy-six Scottish Burghs (actually a count reveals seventy-eight) were using armorial bearings illegally and to the great desirability that they matriculate arms as soon as practicable. Mr. Innes said that action had been taken against Burghs in the past over the use of unregistered arms and instanced the cases of Aberdeen (1637), Edinburgh (1732), Partick (1903) and Dunfermline (1909). He added that in 1916, H.M. Treasury approved "the Lyon Court exercising its powers of taking intensive steps to compel registration of corporation arms, and in the succeeding years practically all educational institutions in the country have been compelled either to register arms or to cease using heraldic insignia. The offending County Councils were dealt with in 1926–27 and the next step will be to clear up the Burgh arms."

The article leaves us in no doubt that, in the view of its author, every Local Authority ought to matriculate arms but it also makes it quite clear that it was not obligatory for a Burgh to have armorial bearings, and that in many cases the offences were quite minor ones, e.g. depicting a landscape or other non-heraldic design on a shield; "a few strokes by an engraver would bring such burgh devices into the lawful 'non-heraldic' class". It also observed that "if a public authority cannot afford the fee for recording a coat-of-arms, the only proper course is to display the patron saint or other conventional non-armorial device (viz. not upon a shield, wreath, coronet, etc.)", adding that this is what was done by several Burghs.

Two days later, Mr. Innes wrote to the Editors of *The Scotsman* and *The Glasgow Herald* (the letters appeared in the issues of 6 April 1929) and in them he referred to enquiries received since the publication of his article and to the procedure for conforming to the law. This letter is of such interest that I quote it in full:

SCOTS BURGH ARMS

THE HERALDIC LAW

HOW TO CONFORM WITH IT

To the Editor of "The Scotsman"

April 4, 1929

SIR,—Since the article on this subject appeared on Tuesday, I have had the pleasure of interviewing a number of Burgh Provosts, who are desirous that their municipal seals and insignia should be correct and in conformity with the dignity of public authorities.

Two points usually present themselves:—

(1) In rectifying any existing seal or insignia, a corporation is naturally anxious to know how far a new design would conflict with that which may have been in use, or involve extensive alterations upon badges and seals which may have been prepared or presented at considerable cost.

I have had pleasure in pointing out that where a corporation voluntarily approaches the Lyon Court with a view to putting its corporate insignia on a proper legal basis, it is almost always possible to arrange this without any appreciable alteration of the existing badges. An expert herald usually has little difficulty in converting the charges which may have been "appropriated" into such a design as the Lord Lyon can be asked to register (of course the Lord Lyon has an absolute discretion in what he will do, but a King-of-Arms is usually disposed to be as considerate as possible). Where a non-heraldic device is desired, it is similarly quite easy to suggest means by which the seal or badge can be rendered lawful in that way.

Of course Lyon cannot be expected to sanction the use of peers' coronets, baronets' badges, &c., but even these can be converted into permissible objects involving only minor alterations to existing designs.

(2) The other matter which I am asked is, how the Lyon Court is to be approached. Naturally, this may be done by letter to the Lord Lyon or the Lyon Clerk, addressed to the Court of the Lord Lyon, H.M. Register House, Edinburgh, and any of the Scots Heralds or Pursuivants will advise if asked; but it will be of interest to Burgh Councillors, and indeed to the public in general, to know that an application for a coat-of-arms is, in Scotland, virtually the same as an application to any other Court of the realm, such as the Sheriff Court or Court of Session, and originates in a petition, which will be in the following form:—

(a) Where arms are claimed in consequence of use prior to 1672, and where only matriculation (Treasury fees, £20) is required:—

Unto the Lord Lyon King of Arms.

The Petition of the Provost, Magistrates, and Councillors of the Burgh of X. . . .

Humbly Sheweth.

That the Burgh of X. . . . has borne certain ensigns armorial from a period anterior to the year 1672, but that the same have never been matriculated in the Public Register of All Arms and Bearings in Scotland in accordance with the statute 1672, cap. 47 (Car. II)

That the petitioners are desirous that the foresaid ensigns armorial should now be matriculated in terms of the said statute.

May it therefore please your Lordship to grant warrant to the Lyon Clerk to matriculate the foresaid ensigns armorial in the Public Register of All Arms and Bearings in Scotland, in names of the Petitioners and of the Burgh of X. . . .

And your Petitioners will ever pray.

Signatures of Provost and Town-Clerk.

(b) Where no arms have been used prior to 1672, or where the burgh is of recent origin, a grant of arms (Treasury fee, £47) is necessary, and for this the petition will run:—

Humbly Sheweth,

That the Petitioners are desirous of bearing and using such ensigns armorial as may be found suitable and according to the Laws of Arms.

May it therefore please your Lordship to grant warrant to the Lyon Clerk to prepare Letters Patent granting licence and authority unto the Petitioners and unto the said Burgh of X. . . . to bear and use such ensigns armorial as shall be found suitable and according to the Laws of Arms.

In the first case the burgh obtains an illuminated "extract" from the Lyon Register, and in the second case, illuminated Letters Patent (of which a duplicate is entered on the Register), each of which are issued under the Seal of the Lyon Office fully emblazoned upon parchment, and suitable for framing in the burgh chambers.—I am, &c.

THOMAS INNES OF LEARNEY,
Carrick Pursuivant.

The seventy-eight Burghs listed in the article were as follows:

21 Royal and Parliamentary: Airdrie, Brechin, Campbeltown, Cromarty*, Cupar, Dornoch, Dumfries, Forfar*, Hawick, Inverkeithing, Inverurie, Kilmarnock, Kilrenny & Anstruther, Kinghorn, Lanark, New Galloway*, North Berwick*, Peterhead, Port Glasgow, Sanquhar, Selkirk.

57 Police: Aberlour*, Auchterarder, Barrhead*, Biggar, Blairgowrie, Bonnyrigg, Bo'ness, Castle Douglas, Clydebank, Cockenzie & Port Seton, Cove & Kilcreggan, Dalbeattie, Dalkeith, Darvel*, Dufftown, Dunoon, Duns, Elie, Ellon, Fort William, Fraserburgh, Galston*, Girvan, Gourock*, Grangemouth, Grantown-on-Spey, Helensburgh, Innerleithen, Johnstone*, Kelso*, Kilsyth, Kingussie*, Kirriemuir, Ladybank, Langholm, Leslie, Leven*, Lockerbie, Lochgelly*, Macduff, Maxwelltown, Maybole, Melrose, Millport*, Moffat, Monifieth*, Motherwell & Wishaw, Newburgh*, Newmilns & Greenholm*, Newport-Fife*, Rattray, Rosehearty, Rothes, Saltcoats*, Stonehaven, Tillicoultry, Tobermory*.

And to these were later added as further defaulters:

4 Royal and Parliamentary: Auchtermuchty*, Crail*, Forres, Galashiels.

3 Police: Largs, Portsoy, Stornoway*

making in all twenty-five Royal and Parliamentary Burghs and sixty Police Burghs, this last figure being reduced by mergers to fifty-eight.† Kinross and two minor offenders, Burghead and Stewarton, seem to have escaped notice at this time.

The matter was pursued vigorously by the Lyon Office and by the end of 1931,

† Blairgowrie united with Rattray in 1929 and Maxwelltown with Dumfries in 1931.

all the above-mentioned Royal and Parliamentary Burghs had matriculated except the six marked *, and of these, Cromarty had agreed to adopt a plain seal and New Galloway had expressed a wish to record arms but had asked for time to raise the money for the matriculation fees. Of the fifty-eight Police Burghs, twenty-eight had recorded arms, eleven (Auchterarder, Blairgowrie & Rattray, Bonnyrigg & Lasswade (united 1929), Cockenzie & Port Seton, Cove & Kilcreggan, Dufftown, Duns, Ellon, Kilsyth, Ladybank and Tillicoultry) had adopted either non-armorial or plain seals, and the eighteen marked * were still in default, though both Aberlour and Kingussie had expressed their intention to comply with the law. The new Burgh of Elie & Earlsferry, which was accepted as a Royal Burgh, matriculated its arms in 1930. In the cases of Dornoch, Blairgowrie, Cockenzie & Port Seton, Innerleithen, Melrose and Rattray, offending seal matrices were handed in to the Lyon Office where they have been retained.

In 1929, the Royal Burgh of Inverbervie, which had not been using an armorial seal, recorded arms so that they could appear on the University War Memorial in King's College Chapel, Aberdeen.[27] Coatbridge registered in 1930 so that its arms could appear with those of the other Lanarkshire Burghs on an armorial window in new County Headquarters in Glasgow. Saltcoats matriculated in 1932 and Kinross, which had brought its own case to attention, in 1934. Ellon, which had previously altered its seal, followed in 1935; Huntly, which had used a non-armorial seal; and Kelso in 1936: these three all arose in connection with Chains-of-Office for their Provosts.[28]

This onslaught on the Burghs by the Lyon Office, mainly through Carrick Pursuivant, did not pass unchallenged and there were hard things said about the Lord Lyon, and the Carrick Pursuivant, in more than one Town Council. Several Burghs were initially most indignant when their coats of arms were brought into question and were against registering even exact replicas; in some Burghs, especially smaller ones, the offending seals were very seldom used and there is even an indication that the action taken by the Lyon Office from 1916 onwards against various non-municipal corporate bodies may have caused one or two Burghs to stop using their seals altogether. In October 1929, Selkirk, with the support of several other Burghs which were also holding off, raised the matter at the Annual Committee of the Convention of Royal Burghs "with a view to opposing the demand that their coats of arms be now registered or to ascertain the views of the Convention on the subject". The Convention was reminded of the 1905 Resolution about the Matriculation of the Arms of Burghs, i.e. "that the Convention take no further action in the matter". The Annual Committee left Selkirk to decide for itself whether to raise the matter at the 1930 Convention "as in view of the Resolution referred to above it was not open to the Committee to take any action meantime".[29] Selkirk decided not to pursue the matter and matriculated its arms in June 1930, the Provost remarking at the February Town Council meeting, when the matter was approved, that "it was not worth making a fuss about".[30]

During this period, Lord Lyon Grant and his Court showed remarkable for-bearance, tact and skill in accepting devices long used by Burghs and incorporating them in coats of arms. By some alteration of colours, e.g. Kilmarnock, Peterhead, Fraserburgh, Kirriemuir and Stonehaven, Burghs were allowed to retain coats almost identical to those of their original Superiors or in cases, such as Dalbeattie, Rothes and Lockerbie, of families closely connected with them. The acceptance of local designs like Clydebank, which included a sewing machine and a battleship, and Langholm, which included a heather-wreathed spade and a plate of bannocks and herring, must have pushed toleration to the limit. Burghs using crests were permitted to retain them and supporters were allowed to be kept in one or two cases where the Burgh concerned had no claim to special distinction. Whenever possible, the Lord Lyon exercised his privilege to recognise "ancient user", i.e. that a Burgh had used arms before 1672, thus saving the Burghs concerned an appreciable sum in fees. Several interesting proofs were submitted in support of applications for "ancient user"—Bo'ness, Ellon, Kirriemuir and Stonehaven are notable examples—but, as a general rule, all Royal Burghs and Burghs which had been Burghs of Regality and Barony founded before 1672 were accorded it without too much argument. The general principle was set out in a letter from the Lyon Clerk to the Town Clerk of Kirkintilloch in 1938—"The use of Arms may be inferred from the right and the doctrine *omnia rite et solemniter acta esse* and thus the lower scale of fees as 'ancient user' applies."[31]

Lord Lyon Grant and his Officers must be given great credit for facilitating so many additions to the Lyon Register, without ever allowing heraldic standards to be lowered unduly, as has happened in civic arms in other countries. In fact the remarkable thing is that so many fine civic coats of arms have emerged from the years 1929–32.

I have already mentioned the registrations between 1932 and 1936. Towards the end of 1937, there came a new and quite unexpected development, as a result of which several further registrations occurred. In that year, the Lord Provost of Edinburgh, Sir Louis Gumley, conceived the idea of using banners bearing the arms of the Scottish Burghs to decorate Princes Street in the Capital on special occasions and he invited all the Burghs to present banners to Edinburgh at a cost of about £10 each. He received a very good response and out of the ninety-eight Burghs which were armigerous in 1938, eighty-two agreed to present banners; two (Crail and Penicuik) which were in the process of matriculating arms also agreed to do so, and eleven others— Lauder, Burntisland, New Galloway, Falkland, Bathgate, Culross, Kirkintilloch, Whitburn and Milngavie (all 1938) and Lochmaben and Nairn (both 1939)— registered arms so that they could join in the scheme, in which the Lord Lyon would allow only armigerous Burghs to participate. The banners were flown only once—at the opening of the General Assembly of the Church of Scotland in May 1938—but many were damaged by a severe gale which occurred at the time; those which survived were put into store and later were destroyed as unserviceable.[32]

Two further registrations occurred in 1939, Cromarty for a Provost's Chain-of-Office, and Banchory on local initiative.[33]

So, by the end of 1939, all the Burghs on the Innes 1929 list (as enlarged) except three Royal Burghs (Forfar, North Berwick and Auchtermuchty) and sixteen Police

Burghs (Aberlour, Barrhead, Darvel, Galston, Gourock, Johnstone, Kingussie, Leven, Lochgelly, Millport, Monifieth, Newburgh, Newmilns & Greenholm, Newport-Fife, Stornoway, Tobermory) had conformed to the law.† In addition, sixteen other Burghs had, for one reason or another, registered their arms.

9. Consolidation and Achievement, 1940–1972

Since 1939, sixty-five more Burghs have recorded arms in the Lyon Register. For this, much credit must go to Lord Lyon Innes, a distinctive and distinguished national figure who, by the vigilance he and his Officers exercised over the illegal use of armorial bearings, and by the great interest he aroused in Scotland in things heraldic, was able to persuade, cajole and lead where lesser men might have failed. The six new Burghs, Pitlochry, East Kilbride, Bearsden, Stevenston, Bishopbriggs and Cumbernauld, all sought grants of arms in their early days. Other Burghs were interested enough to do likewise, sometimes stimulated by a special civic event or anniversary or by a local antiquary or historian, sometimes by a wish to have a coat of arms to display at the Burgh boundaries. Then several Burghs wished to acquire a Chain-of-Office for their Provosts and this almost invariably led to a Grant of arms, as liaison between the jewellers who made the Chains and the Lyon Office was uncommonly good; the only exception seems to have been Aberchirder, whose Provost's Chain, presented in 1964, bears an emblem similar to the device on the Burgh's non-armorial seal.[34] As far as I have been able to trace, there were only five cases, Keith, Tobermory, Barrhead, Auchterarder and Crieff, where the Lyon Office really took the first steps, but in some other cases example must have played an influential part. The case of Forfar, which had been going on for some twenty years, was revived locally and was satisfactorily resolved in 1948, and in 1966 the other outstanding Royal Burgh on the 1929 list, Auchtermuchty, matriculated its arms. In 1958 the English Borough of Berwick-upon-Tweed successfully established its right to the use of arms as a former Scottish Royal Burgh under the "ancient user" rule and had its arms recorded in the Lyon Register.

All this was progress indeed and it must have been a great satisfaction to Lord Lyon Innes, when he retired in 1969, to know that out of the eighty-three defaulting Burghs which he had listed some forty years previously, seventy-eight had recorded arms, two had adopted non-armorial seals, and only three, Aberlour, Kingussie and Millport, were still not conforming to the law. The only other Burgh then in default was Markinch, a more recent case, which was, however, in a rather special category: the Town Council had expressed a desire to record arms in 1954 and actually paid the

† Newburgh is now accepted as a Royal Burgh by the Convention; Newport-Fife changed its name to Newport-on-Tay in 1956.

C

fees, but for various reasons the case was not settled until 1972, in which year Kilsyth also matriculated its arms.

The historical progression of matriculations is set out in the Appendix. In summary, the position of the two hundred and one Burghs in Scotland in 1972 is as follows:

| | Matriculated | Unmatriculated | |
		Using arms	Not using arms
Royal Burghs	67	–	1
Parliamentary Burghs	14	–	–
Police Burghs	96	3	20
	177	3	21

10.   Some Comments on the Heraldry

The Coats of Arms

In considering the details of the heraldry, it is convenient to discuss the shields first, taking the Royal Burghs separately from the other Burghs and then going on to deal with mottoes, crests, supporters, leaving coronets and the Royal Burgh compartment until the end.

For the Royal Burghs we have seventy-two shields in all—the sixty-seven armigerous Burghs plus four with two shields, plus Berwick-upon-Tweed. These can be classified as shown below:

	Number	Remarks
UNDIVIDED SHIELDS (59)		
Without Ordinaries or Sub-Ordinaries	47	In base the sea appears eight times, a loch once, a rock four times and a mount six times.
With Ordinaries (8)		
Chief	1	Wavy.
Chief and Saltire	1	There is a fess wavy on the Chief.
Chief and Cross	1	Embattled: the cross is quadrate couped.
Chevron and Cross	1	Chevron round-embattled on upper edge and cross patée.
Cross	3	One reversed, one reversed and couped.
Piles (3)	1	—

With Sub-Ordinaries (4)

	Number	Remarks
Inescutcheon	3	—
Inescutcheons (2)	1	—
	59	

Note: In two cases the field is semée and in one, chevronny.

DIVIDED SHIELDS (13)

	Number	Remarks
Quarterly	3	—
Per Fess	2	One wavy.
Per Pale	7	One wavy, one has a mount in base.
Tierced in Pairle reversed	1	—
	13	

Note: The blazons of these can, of course, be further broken down.

The Royal arms appear in four cases (Pittenweem, Linlithgow, Renfrew and Selkirk) and the Royal tressure twice (Aberdeen and Perth). The tinctures used are confined to the metals (or and argent) and the four commoner colours (gules, azure, vert and sable) except for one instance where purpure is used (Queensferry) and one where tenny is used (Rothesay); no furs appear at all. One coat (Inveraray) is blazoned "all Proper".

The commonest single charge on the shield is the representation of a patron saint, of which, if we include the Virgin Mary, there are twenty-one examples. There are several castles and towers, many ships and boats of all kinds, generally on a base of sea. Lions and dogs are the commonest animals, salmon, roses and oak respectively the commonest fish, flower and tree. While many of the charges have clear historical associations, family references are surprisingly few and among the older coats are virtually confined to Stewart and Bruce. The saltire appears as a feature only three times, but there are a good number of cases where it appears on ships' flags or pennons. From a heraldic standpoint, Brechin's three piles conjoined in base, Crail's night-fishing scene with its sable field, and Kintore's oak tree set on a gold background semée of torteaux are particularly interesting.

Turning now to the fourteen Parliamentary and ninety-six Police Burghs whose arms are matriculated and taking into account Leith, Portobello and Govan, we find we have one hundred and thirteen shields in all. These can be analysed as set out below:

	Number	Remarks
UNDIVIDED SHIELDS (67)		
Without Ordinaries	26	In base the sea appears four times, a river or stream twice, a loch once, and a mount once.

With Ordinaries (37)

Chief	15	One indented; one with pale and inescutcheon on chief; one divided (half gyronny).
Chief, Pale and Bend	1	Pale wavy.
Chief, Cross, Chevron and Pile	1	Pile nebuly.
Chief and Piles (2)	1	—
Fess	6	One wavy; one dancetty with pale in chief; one raguly.
Chevron	3	One with lozenge; one engrailed.
Bend	3	One bretessed; one wavy.
Bends (2)	1	—
Saltire	2	—
Cross	3	Two cross quadrate; one with bendlets and with cinquefoil overall.
Pile	1	—

With Sub-Ordinaries (4)

Gyronny of 8	1	With cross moline overall.
Inescutcheon	2	—
Shakefork and Lozenge	1	—

67

Note: In four cases there are special fields: one of five barrulets, one barry of six, one barry dancetty of six, and one semée; in three other cases with chiefs, the main part of the shields have respectively fields of chequy, bendy wavy, and barry wavy.

DIVIDED SHIELDS (46)

Per Chevron	4	One with bordure.
Quarterly	10	One wavy; one with roundel overall; one with rose overall; one with cross fillet overall.
Per Fess	15	One wavy; one wavy with pile (issuing from base); one enarched with bend; one with chief; three with fess; one with fess and a pale overall; one with chevron.
Per Pale	11	One embattled, one wavy with pallet overall, one with cross, one with sea in base, one with shakefork overall, one with bordure and canton.
Per Saltire	2	—
Tierced in Pairle reversed	4	—

46

Note: The blazons of these can, of course, be further broken down.

The Royal arms appear only once (Kelso) and the Royal tressure not at all. The tinctures used are, as in the arms of the Royal Burghs, virtually confined to the metals and the best-known colours, there being only four examples of the use of purpure; furs are used seven times, ermine five times and pean twice. Heraldic features of particular interest are the armorial "points" on the dexter side of Gourock's arms, Bearsden's black rose and Cumbernauld's lozenge chequy of twenty-five panes. Also worthy of special mention are the representations of a tolbooth by an embattled chevronel in Newmilns & Greenholm, of the Cathedral by round embattled chevronels in Dunblane, of the hawthorn trees of the Esk Valley by a pale and a fess raguly respectively in Bonnyrigg & Lasswade and in Loanhead, of a coal pithead by a black chevron bearing a wheel in Cowdenbeath, of an early railway engine by a wheel bearing a pile nebuly in Troon.

The charges on the shields are so many and various that one can only make a few comments upon some of them. There are some references to patron saints—St. Ternan appears in Banchory, St. Ronan in Innerleithen, and St. Kentigern in Penicuik, without a halo as he does in Glasgow's crest. There are many ships and other craft on the sea, one or two castles, references to local landmarks like Callander's Ben Ledi and other mountains, Dufftown's Tower, Kinross' Market Cross with its "jougs", Melrose's Abbey, and, in Falkirk and Kirkintilloch, Antonine's Wall. Naturally there are references to historical events and ceremonies closely connected with a Burgh; the arms of Largs recall the famous battle fought there in 1263 between the Scots and the Norwegians, those of Hawick a notable victory over the English in the dark days after the Battle of Flodden (1513), those of Dalkeith, the safe custody of the Scottish Crown Jewels in its Castle in 1637–38, those of Burghead, the annual tradition of "Burning the Clavie", those of Langholm the annual Common Riding ceremony. Industry is well represented: we find agriculture and shipbuilding, distilling and coal-mining, fishing and iron-smelting, weaving, bonnet-making and explosives, and some others. But the vast majority of the shields of the Parliamentary and Police Burghs bear charges which refer directly to the founder or Superior of the Burgh and sometimes to other notable local families. These allusions cover much of the history of Scotland and are far too numerous to mention.

Mottoes, Crests and Supporters

All the Royal Burghs (and Berwick-upon-Tweed) have *mottoes* except ten; five of them have two mottoes, shown one above and one below the shield—Dundee, Stirling, Kilrenny & Anstruther, Burntisland and Wick—while Linlithgow has a motto for each of its two coats. This makes sixty-four mottoes in all, of which fifty-five are in Latin, six in English, two in Scots and one in French. In two cases, Tain and Linlithgow (2nd coat), the mottoes are not mentioned in the Lyon Register, but both are of such long-standing use that I have accepted them as authentic, which they undoubtedly are.

One hundred and two of the one hundred and thirteen Parliamentary and Police Burghs (including Leith, Portobello and Govan) have mottoes, four—Falkirk, Kilmarnock, Helensburgh and Innerleithen—have two each, again shown one above and one below the shield. Of these one hundred and six mottoes, forty-four are in Latin, twenty-nine in English, twenty-three in Scots, six in Gaelic, two in French, and one each in Welsh and Old Norse, the last two being respectively Penicuik and Hawick.

Lord Lyon Innes frowned upon colourless mottoes, preferring those of a rugged national type like "A Licht Abune" (Alyth), "Bear the Gree" (Bearsden), "Stent nae Stent" (Cowdenbeath), "Duns Dings A'" (Duns), "Prosper But Dreid" (East Kilbride) and "Wick Works Weil" (Wick) which originally proved the subject of much controversy. The very clever punning motto of Tayport "Te Oportet Alte Ferri" referring both to the Tay port and the Tay ferry is well worthy of note, as is Ellon's "Judge Nocht Quhill Ye End" in which the mottoes of Erskine and Kennedy are ingeniously combined.

The use of *crests* in Burgh arms in Scotland is not very extensive. Nowadays it is accepted as completely inappropriate for a Burgh or County or other Corporation to have a crest. So none of the grants is more recent than 1938 (Milngavie and Whitburn),† while seventeen date from the 1929–31 "amnesty" period, during which Lord Lyon Grant adopted a generous attitude to Burghs which wished to have crests.

The ten Royal Burghs which have crests are: Edinburgh (an anchor); Dundee (a lily); Glasgow (St. Kentigern (without a halo)); Montrose (a hand issuing from a cloud and holding a rose garland); Cupar (a demi-lion of Fife); Inverness (a cornucopia); Rutherglen (the Virgin and Child); Sanquhar (a thistle); Dornoch (a wild cat with the Sutherland shield) and Campbeltown (a herring).

Six Parliamentary Burghs have crests, viz. Airdrie (a cock), Coatbridge (a monk with a stone), Hamilton (a cinquefoil pierced), Kilmarnock (a man's hand), Peterhead (a roebuck's head) and Portobello (a tower), and fourteen Police Burghs, viz. Alloa (a griffin's head), Clydebank (a garb), Dalbeattie (a stag in front of a holly bush), Fraserburgh (an ostrich with a key in its beak), Govan (a garb and a salmon on its back), Grangemouth (a steamship on the sea), Helensburgh (a stag's head), Lerwick (a raven), Leslie (a griffin), Macduff (a knight on horseback), Maybole (a dolphin), Milngavie (a mill-wheel between two garbs), Stonehaven (a roebuck's head set in a marquess' coronet) and Whitburn (a stagecoach and four).

As with crests, the use of *supporters* is not very great. Only fifteen Royal Burghs—Edinburgh, Perth (which has an eagle as bearer), Dundee, Aberdeen, Stirling*, Glasgow, Montrose, Inverness, Arbroath, Elgin, Rutherglen, Cullen*, Kintore*, Auchterarder* and Auchtermuchty* (and also Berwick-upon-Tweed*)—have them, and of these the six marked * are very recent grants. Of the Parliamentary Burghs, only three have supporters, Falkirk (which has a crowned lion as bearer), Kilmarnock (which has the unique Boyd squirrels sejant) and Peterhead, and in the Police Burghs we find ten cases, Barrhead, Dalkeith, Duns, Fraserburgh, Govan, Helensburgh, Huntly, Innerleithen, Motherwell & Wishaw, and Stonehaven. I understand that nowadays any Royal Burgh which requested supporters would be granted them, but that otherwise some special reason would have to be proved such as being a Parliamentary Burgh, a County town, or a place of importance like a Large

† Barrhead, which had been using a crest for many years, was offered one in 1948, but decided against it.

Burgh or a comital seat. On this basis, the claims of Barrhead, Helensburgh and Innerleithen are slighter than the others and would probably now be hard to justify. Apart from those already mentioned above, cases of more than ordinary interest are Edinburgh's maid richly attired and St. Giles' doe, Montrose's mermaids, Inverness' elephant and camel, Kintore's bulls, Dalkeith's halberdiers, Duns' lion and ermine goat in their "rugby" stripes, Govan's engineer and ship carpenter and Motherwell & Wishaw's puddler and miner. Elgin, Rutherglen and Fraserburgh have angels, and Peterhead and Stonehaven the stags or roebucks of Keith, the Earl Marischal.

It is of interest that only six Royal Burghs (Edinburgh, Dundee, Glasgow, Montrose, Inverness and Rutherglen), two Parliamentary Burghs (Kilmarnock and Peterhead) and four Police Burghs (Fraserburgh, Govan, Helensburgh and Stonehaven) have full achievements of shield, motto, crest and supporters.

The Burghal Coronet

The Burghal coronet is the same as a mural coronet and was introduced as part of a Burghal coat of arms by Lord Lyon Balfour Paul, the first grant being made to Paisley in 1912. There is clear evidence that it was offered to that Burgh as early as 1907, when the question of matriculation was first under discussion; in 1908, the Town Clerk of Peebles was informed that a mural crown could be part of a Burgh's achievement. It has since become a regular feature of Scottish Burghal arms; just as the coronet of a peer is placed above his shield, so are the arms of a Burgh ensigned with a Burghal coronet. Its use in 1900 in the decoration of the Scottish National Portrait Gallery has been mentioned on page 12 above; it may also be noted that coronets had appeared before 1912 on Provosts' Chains-of-Office, e.g. Rothesay, St. Andrews and Banchory, and on the Burgh seals of Cromarty and Lanark.

The coronets are intended to recall the wall around the Burgh—Fox-Davies records that "abroad e.g. in the arms of Paris, it is very usual to place a mural crown over the shield of a town"; in Germany, a coronet called a "mauerkrone" has been used.[35] In his book on the arms of the Royal and Parliamentary Burghs, Lord Bute put mural coronets above all the shields. I have heard that he thought they should be gold in colour and his intention seems to have been to confine their use to the Royal and Parliamentary Burghs since in his second book on the Baronial and Police Burghs, none of the shields is shown with a coronet.

The introduction of the Burghal coronet was severely criticised by Fox-Davies because "it smashes a very cherished privilege of army grants. Had Lyon, following the continental practice, introduced the walled and turreted crown one meets with in Germany, the matter might have been different but he has matriculated the army crown pure and simple."[36]

The Scottish Burghal coronets are variously described in grants of arms, e.g. a coronet appropriate to a [Royal] Burgh, a Burghal coronet, a Burghal crown, a mural coronet, a mural crown; in one case (Dalbeattie) a mural crown masoned sable, and in another (Innerleithen) a coronet suitable to a Burgh, masoned sable. In the earlier drawings, they are shown with walls of three courses of stone and five towers each of three courses of stone, but successive heraldic painters have varied practice and now usually the towers are drawn with two courses. This is the pattern which has been used throughout the drawings which illustrate this book.

Strictly speaking, Burghs whose arms were registered before 1912 are not entitled to use Burghal coronets unless they have been specially authorised to do so by the Lord Lyon. In fact, the absence of a coronet indicates that the Burgh arms are of long standing, which can be regarded as something of a distinction. Renfrew, Dundee, Montrose and Jedburgh have, however, had coronets added in Extracts of Matriculation dated 1932, 1932, 1953 and 1956 respectively; Linlithgow, Tain and Stranraer have had them added by the Lyon Office Herald Painter in specially commissioned drawings; Peebles and Queensferry use them to a limited extent.

In 1957, Lord Lyon Innes introduced distinctive coronets for Burghs of Barony (Gules masoned Argent) and for Police Burghs (Azure masoned Argent). The first Burgh to be granted a Burgh of Barony coronet was Stornoway in 1958 and the first to be granted a Police Burgh coronet was Cove & Kilcreggan in 1957. The coronet for a Royal Burgh was made "Proper masoned Sable"; this was previously the pattern used for all Burghs. The first to be so granted was to Stirling in 1962; that granted to Berwick-upon-Tweed in 1958 was described as "a coronet proper to a Royal Burgh". It is of special interest that the coronet given to Jedburgh in its Extract of Matriculation in 1956 was specially coloured (as "Proper") to resemble the reddish-brown stone of the district.

Since the introduction of the specially coloured coronets, two Burghs of Barony, which had matriculated before 1957, have asked for their coronets to be changed to the new pattern—Cockenzie & Port Seton (1958) and Alyth (1962). None of the other Burghs has so far asked for its coronet to be altered.

I have been shown in the Lyon Office a scheme for extending the system of special coronets, including special designs for Edinburgh (the Capital City), Perth (the second City), Burghs of Regality and "Honest Touns", but this has not yet been implemented.

The Royal Burgh Compartment

Something quite unique heraldically is the Royal Burgh compartment. This can be described as a turreted and embattled compartment; the motto is usually set in the battlement below the shield. The whole effect is very pleasing and distinctive and it is a pity that more Royal Burghs do not have one added to their achievements, since only a small fee is involved.

The Royal Burgh compartment was first used in the case of Elgin (1678), a matriculation which through mischance was not entered in the Lyon Register until the omission was discovered and proved in 1888. So no one knows what the compartment originally looked like; the version used for Elgin is a Victorian conception. And since the Register was apparently not as well maintained as it might have been in the seventeenth century, there may have been grants of Royal Burgh compartments to other towns.

The use of the Royal Burgh compartment was revived by Lord Lyon Innes in the case of Forfar (1948), and since then seven Royal Burghs have sought and have been granted the Royal Burgh compartment: Montrose (1953), Fortrose (1954), Wick (1954), Cullen (1956), Berwick-upon-Tweed (1958), Kintore (1959) and Stirling (1962). It is, however, possible that the compartment granted to Rutherglen in 1889—the year after Elgin's matriculation was rediscovered—was intended to be a Royal Burgh compartment, since it is of a wall-like type as compared with the metal-bracket type granted to Glasgow twenty-three years previously.

PART II

County Heraldry
in
Scotland

1.   The Scottish Counties

There are thirty-three Counties in Scotland, most of them originating in the old Sheriffdoms, of which there are some which date from the reign of King David I (1124–1153) and twenty-five which are mentioned in an ordinance of 1305.[1] The number and grouping of the Sheriffdoms were changed from time to time, but by the nineteenth century the thirty-three Counties we now know were well established, though Ross and Cromarty were still formally separate and Orkney and Shetland were frequently regarded as one.

By the end of the nineteenth century, the administration of the Counties (outside the Burghs) presented a confused picture. Much of it was carried out by Commissioners of Supply (originally appointed in 1667 to collect national revenue) who levied rates, managed the County expenditure and controlled the County Police. Matters such as roads, lunacy and prisons were dealt with by specially-created Authorities, poor law, water supply and public health by Parochial Boards (from 1894 Parish Councils), education by School Boards (Education Authorities were not set up until 1918), and various sundry matters by Justices of the Peace.

The setting up of the thirty-three County Councils by the Local Government (Scotland) Act, 1889, was a first step towards a more co-ordinated system of County administration. The new Councils had transferred to them the powers of the Commissioners of Supply (except Police), of the Justices of the Peace, and jurisdiction over roads, water supplies and many public health matters. Ross and Cromarty were united; Shetland divorced from Orkney and renamed Zetland; and various boundary anomalies between Counties sorted out, leaving Dunbarton as the only County with a "detached" part. A Standing Joint Committee, on which the County Council members and the Commissioners of Supply were equally represented, was created to be the Police Authority and to supervise the County's capital expenditure.

Forty years later, the Local Government (Scotland) Act, 1929, made sweeping changes in local administration. County Councils, Town Councils (divided into Counties of Cities, Large Burghs and Small Burghs as mentioned on page 5 above) and District Councils were henceforward to be the only Local Authorities; all others were abolished. The Counties of Perth and Kinross, and the Counties of Moray and Nairn, were united for all major purposes, although the individual County Councils were allowed to retain their identity for "Small Burgh" functions. Professor Pryde admirably sums up the new position thus:

On the councils of thirty-one counties and four counties of cities were conferred all branches of administration, including education. Police went to counties and cities, and to large burghs if they were over 50,000 in population or had a police force in being at the time. Other major public services, and more especially public health and public assistance, were entrusted to the large burghs, while the small burghs became responsible for housing and such local services as lighting, cleansing and drainage. The district councils acquired some of the functions of the extinguished parish councils, but were limited in finance to a rate of one shilling in the pound.[2]

Subsequent legislation, especially that passed since the 1939–1945 World War, has altered many of these administrative arrangements, in particular those relating to welfare, medical and police services. But these are really points of detail with which we need not concern ourselves here.

The Association of County Councils in Scotland was formed by nineteen of the County Councils in 1894. Since then all the thirty-three Councils have become members.

2.   County Heraldry before 1927

Apart from the four Counties of Cities (Edinburgh, Dundee, Aberdeen and Glasgow) which have been dealt with under the Burghs, the heraldry associated with the Counties, whether *per se*, or through the Commissioners of Supply, or through the County Councils, is of comparatively recent origin. It seems probable that such County heraldry as existed by the early nineteenth century had originated in connection with the local Militia and Volunteer Forces.

The Caledonian Mercury of 21 April 1798 contains the following note about County coats of arms:

We understand that when the Militia of Scotland are embodied, the colours of the different Counties are to be ornamented, like those of the English militia and fencibles, with their respective coats of arms. Several applications for these have been made to the Lyon Office, from which they are to be granted, on an order from the Lords Lieutenants, with the sanction of the approaching meetings of the Counties on the 30th instant.

But in the event, only two of the Counties appear to have applied for grants of arms.

In 1798, Robert, 10th Earl of Kinnoull and Lord Lyon King of Arms, granted arms to the County of Roxburgh and two years later, in 1800, he presented a coat of arms, which he had personally designed,[3] to his own County, the County of Perth. Both these coats have been inherited by the County Councils and are still in use.

There are, however, some instances of the use of "unofficial" arms which in due course of time became features of officially matriculated County (Council) achievements. Selkirkshire used a device, said to have been connected with Sir Walter Scott, which showed a stag at rest beneath a tree;[4] there is an example on a Selkirkshire Volunteers medal dated 1807. "The Thane of Fife" (a crest of Earl Fife) appears on a colour of the Fife Fencible Cavalry (disbanded in 1797) and the same emblem was used by the Fife Yeomanry in the nineteenth century.[5] From 1826 onwards, the Lanarkshire Yeomanry used a device showing a double-headed eagle with a hand-bell on its dexter claw;[6] this emblem, which obviously was taken from the seal of the Royal Burgh of Lanark, was also used by the Clerk of Supply on his official notepaper. This is in no way meant to be an exhaustive list and there may well be examples from one or two other Counties.† In passing, I would also mention that there must be a long association between the County of Berwick and the emblem of a bear chained to a tree (the ancient arms of Berwick-upon-Tweed) and that there is some reason to suppose that in Kinross-shire, by the later part of the nineteenth century, a representation of Loch Leven Castle was regarded as a County symbol.

In 1886, the Commissioners of Supply for the County of Lanark were granted arms and so were the Commissioners for the County of Renfrew three years later. These coats of arms were taken over by the County Councils when they were formed in 1890 under the Local Government (Scotland) Act, 1889.

This Act required each County Council to adopt a Common Seal, for which purpose the County Councils of Aberdeen, Ayr, Berwick and Stirling recorded arms in 1890. The Lyon Office letter books for 1889–90 show that several of the other County Councils received advice on possible coats of arms or on the designing of their seals, always accompanied by a warning against the illegal use of armorial bearings, but the advice was not always followed by the newly-elected Councils. Although nine Councils (using the modern names)—Caithness, Moray, Bute, Fife, Midlothian, West Lothian, Wigtown, Kirkcudbright and Dumfries—adopted seals which, by 1929 Lyon Office standards, were definitely armorial or were otherwise open to objection, no action appears to have been taken against them, even though the Lord Lyon must have been well aware of what had happened and, in the cases of West Lothian, Kirkcudbright and Dumfries, had specifically warned the Councils against breaches of the law.

3.   The Lyon and the Counties, 1927–1928

In the next thirty-five years, I have only been able to trace two items and these are only of passing interest. In 1922, Ross & Cromarty made a very tentative approach about a coat of arms following an enquiry about a suitable crest for H.M.S. *Ross*, and

† I have confined my list to what can be found in the Scottish United Services Museum at Edinburgh Castle and in the Journal of the Society for Army Historical Research. The other surviving relics of the Scottish Militia and Local Volunteer Forces are scattered all over Scotland in churches, civic and county buildings, family seats, etc. It would take years to track them all down.

in the following year, the Lyon Office remonstrated with Fife County Council about its improper use of the crest of H.R.H. The Duchess of Fife.

But there were some important developments in 1927 when the Scottish National War Memorial at Edinburgh Castle was nearing completion. As part of his scheme of internal decoration, the architect, Sir Robert Lorimer, proposed to use shields bearing the arms of many of the Counties and some of the Burghs. Not all the Counties were selected: Midlothian was very upset at being left out and having to be represented by Edinburgh's arms.[7] It appears that there was lack of consultation between the architect and the Lyon Office with the result that stone carvings of some unmatriculated County and Burgh arms were placed on the Memorial. When he became Lord Lyon in 1927, Captain G. S. C. Swinton, who was Secretary of the War Memorial Committee, had to make it perfectly clear that only arms which had been duly matriculated would be allowed to appear on the Memorial, and he so informed the County Councils and Burghs concerned. According to Lord Lyon Innes, some unauthorised arms had to be removed from the Memorial, but I have been unable to trace any details as to which these were.[8]

All this seems to have caused less fuss than it might have done, probably because there was so little time left before the Memorial was due to be opened. Nevertheless, there were not only some mild complaints from County Conveners that the matter was being unduly rushed, but the question was raised by the Duke of Buccleuch (probably on behalf of Dumfries-shire) as the subject of a House of Lords debate, on 28 June 1927, during which the Duke of Sutherland, for the Government, said: "It was the statutory duty of the Lord Lyon to see that arms were not irregularly displayed, and the action taken seemed to the Government to be right and proper."[9]

The general position seems to have been that the following County Councils (and the Royal Burghs of Haddington and Inveraray) naturally wished to be represented in the National War Memorial and agreed, with little demur, to record arms:

Inverness, Nairn, Moray, Kincardine, Angus, Bute, Clackmannan, Kinross, Fife and Selkirk.

In addition, Dunbarton and East Lothian, neither of which appears to have been included in the original scheme of decoration, recorded arms so that they too could be represented in the Memorial.†

In several instances, the device on the Council seal was accepted as the basis of the arms, but there were some interesting new grants like Moray, where the ancient arms of the Province were combined with those of Thomas Randolph, the famous nephew and Lieutenant of King Robert I (The Bruce), East Lothian, based on the rather unique red and ermine achievement of the Giffords of Yester, and Clackmannan, where the arms make reference to a local legend also about King Robert I.

† As both these County Councils were using non-armorial seals, it had apparently been originally decided that the two Counties should be respectively represented by the arms of the Royal Burghs of Dumbarton and Haddington; the latter were, however, retained.

In 1928, the County Council of Dumfries, which had previously refused to record its arms, and which seems to have been responsible for initiating the House of Lords' debate mentioned above, agreed to do so, and its arms were added to the Memorial. The non-armigerous Counties were represented either by the arms of their County towns, i.e. Zetland by Lerwick, Ross & Cromarty by Dingwall, Banffshire by Banff, Argyll by Inveraray, West Lothian by Linlithgow, Peebles-shire by Peebles, or by ancient territorial arms, i.e. Orkney, Caithness and Sutherland by the arms of those three ancient Earldoms, and Wigtown and Kirkcudbright by the arms of the Lords of Galloway.

4. The Local Government (Scotland) Act, 1929

As mentioned above, the passing of the important Local Government (Scotland) Act, 1929, gave greatly increased powers to the County Councils. The changes were regarded as so important by Ayr County Council that it sought a new grant of arms in 1931 to replace those granted in 1890 which were not thought to be sufficiently representative of the County. Peebles County Council decided to record arms in the same year and for the same reason, while Orkney County Council, through the good offices of a local benefactor, also matriculated arms in 1931. This last was a most interesting case as the Council was able to prove that it was the legal descendant of the Communitas Orcadiae whose armorial seal could be traced back to 1425. Thus Orkney became the only County Council to qualify for "ancient user" privileges under the 1672 Act.

In 1935, Caithness County Council, which had begun considering the matter in 1931, but had deferred a decision on economic grounds, recorded arms and became the twenty-fourth of the thirty-three Counties to do so.

5. Consolidation and Achievement, 1951–1957

The remaining nine all recorded arms between 1951 and 1957—Kirkcudbright (when Lord Lyon Innes introduced the County Council coronet) and Midlothian in 1951, West Lothian in 1952, Banff and Argyll in 1953, Wigtown in 1955, Zetland in 1956 and finally Ross & Cromarty and Sutherland in 1957. While the earlier three of these were certainly influenced by the watchfulness of the Lyon Office, and Banff arose out of the Queen's coronation, two events exerted their influence over the situation generally. The rebuilding of St. Columba's Church of Scotland in London, which

D

began in 1950–51, included a scheme for the display of all the County arms in the new church. Soon afterwards, Midlothian County Council decided to seek from the Lord Lyon a Brieve of Precedency confirming Midlothian as the Premier County of the Realm of Scotland and on the Brieve each County was to be shown in order of precedence and with its coat of arms. The Brieve was sealed by the Lord Lyon on 21 June 1956, the order of precedence of the Counties being as follows:

1. Midlothian, 2. East Lothian, 3. Berwick, 4. Roxburgh, 5. Selkirk, 6. Peebles, 7. Lanark, 8. Dumfries, 9. Wigtown, 10. Ayr, 11. Dunbarton, 12. Bute, 13. Renfrew, 14. Stirling, 15. West Lothian, 16. Perth, 17. Kincardine, 18. Aberdeen, 19. Inverness, 20. Nairn, 21. Ross & Cromarty, 22. Argyll, 23. Fife, 24. Angus, 25. Banff, 26. Kirkcudbright, 27. Sutherland, 28. Caithness, 29. Moray, 30. Orkney, 31. Clackmannan, 32. Kinross, 33. Zetland.

Despite its date, the Brieve was not completed until well into 1957, as it was only then that the Ross & Cromarty and Sutherland arms had been settled, and all the Scottish County Councils had their arms duly recorded in the Public Register of All Arms and Bearings in Scotland. Since then only one change has occurred—the addition of a motto by Banffshire in 1971.

6.   Some Comments on the Heraldry

The Coats of Arms

The coats of arms of the County Councils total only thirty-three in number and thus any analysis of them can only be a very limited exercise. Nevertheless, the following points may be of some interest.

In twenty-one cases, the shields are undivided; eight bear no ordinaries or sub-ordinaries, but the sea appears in base once, a loch once and a mount thrice; ten bear ordinaries—chief (1), chief and saltire (2), fess (3), chevron (1), saltire (2), bordure (1)—and three sub-ordinaries—canton (1) and inescutcheon (2). Of the twelve cases with divided shields, one is parted per chevron, six are quartered (one with a pale overall), two parted per fess (one with a fess wavy as well as a chief parted per pale, half of which is gyronny of eight, and one with a base parted per pale) and three per pale (one indented and with a chief). In some instances the blazons can be further broken down.

In addition to the two metals, only the four commonest colours (gules, azure, vert and sable) are used as tinctures, and just one fur, ermine, which appears twice, once as a fimbriation.

As might be expected, the lion is the commonest charge and most of the sea-board Counties of the north and west have ships of one kind or another. The

Royal tressure appears twice (Moray and Perth). Industry is not particularly widely represented, there being only two references to agriculture, one to fishing and one to woollen manufacturing. In the main, the charges on each shield recall the historical associations, particularly family associations, with the area it represents; there are several references to the ancient Scottish Earldoms. In the shields which have concentrated on the family or clan connections, there are some good examples of heraldic shorthand: the simple shield of Inverness refers to eight clans, that of East Lothian to five families and that of Dumfries to as many as ten. One feature of particular heraldic interest is the use, in Argyll, of a winged claw holding a crowned sword to represent the Lordship of the Isles. There are also a few examples where the arms recall historical events connected with the County: Orkney's coat alludes to the ancient Norwegian connection, Stirling's to the Battle of Bannockburn (1314), and Kincardine's to the saving of the Scottish Crown Jewels from Dunnottar Castle in 1651–52. Landmarks also are used: Kinross has Loch Leven Castle; Perth, Scone Palace; and Selkirk, Ettrick Forrest, and in eight cases, the arms of the County have a direct reference to the County town, usually by inclusion of a feature from the Burgh arms.

Mottoes, Crests and Supporters

Ten of the thirty-three County Councils do not have *mottoes*: these include important Counties like Midlothian, Aberdeen, Dumfries and Stirling. Lord Lyon Innes was rather against mottoes for County Councils, even hinting that some of those granted in 1927 had only been allowed because they had already been carved on public buildings and it would have cost public money to remove them.[10] Of the twenty-three mottoes which have been granted, nine are in Latin, five in Scots, five in English, three in Gaelic and one in Old Norse.

Only six of the Counties have *crests*—Roxburgh, Perth, Lanark, Renfrew, Peebles and Caithness. None of these is a recent grant. Roxburgh and Perth are both old and unusual, Lanark and Renfrew date from a time when the Lyon Office granted crests to corporations without any difficulty and Peebles and Caithness from the 1930's when similar achievements were still being allowed to Burghs which wished to have them. But, strictly speaking, if it is incorrect for a Burgh to have a crest, it is equally incorrect for a County Council to have one.

Supporters have been granted only three times: Perth, a very special case, Orkney, which was able to prove its ancient right to use them, and Peebles, presumably because it asked for them. Taking an analogy from the Royal Burghs, it would appear a reasonable assumption that any County Council which wished to apply for supporters would now be granted them.

The County Council Coronet

The County Council coronet—"Issuant from a circlet Vert, five paling piles also Vert alternately with four garbs Or, banded Sable"—was introduced by Lord Lyon Innes in 1951 and first used for Kirkcudbright. Its design, which was probably inspired by the open crown on the border of that County's seal, is intended to reflect the rural aspects of a County as compared with the urban characteristics associated with the mural coronets granted to Burghs. A County Council which matriculated its arms before 1951 and which wishes to use the County coronet must seek authority from the Lord Lyon to do so; so far, Roxburgh is the only County which has had the coronet added to its arms.

PART III

The Arms of the Burghs and County Councils

(arranged by Counties)

I

INTRODUCTORY

We now come to the main part of this book and look in detail at the coats of arms of the individual Burghs and County Councils. As mentioned on pages 22 and 38 above, one hundred and seventy-seven out of the two hundred and one Burghs and all the thirty-three County Councils have recorded arms and these are all described and illustrated. For the sake of completeness, I have also included brief details, but not drawings, of the seals used by the twenty-four non-armigerous Burghs.

The various individual articles have been arranged under Counties, the group of Counties of Cities coming first and then the Counties proper, going from Zetland in the North to Berwickshire in the South. The Burghs are given in the order used by the Convention of Royal Burghs; Royal Burghs come first, then Parliamentary Burghs and then Police Burghs; at the end of each County chapter come the arms of the County Council. In a final chapter or postscript, there is reference to the arms of Berwick-upon-Tweed, and to the arms of the three armigerous Burghs which have been merged with adjacent Cities, together with notes on the changes in the number of Burghs which have occurred since 1905, and on the forthcoming Reform of Local Government in Scotland.

As this part of the book must inevitably be very much like a catalogue, I make no apology for the frequency with which certain words and phrases keep recurring. When referring to the coats of arms, I have regarded the verbs "matriculate", "register" and "record" as synonymous and, therefore, interchangeable. The many references to devices on Burgh seals dated 1892 or earlier are unavoidable since I have tried to make each article complete in itself. I have endeavoured to explain the use of the word "City" in Scotland on pages 4–5 above and in the following articles I have confined its use to the four Counties of Cities and to Perth since it has precedence over three of the Counties of Cities.

Each Burgh article is prefaced by a short note generally on the constitutional history of the Burgh, more often than not to give information which helps to explain the coat of arms. Most of the basic information about the foundation of the Royal and feudal Burghs has come straight from the late Professor G. S. Pryde's *The Burghs of Scotland* (1965) and I would again express my indebtedness and gratitude to him and to his editor, Professor A. A. M. Duncan, because all this information was so recently published and thus so very easily accessible. The dates of the Police Burghs have been checked as carefully as possible but no definitive list appears to exist. Then when

explaining many of the coats of arms, I have been able to draw freely on the last published works on the subject: Lord Bute's *The Arms of the Royal and Parliamentary Burghs
of Scotland* (1897) and *The Arms of the Baronial and Police Burghs of Scotland* (1903) and
Alexander Porteous' *The Town Council Seals of Scotland* (1906).

In each County Council article, I have included a brief description of the device
on the seal adopted by the Council in 1890, except in those cases where the Council
had already either recorded or inherited arms.

There are many references to Scottish kings. Apart from Kenneth MacAlpin,
William the Lion and John Balliol, all the kings are called by their official number.
Thus Malcolm Canmore is King Malcolm III, and Robert the Bruce, King Robert I.
Queen Mary is referred to by her customary style of Mary, Queen of Scots.

The drawings are all new and have been specially drawn for this book by Miss
Mary Gordon, the Herald Painter to the Lyon Court. They are intended to stand
together as an effective set and we have tried to make them as consistent as possible.
Where a Burgh has two coats, the sacred bearings have been put on a flag. The
hatchings employed to depict the various metals, colours and furs are shown in the
diagram below; these hatchings have been used wherever the scale of drawing has
permitted. All coronets have been drawn to the pattern now used by the Lyon Office.

One or two additions, shown in square brackets, have been made to the seventeenth-century blazons and some archaisms in them have been modernised; where
coronets have been added in this century this is mentioned either in a note to the
blazon or in the explanatory text. Additions have also been made to some of the more
recent blazons, again shown in square brackets; these are mostly minor changes and
the majority of them relate to coronets.

2

THE COUNTIES OF CITIES

In Scotland, there are four Counties of Cities, Edinburgh, Dundee, Aberdeen and Glasgow.

CITY OF EDINBURGH

Argent, a castle triple-towered and embattled Sable, masoned of the First, and topped with three fans Gules, windows and portcullis shut of the Last, situate on a rock Proper.

[Above the Shield is placed a suitable Helmet with a Mantling Sable doubled Argent,] and on a Wreath of the Colours is set for *Crest* an anchor wreathed about with a cable all Proper. *Motto*, in an Escrol above, "Nisi Dominus Frustra". *Supported*, on the dexter by a maid richly attired with her hair hanging down on her shoulders, and on the sinister by a doe, [both] Proper.

(Lyon Register, i, 455: 23 November 1774, but granted 21 April 1732)

EDINBURGH, the Capital of Scotland, has been a Royal Burgh since the reign of King David I, dating from between 1124 and 1127.[1] It was one of the original members of the Curia Quattuor Burgorum (Berwick, Edinburgh, Stirling and Roxburgh) out of which developed the Convention of Royal Burghs.

The arms resemble, but are not identical to, the device on the earliest known seals of the City of which fourteenth- and fifteenth-century impressions are on record. The first example of the arms on a shield is dated 1496 and appears on a seal of St. Giles' Church.[2] The principal charge is Edinburgh Castle on its rock; the red masoning, fans and portcullis denote that it is a Royal castle but the reason for the silver and black livery colours is not known. The anchor crest is said to refer to the *ex-officio* title of Admiral of the Forth held by the Lord Provost. The dexter supporter may be a Pictish princess in reference to the legend that in ancient days, during a battle, the Pictish Kings used to shut up their daughters inside the castle for safety, hence Edinburgh's former name "Castrum Puellarum"; alternatively, as Lord Lyon Balfour Paul has suggested, she may be "simply emblematical of the fair beauty of the city itself". The sinister supporter is the doe of St. Giles, the patron saint of Edinburgh. The Latin motto is an abridgement of Psalm 127:1: "Except the Lord keep the city, the watchman waketh but in vain." The matriculation of the arms, though originally agreed to by the Town Council in 1710, was the subject of protracted argument between the Council and successive Lords Lyon between 1732 and 1774, during which the Council disputed the need to matriculate at all. In 1774, it was discovered that matriculation had actually occurred in 1732 though the fact had not been recorded in the Lyon Register.[3] There is an interesting article by Lord Lyon Balfour Paul about the arms of Edinburgh in *The Book of the Old Edinburgh Club*, Vol. *iii*, 1–12, and it may be noted that the helmet with its black and silver mantling is a subsequent early twentieth-century addition, to which the Lyon Office raised no objection at the time.

DUNDEE is dated as a Royal Burgh created between 1191 and 1195 by King William the Lion. By 1195, it had become a burgh of the King's brother, David, Earl of Huntingdon, in whose family it appears to have remained until 1237 or even 1290. Nevertheless, it had all the privileges of a Royal Burgh and these were confirmed by King Robert I in 1327.[4]

The arms follow very closely the heraldic device on an old seal of the City, of which an impression dated 1416 is on record; the supporters to the shield bearing the pot of lilies are described as wyverns.[5] The lilies and the blue field are for the Virgin Mary, to whom the parish church of Dundee is dedicated; the white lily is one of the flowers specially associated with her. It has been thought that the dragons symbolised the sea and the City's overseas trade, but Lord Bute has suggested that they may be derived from the lions' heads and legs of the faldstool on which St. Clement sits on the obverse of the old Burgh seal.[6] The first Latin motto is said to be connected with a legend which tells how David, Earl of Huntingdon, landed here after a storm on his return from the Crusades about 1190 and called the place "Donum Dei"—"God's Gift"; this, however, has nothing whatever to do with the name Dundee which almost certainly comes from the Gaelic and means "fort on the Tay".

In 1932, the City Council agreed to a request that the City's arms should be displayed in a tapestry panel as part of the decoration of the board room at the Head Office of the Midland Bank in London.[7] As some doubts existed about the correct form of the arms, the Lyon Office was consulted, whereupon Lord Lyon Grant drew

CITY OF DUNDEE

Azure, a pot of three growing lilies Argent.

Above the Shield is placed a mural coronet and a Helmet befitting the degree of a Royal Burgh with a Mantling Azure doubled Argent, and on a Wreath of the same Liveries is set for *Crest* a lily Argent, and in an Escrol over the same this *Motto* "Dei Donum"; in another Escrol below the Shield this *Motto* "Prudentia et Candore", the said Shield having for *Supporters* two dragons, wings elevated, their tails nowed together underneath Vert.

(Lyon Register, xxx, 38: 6 October 1932)
(Previously matriculated Lyon Register, i, 455: 30 July 1673)

the Council's attention to the fact that the arms being used differed in detail from those granted in 1673 since the supporters had been changed from dragons to wyverns, the lily crest did not grow out of the top of the shield, and a second motto "Prudentia et Candore"—"With Thought and Purity" (possibly a further reference to the Virgin Mary)—had been added. After some discussion, the Council decided that it wished to adhere to the original form of the arms and to add the second motto; at the same time it was requested that "three lilies" be mentioned in the blazon and that the dragons' wings be elevated. In the re-matriculation of the arms, these and one or two other small changes were made in the blazoning, and the coronet, helmet and mantling were added above the shield.

ABERDEEN became a Royal Burgh between 1124 and 1153 in the reign of King David I.[8] This creation, however, related to the fishing and trading community which developed at the mouth of the river Dee. During the War of Independence, the Burgh rendered distinguished service to King Robert I but in 1336 was sacked by the English King Edward III; when rebuilt, the name "New" Aberdeen became associated with it. Another town, known as the Ville of Aberdon, grew up, under the patronage of the Bishops, around the cathedral and near the estuary of the river Don; it was created a Burgh of Barony (with the name Old Aberdeen) in favour of the Bishop of Aberdeen in 1489[9] and retained its separate burghal identity until 1891 when "with much heartburning and reluctance", it was amalgamated with "New" Aberdeen.

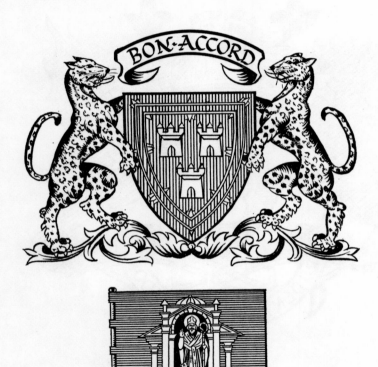

CITY OF ABERDEEN

Gules, three towers triple-towered within a double tressure [flowered and] counterflowered Argent.

Supported by two leopards Proper; the *Motto* in an Escrol above "Bon Accord".

And upon the reverse of the seal is insculped in a field Azure, a temple Argent, Saint Nicholas standing in the porch mitred and vested Proper, with his dexter hand lifted up to heaven praying over three children in a boiling cauldron of the First, and holding in the sinister a crosier Or.

(Lyon Register, i, 455: 25 February 1674)

The arms are a development of early (but not the oldest) seals of the City of which impressions dated 1430 and 1440 are on record.[10] It is known that Aberdeen had some armorial problems to sort out with the Lyon Court in 1637;[11] it is one of the four Scottish Burghs with two coats of arms recognised by the Lyon Office. The first coat is that most commonly used and its three triple-towered towers (originally one) are said to refer to the three fortified hills, Castle, Port and St. Catherine's, on which the City had its origins. The Royal tressure is traditionally regarded as having been granted in 1308 by King Robert I in recognition of the outstanding services given by the burghers in capturing Aberdeen Castle and expelling the English from the City; but there appears to be good historical evidence to support the view that it only dates from the reign of King James I (1406–1437) and may have been granted by him, along with the supporters (originally more like lions and similar to those used by King James himself), because Aberdeen was one of the Burghs which agreed to underwrite his expenses during his exile in England.[12] The motto, however, may well have originated during the 1308 siege: the 1674 Patent states that "the word 'Bon Accord' was given them (the citizens) by King Robert Bruce for killing all the English in one night in their town, their word being that night 'Bon Accord' ".[13] The second coat of arms shows St. Nicholas, the City's patron saint, performing his famous miracle of restoring the dead children to life.

It is of interest to note that the drawing issued by the Lyon Office in 1674 was incorrect as the towers were not triple-towered and it showed the leopard supporters in different stances, the dexter full-faced and the sinister in profile. "This has led to much diversity and inaccuracy in the representation of the arms of the City" and the error was not put right until a new drawing was obtained in 1883. At the same time, an error in the Lyon Register in the blazon of the second coat, where St. Michael had been mentioned instead of St. Nicholas, was put right. The blazon in the Patent issued to the City had been correct.

Much interesting detail about the arms of Aberdeen can be found in *The Armorial Ensigns of the Royal Burgh of Aberdeen*, by John Cruickshank (1888).

GLASGOW, the cathedral town of the old diocese of the same name, was made a Burgh of the Bishop of Glasgow by King William the Lion between 1175 and 1178. In 1587, it was created a Burgh of Regality in favour of Walter Stewart of Cardonald, Commendator of Blantyre, who became Lord High Treasurer in 1596 and later Lord Blantyre. In 1611, after many years as a *de facto* Royal Burgh, it was created a Royal Burgh *de jure* by King James VI.[14]

The arms were the subject of a detailed study by Andrew Macgeorge in his book *An Inquiry as to the Armorial Insignia of the City of Glasgow* (1866). He makes it clear that they have appeared in many versions and traces their development from a seal of 1268 which showed the head of St. Kentigern, through one which he dates as 1325 showing the Saint's head with a robin perched on a branch on the dexter and a bell and a salmon with a ring in its mouth on the sinister, to a seal of 1647 which omits the Saint's head, but rearranges the other features in the manner now familiar.[15] The salmon supporters he regards as a nineteenth-century, but not inappropriate, addition and he refers to one seventeenth-century example of a carving of an unauthorised version of the City's arms and to others in the achievements of the Bishops, where salmon form a kind of ornamental backcloth to the arms. In granting the arms, Lord Lyon Burnett followed, as Mr. Macgeorge had suggested, the description given by Alexander Nisbet in his *System of Heraldry* and placed the tree on a mount.[16]

The charges on the shield recall three legendary miracles connected with St. Kentigern (or St. Mungo), the City's patron saint: the tree, said to be a hazel tree, recalls how he produced fire from a hazel branch; the redbreast recalls the robin he restored to life; the salmon and the ring recall his intervention to help the Queen of Cadzow who was suspected of unfaithfulness by her husband. The handbell is his

CITY OF GLASGOW

Argent, on a mount in base Vert an oak tree Proper, the stem at the base thereof surmounted by a salmon on its back also Proper, with a signet ring in its mouth Or; on the top of the tree a redbreast, and in the sinister fess point an ancient hand bell, both also Proper.

Above the Shield is placed a suitable Helmet, with a Mantling Gules doubled Argent, and, issuing out of a Wreath of the proper Liveries, is set for *Crest* the half-length figure of Saint Kentigern affrontée vested and mitred, his right hand raised in the act of benediction, and having in his left hand a crosier, all Proper; in a Compartment below the Shield are placed for *Supporters* two salmon Proper, each holding in its mouth a signet ring Or; and in an Escrol entwined with the Compartment this *Motto* "Let Glasgow Flourish".

(Lyon Register, vii, 48: 25 October 1866)

much venerated bell (cf. Lanark). The colours seem to have no special significance; at one time the field appears to have been "parted per fess Argent and Gules", and is so shown on the mace of Glasgow University. The salmon supporters refer to the legend mentioned above and could also allude to the river Clyde and to salmon-fishing, which was the City's staple industry in the eighteenth century. The crest is St. Kentigern himself—but without a halo—thus harking back to the 1268 seal. The motto is a shortened version of "Lord, let Glasgow flourish by the preaching of Thy Word and the praising of Thy Name".

3

COUNTY OF ZETLAND

The County of Zetland has one Burgh, the Police Burgh of Lerwick, also the County town.

BURGH OF LERWICK

Or, in the sea Proper, a dragon ship Vert under sail, oars in action; on a chief Gules, a battle-axe fessways Argent.

Above the Shield is placed a suitable Helmet with a Mantling Gules doubled Argent, and on a Wreath of their proper Liveries is set for *Crest* a raven Proper, and in an Escrol over the same this *Motto* "Dispecta est Thule".

(Lyon Register, xi, 6: 20 April 1882)

LERWICK was created a Burgh of Barony in 1818 on the application of the burgesses[1] and became a Police Burgh in 1833.

The Burgh's arms recall its early history, the Viking ship commemorating the Norwegian origin and the red chief with its silver battle-axe, the connection with Denmark. The raven is the crest of the Jarls of Orkney, whose lands include the Shetland Isles. The Latin motto—"Thule was sighted"—is a quotation, referring to the Shetlands, from Tacitus' account (*Agricola*, Book 10) of the Roman fleet's voyage to the Orkneys about A.D. 84; it was chosen as "the earliest reference to our Islands to be found in literature". The arms were registered in connection with the new Town Hall which was completed in 1883; the costs were met by subscriptions collected by the Decoration Fund Committee for the new Hall.[2]

ZETLAND COUNTY COUNCIL

Azure, a base invected barry Argent and Sable, the alternate party lines being engrailed and plain, a dragon ship Or, under sail spread to starboard Argent, oars in action [Or], flag and mast Gules.

Which Shield is ensigned with the proper coronet of a County Council, and in an Escrol below the same this *Motto* "Med Lögum Skal Land Byggja".

(Lyon Register, xli, 35: 14 February 1956)

The County Council of THE COUNTY OF ZETLAND bears arms which retain the main feature of the obverse of the seal adopted in 1890, a Viking warship which recalls the old link with Norway and Denmark. The ship and its oars are coloured gold and set on a blue field since these are the colours of the ancient Earldom (or Jarldom) of Orkney of which the Shetlands were once part. This Earldom in 1379 passed into the family of Sinclair (or St. Clair) of Roslin, as heirs by marriage of the Norse Jarls, and so the sea has been coloured silver and black and given an engrailed pattern in reference to them; the black colour also recalls the black raven which was the badge of the Jarls. The motto, in Old Norse, appears on the reverse of the 1890 seal and comes from a speech in *Njal's Saga* (Chapter 70);[3] it means "By law shall the land be built up".

4

COUNTY OF ORKNEY

The County of Orkney has two Burghs, the Royal Burgh of Kirkwall, the County town, and the Police Burgh of Stromness.

ROYAL BURGH OF KIRKWALL

Party per fess wavy Or and Azure: an ancient three-masted ship of the First, sails furled, masts and rigging Proper, flags and pennons Gules, each having a canton of the second charged with a Saint Andrew's cross Argent.

In an Escrol below the Shield is placed this *Motto* "Si Deus Nobiscum".

(Lyon Register, xi, 92: 11 November 1886)

KIRKWALL, the cathedral town of the old diocese of Orkney, was created a Royal Burgh by King James III in 1486.[1] The arms, which follow the device on the 1675 Burgh seal,[2a] use the blue and gold colours of the ancient Earldom of Orkney. The three-masted ship denotes that Kirkwall is an important seaport. The Latin motto—"If God be for us"—is evidently taken from Romans 8:31. The arms were matriculated on the occasion of the quatercentenary of the Burgh.

STROMNESS became a Burgh of Barony in 1817 on the application of the freeholders.[2b] This followed prolonged litigation with Kirkwall over taxes levied by the latter and the eventual House of Lords judgement in favour of Stromness freed all small towns and villages in Scotland from being tributaries of the Royal Burghs. Stromness became a Police Burgh in 1856 but has not registered arms; its seal shows a Norse dragon-ship, with the motto "Per Mare" and the date 1817 below, and also a small pair of scales to recall the successful legal battle mentioned above.

ORKNEY COUNTY COUNCIL

Parted per pale Azure and Gules: in the dexter a dragon galley Or, sails furled Argent, and in the sinister a lion rampant imperially crowned Or, armed and langued Azure, holding in its forepaws a battle-axe erect in pale Gold.

On a Compartment below the Shield with this *Motto* "Boreas Domus Mare Amicus" are set for *Supporters* two udallers habited of the fifteenth century.

(Lyon Register, xxix, 66: 3 March 1931)

The County Council of THE COUNTY OF ORKNEY bears arms which show on the dexter side the blue field and gold galley of the ancient Earldom of Orkney and on the sinister the red field and golden crowned lion from the Royal Arms of Norway, recalling that Orkney was once Norwegian territory. The battle-axe held by the lion has been coloured gold for difference. The Latin motto—"The North our home, the sea our friend"—was chosen in 1931. The supporters are udallers, a term which, under the udal system of land tenure which still applies in Orkney and Shetland, covers the whole of the landowning class, and they are appropriately dressed in their "braws" (best clothes) for the important task of supporting the County Arms. The arms are partly based on an old seal of the Communitas Orcadiae of which a 1425 impression is on record and which showed the Norwegian Royal Arms with two supporters; this old seal had been reconstructed by a Danish Herald, Herr A. Thiset.[3] In view of this clear evidence from past centuries, Lord Lyon Grant accepted the County Council as the legal descendant of the Communitas Orcadiae and allowed it to matriculate arms as "ancient user" under the Act of 1672, thus making it unique among the County Councils. Mr. J. Storer Clouston, the author and historian, who was County Convener at the time, took a leading part in the discussions about the coat of arms, and the cost of the fees for registration of the arms was met by an Orkney gentleman who wished to remain anonymous.[4] The seal adopted by the County Council in 1890 had a device showing the traditional Orkney galley with furled sails; it was designed by Mr. T. S. Peace, a local architect.[5]

5

COUNTY OF CAITHNESS

The County of Caithness has two Burghs, the Royal Burgh of Wick, the County town, and the Police Burgh of Thurso.

ROYAL BURGH OF WICK

Azure, a chevron round-embattled on the upper edge and ensigned of a cross patée at the apex close-fitched Argent, between two lymphads Or, sails of the Second, flagged Gules, in chief, and in base upon the sea barry wavy Argent and Vert, an ancient boat of the Third, therein two naked men Proper handling oars in action Sable, and a bishop erect attired of the Second, mitred of the Third, holding in his sinister hand a book of the Last, his dexter hand raised in act of blessing, and in the base of the shield, a crosier-head also of the Third.

Above the Shield which is ensigned of the Burghal coronet is placed in an Escrol this *Motto* "Nisi Dominus Frustra", and below the Shield is placed a Compartment suitable to a Burgh Royal, its turrets having string-courses engrailed and thereon this *Motto* "Wick Works Weil".

(Lyon Register, xl, 21: 21 July 1954)

WICK, which had probably been a Burgh of Barony from about 1400, was created a Royal Burgh by King James VI in 1589,[1] at the request, it is thought, of the 4th Earl of Caithness, George Sinclair, who was Chancellor of the jury which in 1567 tried the Earl of Bothwell for the murder of Henry, Lord Darnley, second husband of Mary, Queen of Scots.

The Burgh arms combine the features of two seals which it has used. The blue and gold colours recall the ancient Earldom of Caithness and the round-embattled chevron with the cross, the old Church of St. Fergus, patron saint of Wick, which was a prominent landmark from the sea. The two ships in chief refer to the town's important connections with shipping and fishing. Below the chevron there is a bishop (St. Fergus) in a boat with a crosier-head underneath; the Saint is reported to have come by sea from Ireland to Scotland. The two mottoes caused much discussion. The Latin one, which Wick had long used on one of its seals, was allowed after Edinburgh (q.v.) which also uses it, had agreed "that it be assigned to the Burgh of Wick". The second motto is intended to echo the motto "Commit Thy Wark to God" of the Sinclair Earls of Caithness (cf. Thurso and Caithness) but was only accepted by the Town Council after prolonged negotiation and much press publicity. At the end of it all, the local newspaper commented: "Few Wickers may have heard of the original Motto 'Nisi Dominus Frustra' but most will be familiar with 'Wick Works Weil'."[2]

BURGH OF THURSO

Argent, five barrulets Sable, engrailed on their under edges, the figure of Saint Peter enhaloed Proper, vested Azure and Or, in his dexter hand two keys in saltire of the Last and of the First, in his sinister a patriarchal cross of the Fourth.

Above the Shield is placed a coronet appropriate to a Burgh and in an Escrol below the same this *Motto* "Wark to God".

(Lyon Register, xxxix, 40: 24 November 1952)

THURSO was erected into a Burgh of Barony in 1633 in favour of John Sinclair, Master of Berriedale and father of George, 6th Earl of Caithness,[3] and became a Police Burgh in 1841.

The arms show St. Peter, the patron saint, who also appears on the Burgh seal (of which an impression dated c. 1633 is on record),[4] set on a background of silver with black engrailed barrulets, these colours and the engrailing alluding directly to the Sinclair arms. The motto is the second part of that of the Sinclair Earls of Caithness. The arms were matriculated following a decision by the Town Council to provide a Chain-of-Office for the Provost; the cost was met by a memorial gift to the Burgh by the family of Sir Charles and Lady Findlay.[5]

CAITHNESS COUNTY COUNCIL

Azure, a galley Or, the sail thereof Argent, charged with a raven Sable.

Above the Shield is placed a Helmet of befitting degree with a Mantling Azure doubled Or, and on a Wreath of their Liveries is set for *Crest* a cock Proper, armed and beaked Or, and in an Escrol over the same this *Motto* "Commit thy Work to God".

(Lyon Register, xxxi, 32: 10 January 1935)

The County Council of THE COUNTY OF CAITHNESS bears arms which display the golden galley on a blue field of the ancient Earldom of Caithness; and on its sail is the black raven of the Norse Jarls whose territory covered not only Orkney and Shetland but also Caithness and Sutherland. The crest of a cock and the motto are those of the Sinclair Earls of Caithness; these were used on the seal adopted by the County Council in 1890.

6

COUNTY OF SUTHERLAND

The County of Sutherland has one Burgh, the Royal Burgh of Dornoch. The County town, Golspie, is not a Burgh.

ROYAL BURGH OF DORNOCH

Argent, a horseshoe Azure, having seven horsenails Or.

Above the Shield is placed a mural crown masoned Proper, thereon a Helmet befitting their degree with a Mantling Azure doubled Argent, and on a Wreath of their Liveries is set for *Crest* a cat-a-mountain sejant Proper, holding in his dexter paw an escutcheon Gules charged with three mullets Or, and in an Escrol over the same this *Motto* "Without Feare".

(Lyon Register, xxviii, 41 : 20 June 1929)

DORNOCH, the cathedral town of the old diocese of Caithness, was originally a Burgh of the Bishop of Caithness. In 1628, it was created a Royal Burgh by King Charles I, but with some reservation of rights to the Earl of Sutherland, the hereditary Superior.[1]

The arms are based on an old Burgh seal of which a 1786 impression is on record.[2] The silver and blue colours are those traditionally used by the town and the horse-shoe recalls the victory of William, Thane or Earl of Sutherland, over the Danes and Norwegians at nearby Embo in about 1259. In this battle, the Thane is said to have slain the Danish General with a horse's leg he had picked up on the battlefield, and there has grown up a tradition that, in honour of his triumph, the place was given the name Dorneich, being the Gaelic for a horse's foot or hoof; this, however, is not so, as the name Dornoch is mentioned in a Mandate of King David I dated about 1136.[3] The wild cat in the crest is the Sutherland crest and it holds a shield with the arms of the ancient Earldom of Sutherland. The motto is an English version of the French motto "Sans Peur" of the Earls of Sutherland; it appears on the fountain presented by Miss Georgina Anderson to the Burgh in 1892 and on the Carnegie Free Library which was opened in 1906.

SUTHERLAND COUNTY COUNCIL

Gules, on a fess Argent, between three mullets Or, a raven displayed Sable.

Below the Shield, which is ensigned of the coronet proper to a County Council, is placed in an Escrol this *Motto* "Dluth Lean Do Dhuthchas Le Durachd".

(Lyon Register, xli, 68: 27 July 1957)

The County Council of THE COUNTY OF SUTHERLAND bears arms which are the arms of the ancient Earldom of Sutherland differenced by a silver fess with a black raven to recall the old connection with the Norse Jarls of Orkney whose territory came down to the County lands. The Gaelic motto—"Cling close to thy heritage with diligence"—was allowed, after some discussion, so that the western Celtic aspect of the County could be represented in the arms. This motto was suggested by the Rev. William MacLeod of Dornoch, who later became Convener of the County.[4] The wording on the plain seal adopted by the County Council in 1890 was entirely in Gaelic and, as well as the name of the County Council, included the words "Caidheal na Gaidheal an Gualaibh a Cheile" (Children of the Gael shoulder to shoulder).

7

COUNTY OF ROSS & CROMARTY

The County of Ross & Cromarty has six Burghs, the Royal Burghs of Tain, Dingwall (the County town) and Fortrose, the Parliamentary Burgh of Cromarty, and the Police Burghs of Invergordon and Stornoway.

ROYAL BURGH OF TAIN

Gules, Saint Duthacus in long garments Argent, holding in his dexter hand a staff garnished with ivy, in the sinister laid on his breast a book expanded Proper.

[The *Motto* in an Escrol "St. Beatus est Duthacus".]

(Lyon Register, i, 462: c. 1673)

TAIN is a place of great antiquity which could justifiably claim in 1966 that King Malcolm III had granted it trading privileges 900 years previously. Professor Pryde dates it as a Royal Burgh of King James II created in 1439, but adds that its origin as a Burgh presents unanswerable problems.[1]

The arms, which either by accident or by design have the red and silver colours of the ancient Earldom of Ross, show "the kind confessor blessed St. Duthac", said to have been born at Tain about A.D. 1000 and to have died at Armagh in Ireland in

1065. His relics were brought back to Tain in 1253 and his shrine became a famous place of pilgrimage to which many people, including kings, came. St. Duthacus is vested as a bishop, which according to tradition he was, and his long garments may refer to his shirt which was a celebrated relic at Tain. Lord Bute has suggested that it may have been the custom of pilgrims to Tain to fasten a sprig of ivy to their staves and I have found no other possible explanation for the saint's ivy-garnished staff.[2] The Latin motto—"Blessed is St. Duthacus"—is not mentioned in the Lyon Register but has long accompanied the figure of St. Duthacus on Tain's seal: there is a seventeenth-century impression on record.[3] The motto was included and a coronet added in a drawing specially commissioned from the Lyon Office Herald Painter in 1949.

ROYAL BURGH OF DINGWALL

Azure, the sun in its splendour between five mullets Or.

And in an Escrol below the Shield is placed this *Motto* "Salve Corona".

(Lyon Register, xiv, 57: 31 March 1897)

DINGWALL was created a Royal Burgh by King Alexander II in 1226–27 but from 1321 to 1475 was under the Earls of Ross. It was re-established as a Royal Burgh by King James IV in 1497–98.[4]

The arms are taken from the device used on the Burgh seal from time immemorial; there is a 1438–39 impression on record and the matrix is thought to be of thirteenth-century manufacture.[5] This device had long been thought locally to represent a starfish, of which there are many in the adjacent Cromarty Firth, but in 1897 Lord Lyon Balfour Paul had no hesitation in identifying it as the sun in its splendour. By happy chance, the gold and blue colours which were the natural choice for the sun and the firmament are also the livery colours of the Mackenzies of Tarbat (now represented by the Earl of Cromartie) whose seat, Castle Leod, is a few miles outside the Burgh, and who have a very long connection with it; nevertheless, it would be going too far to suggest that Dingwall's arms were inspired by the sun crest of the Tarbat Mackenzies. The Latin motto—"Hail the Crown"—was chosen in honour of Queen Victoria's Diamond Jubilee in 1897, the year the arms were matriculated. The fees were paid by Mr. Alexander Littlejohn of Invercharron, a benefactor of the Burgh, originally so that the arms could be displayed on a small building he was giving to the town; Mr. Littlejohn presented the Extract of Matriculation to the Burgh in an ornate silver casket which he had specially designed for the purpose.[6]

ROYAL BURGH OF FORTROSE

Per pale wavy: dexter, per fess embattled Vert and Azure, a barrulet embattled Or, between a rose Argent, barbed and seeded of the Third, in chief, and a stag's head cabossed also of the Third in base; sinister, Gules, a demi-lion rampant guardant Argent, mitred Or, issuant from a rose also Argent, barbed and seeded Vert.

Below the Shield, which is ensigned with a Burghal coronet, is placed upon a Compartment suitable to a Burgh Royal this *Motto* "From Age to Age Endure".

(Lyon Register, xl, 9: 17 June 1954)

FORTROSE, the cathedral town of the old diocese of Ross, has a long and complicated burghal history, much of it connected with the adjacent town of Rosemarkie, the original see of the diocese and a Bishop's Burgh from the thirteenth century.[7] Fortrose or Chanonry was in 1455 made a Burgh in favour of the Bishops of Ross and annexed to the Burgh of Rosemarkie; Rosemarkie itself was later made a Burgh of Barony in favour of the Bishop of Ross in 1553–54. In 1592, King James VI confirmed the union of Rosemarkie and Fortrose as the Royal Burgh of Rosemarkie, thus setting aside a 1590 Charter which had made Fortrose a Royal Burgh on its own. Subsequent Charters of 1612 and 1641 confirmed Rosemarkie's position, but in 1661 Parliament finally transferred the burghal rights to Fortrose and enacted that thenceforward the two towns should comprise the Royal Burgh of Fortrose.[8]

The Burgh arms, which were matriculated in honour of its quincentenary, refer to several important points in its history. The silver and gold rose on its green field recalls St. Moluag of Lismore, one of the famous Celtic missionaries, with whom the foundation of the Church at Rosemarkie is reputed to have been connected; the gold embattled barrulet is for the fort or Castle of Fortrose, and the golden stag's head on the blue field for the Mackenzie Earls of Seaforth who lived there. On the other side of the shield is the silver lion of the Ross Earldom on its red field wearing a mitre to recall the former diocese of Ross; the lion issues from a second rose which was added as two roses appear on an old seal of the Bishopric of Ross;[9] the two roses also make a pleasing heraldic pun on the names Fortrose and Rosemarkie, which have, however, no floral connections, but are derived from a Gaelic word meaning "a headland".

The wavy line down the centre of the shield stands for the Firth and the old Chanonry Ferry across it which was once an important north/south link. The motto was a local suggestion, chosen to indicate the long heritage of the Burgh and the fact that so many of its citizens bear the same surnames as those of the seventeenth century or earlier.

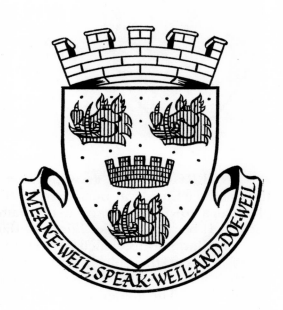

BURGH OF CROMARTY

Or, three boars' heads erased Gules, armed and langued Azure, in the centre of the shield a mural coronet of the Second.

Above the Shield is placed a mural coronet suitable to a Burgh and in an Escrol below the Shield this *Motto* "Meane Weil, Speak Weil, and Doe Weil".

(Lyon Register, xxxiii, 47: 11 January 1939)

CROMARTY seems to have been a Royal Burgh by 1264 but was associated with the Earls of Ross from 1315 to 1475. After a period of obscurity, it was re-erected as a Royal Burgh by King James VI in 1593 but was disenfranchised by the Privy Council in 1672. In 1685, it was created a Burgh of Barony (being so ranked from 1681) in favour of Sir George Mackenzie of Tarbat, who became in 1702–3, 1st Earl of Cromartie.[10] It became a Parliamentary Burgh under the 1832 Reform Act.

The arms are a slightly-differenced version of the arms of Urquhart of Cromartie, which the Burgh had used on the seal it adopted in 1892. The mural coronet, which has been added, was shown above the shield on this old seal and by being coloured red appropriately recalls the "old red sandstone" of the district well known by the writings of Hugh Miller (1802–1856), a distinguished son of Cromarty. The motto is the Urquhart one. The fees for matriculation of the arms were met by public subscription on the occasion of the presentation of a Chain-of-Office to the Provost, a ceremony which was coupled with the unveiling of a memorial plaque to Sir Thomas Urquhart of Cromartie (c. 1611–1660), the celebrated translator of Rabelais, and the handing over of Hugh Miller's Cottage to the National Trust for Scotland.[11]

BURGH OF INVERGORDON

Per fess Azure and Purpure: on a fess wavy Argent, four lymphads Gules, under full sail Vert, pennons of the Fourth, between three boars' heads couped Or, armed Proper and langued Gules in chief, and in base two roses Or, along with a base dancetty of barry undy Argent and Vert.

The Shield being ensigned of a coronet befitting a Police Burgh (videlicet: Azure masoned Argent).

(Lyon Register, xlv, 110: 26 August 1964)

INVERGORDON grew up after its Castle, which originally dates from the thirteenth century, was purchased by Sir William Gordon of Embo in the 1700's. He planned a town and changed the name of the place from Inverbreakie to Invergordon. It became a Police Burgh in 1864.

The Burgh arms, which were registered to mark its centenary, show three golden boars' heads on their blue field to recall Sir William Gordon. The wavy lines are for the river and the sea and the red ships refer to the Burgh's long connection with the Royal Navy. The golden roses and the dancetty in base come from the arms of Sir Max Rayne, Chairman of Invergordon Distillers Limited at the time, who met the cost of the grant of arms and asked for some feature of his own arms to be included in those granted to the Burgh. The use of the colour purple is appropriate for a Highland town where in late summer and autumn, one is never far away from a heather-clad moor.

BURGH OF STORNOWAY

Tierced in pairle reversed: 1st, per fess wavy: in chief Or, in base undy Azure and Argent, a two-masted ship Proper, her jib and mainsail Argent, pennons Gules; 2nd, Azure, three fish naiant Or; 3rd, Gules, a castle of two towers upon a rock in base Or.

Below the Shield which is ensigned of a mural coronet proper to a Burgh of Barony (videlicet: Gules masoned Argent) is placed in an Escrol this *Motto* "God's Providence is our Inheritance".

(Lyon Register, xli, 80: 14 January 1958)

STORNOWAY, which was created a Burgh of Barony in 1607 in favour of Sir James Elphinstone, 1st Lord Balmerino, who as Lord Invernochty was President of the College of Justice, and others,[12] became a Police Burgh in 1863.

The arms retain the main features of the Burgh seal; the ship and the fish are for the fishing industry and the castle is the old Castle of Stornoway. The colours used recall the three main families who have owned the Island of Lewis, and thus in the first part we have the gold and blue of the MacLeods, in the second the blue and gold of the Mackenzies and in the third, the red and gold of the Mathesons of Achany also recalling that Sir James Matheson bought the Island in 1844 from the Mackenzies and erected the present Castle of Stornoway. The castle rock was coloured gold in accordance with a late nineteenth-century document in the Burgh archives. The motto comes from the most remarkable achievement (ten coats, 3, 3, 3 and one in base) registered in 1772 for The Incorporated Trades of Stornoway. The arms, which include the first example of a Burgh of Barony coronet, were matriculated to mark the 350th anniversary of the Burgh Charter.[13]

ROSS & CROMARTY COUNTY COUNCIL

Per fess and in base per pale: 1st, Gules, three lions rampant Argent; 2nd, Azure, a stag's head cabossed Or; 3rd, Or, a beacon Azure, masoned Argent and enflamed Gules.

Below the Shield which is ensigned with the coronet appropriate to a County Council, is placed in an Escrol this *Motto* "Dread God and Do Well".

(Lyon Register, xli, 65: 19 June 1957)

The County Council of THE COUNTY OF ROSS & CROMARTY bears arms which recall the five main clans or families connected with the County. The silver lions on their red field are for Ross and the ancient Earldom, the gold caber-feidh on blue for Mackenzie and the flaming beacon on gold for MacLeod of Lewis. The motto combines very effectively the Munro "Dread God" with the last part of the Urquhart "Meane Weil, Speak Weil and Doe Weil". The seal which the County Council adopted in 1890 was of the "landscape" type, showing a kilted Highlander with his cow and sheep standing by a sea loch with a herring fleet and mountains in the distance.

8

COUNTY OF INVERNESS

The County of INVERNESS has three Burghs, the Royal Burgh of Inverness, the County town, and the Police Burghs of Fort William and Kingussie.

ROYAL BURGH OF INVERNESS

Gules, Our Lord upon the Cross Proper.

Above the Shield is placed a suitable Helmet with a Mantling Gules doubled Or, and upon a Wreath of their proper Liveries is set for *Crest* a cornucopia Proper, and in an Escrol over the same this *Motto* "Concordia et Fidelitas", and upon a Compartment below the Shield are placed for *Supporters*, on the dexter side a dromedary and on the sinister side an elephant, both Proper.

(Lyon Register, xv, 74: 9 February 1900)

INVERNESS appears to have been made a Royal Burgh by King David I some time between 1130 and 1153.[1] The Burgh arms are based on the obverse of the oldest known Burgh seal of which a 1439 impression is on record.[2]

The oldest known representation of the Burgh arms appears on a panel painted in the reign of King Charles I, and now preserved in the Town House, which shows "Gules, a camel statant contournée Or" with two elephants as supporters and crest and motto as in the present arms. Nevertheless, in 1685, James Smith, Master Mason, Edinburgh, was instructed to carve the town's arms on the new Ness Bridge, such arms to show "Our Saviour on the Cross, supported by a dromedary on the dexter and an elephant on the sinister". It is not known why such a change was decided upon, but it is known that in the following year an effort was made to alter the instructions so that the carving would show "a dromedary supported by two elephants". By that time, however, Smith had completed his work (incidentally, showing the supporters as *statant*) and he naturally demanded an extra fee for a new carving. This the Town Council was unwilling to pay, and so the stone with the incorrect arms was allowed to remain.[3] When, some two hundred years later, it was decided to matriculate the arms, the crucifix design was so well-established that no amount of persuasion from Lord Lyon Balfour Paul or other authorities could persuade the Council to revert to the blazon shown on the Charles I panel. James Smith's carving, which had been preserved when the Ness Bridge was destroyed by flood in 1849, and had later been built into the Castle Wynd gable of the Town House, had come to be regarded as authoritative.

The meaning of the arms is not wholly clear. The representation of Our Lord on the Cross probably refers to the important side altar of The Holy Cross in the pre-Reformation parish church which was dedicated to the Virgin Mary, but the elephant and the camel have never been satisfactorily explained though they may refer to the considerable trade Inverness carried on with the East in medieval times; the legend that they were granted to the town by King William the Lion (1165–1214) is certainly groundless as the use of supporters in Scots heraldry cannot be traced further back than the end of the thirteenth century. The cornucopia crest is also probably symbolic of the Burgh's trade and prosperity, while the Latin motto—"Concord and Fidelity"—is a noble sentiment worthy of a Burgh which is capital of the Highlands. There is some evidence, not entirely conclusive, that the Town Council decided to matriculate its arms in 1680;[4] registration in 1900 was the result of the initiative of Dr. Charles Fraser-Mackintosh of Drummond, some time M.P. for Inverness-shire and a noted antiquarian, who also met the fees involved.[5] But much of the credit for this must go to Mr. P. J. Anderson, the distinguished Librarian of Aberdeen University and a native of Inverness, who had, for many years, pressed for the matriculation of the Town's arms. His articles about them in *Scottish Notes and Queries* (1891) and (1902) are of particular interest.

FORT WILLIAM, as Gordonsburgh, was created a Burgh of Barony in 1618 in favour of George, Lord Gordon and Badenoch, later 2nd Marquess of Huntly,[6] and later, during the reign of William and Mary, it was, as Maryburgh (according to Burt), created a Burgh of Barony in favour of the Governor of the Fort, originally built by General George Monk and named Inverlochy.[7] It became a Police Burgh in 1875.

BURGH OF FORT WILLIAM

Argent, two Lochaber axes, heads upwards and blades outwards, saltirewise, intertwined with a chaplet of oak; in chief an imperial crown, all Proper.

[Above the Shield is placed a Burghal coronet] and in an Escrol under the Shield this *Motto* "A D'h Aindeoin Co Theireadhe".

(Lyon Register, xxix, 25: 17 June 1930)

The arms are virtually a replica of the device on the Burgh seal and were matriculated in 1930 not only because of pressure from the Lyon Office but also in connection with the presentation of a Provost's Chain-of-Office by Sir Henry and Lady Fairfax-Lucy, the latter being the Superior of the Burgh.[8] The crossed Lochaber axes recall that Fort William is the capital of that district and also the Battle of Inverlochy fought near by in 1645. The oak branches are the plant badge of Clan Cameron in whose lands the Burgh is situated and the Crown recalls the two royal names it has borne. If, however, the axes are removed, the device bears a marked resemblance to the shoulder-belt plate of the Lochaber Fencibles, who were embodied in 1798 and disbanded in 1802, after service mostly in Ireland; their Colonel was Donald Cameron, 22nd of Lochiel.[9] The Gaelic motto means "Gainsay it who dare" and is the same as that of Macdonald of Clanranald; it is said to have been associated with the Lochaber Fencibles because one of their Captains was a Ronald Macdonald.[10]

KINGUSSIE was made a Burgh of Barony in 1464 in favour of Alexander, Lord of Badenoch and 1st Earl of Huntly.[11] It became a Police Burgh in 1867. The Burgh has not registered arms, but its seal, which was designed by Mr. Alexander Mackenzie, C.E., a well-known citizen,[12] shows a pine-tree on a wreath supported by two wild cats, with the name of the town above in Gaelic and below in English. In the device used by the Burgh on its notepaper and for other purposes, the wreath has been replaced by a mound. Around the edge of the seal is the Gaelic motto "Lean Gu Dluth Ri Cliu Do Shinnsear", a quotation from Ossian's *Fingal*, whose editor James Macpherson was born in Kingussie. In English, it means "Follow closely the fame of your forefathers".

F

INVERNESS COUNTY COUNCIL

Azure, in dexter chief a stag's head and in sinister chief a bull's head both erased, and in base a galley, sails furled, oars in action, and flagged, all Or.

And in an Escrol under the Shield this *Motto* "Air Son Math Na Siorrachd".

(Lyon Register, xxvii, 41: 10 June 1927)

The County Council of THE COUNTY OF INVERNESS bears arms which, though simple in themselves, allude to no less than eight clans or families closely connected with Scotland's largest County. The stag's head and the bull's head are respectively the crests of Fraser of Lovat and MacLeod of MacLeod, while the galley appears in the arms of the Mackintosh, Clan Chattan, and Macdonald of Macdonald as well as in those of the Chiefs of Macpherson, Mackinnon and Macneil. The blue field is in the principal colour of Fraser and MacLeod and the gold charges are in the principal metal of Mackintosh and Macdonald. The arms are based on the device on the seal adopted by the County in 1890 from which also comes the Gaelic motto—"For the good of the County"; this seal was designed by Mr. J. H. Gall, an Inverness architect.[13]

9

COUNTY OF NAIRN

The County of NAIRN has one Burgh, the Royal Burgh of Nairn, also the County town.

ROYAL BURGH OF NAIRN

Azure, the figure of Saint Ninian holding in his dexter hand an open book, his crosier in his sinister hand, and pendant from the wrist thereof a manacle all Proper.

Above the Shield is placed a mural coronet and in an Escrol below the same this *Motto* "Sole Valemus".

(Lyon Register, xxxiii, 71: 31 July 1939)

NAIRN dates as a Royal Burgh from about 1190 (King William the Lion) but from 1312 to 1475 came for a short time under the Earls of Moray and then under the Earls of Ross. It appears to have regained its Royal Burgh status in 1476 in the reign of King James III.[1]

The arms show St. Ninian, the patron saint of the Burgh, who appears on the oldest known Burgh seal of which a 1479 impression is on record.[2] The influence of Fearn Abbey, on the opposite side of the Moray Firth, whose first Abbot came from Whithorn, and which possessed some of St. Ninian's relics, led to his adoption as Nairn's patron saint. The blue field is for the sea, but blue is also a colour associated with St. Ninian. The Latin motto—"We prosper by the sun"—was chosen because of the town's very fine sunshine record and has been freely translated by its author, Mr. W. Ray, Headmaster of Alton Burn School, Nairn, as "The sun is our strong point at Nairn". The fees due on matriculation were raised by public subscription and included a substantial donation from the Edinburgh Nairnshire Association.[3]

NAIRN COUNTY COUNCIL

Or, on a chevron Gules, between two water budgets in chief and in base a stag's head cabossed Sable, three mullets Argent.

And in an Escrol under the Shield this *Motto* "Unite and be Mindful".

(Lyon Register, xxvii, 43: 21 July 1927)

The County Council of THE COUNTY OF NAIRN bears arms which include features from the arms of the four well-known local families whose crests had appeared on the seal adopted by the Council in 1890. The black water budgets are for Rose of Kilravock, the black stag's head for Campbell of Cawdor, the red chevron for Brodie of Brodie and the silver stars for Baillie of Lochloy. The motto combines those of Brodie of Brodie and Campbell of Cawdor.

10

COUNTY OF MORAY

The County of MORAY has six Burghs, the Royal Burghs of Elgin (the County town) and Forres, and the Police Burghs of Burghead, Grantown-on-Spey, Lossiemouth & Branderburgh, and Rothes.

ROYAL BURGH OF ELGIN

Argent, Sanctus Aegidius habited in his robes and mitred, holding in his dexter hand a pastoral staff and in his left hand a clasped book all Proper.

Supported by two angels Proper winged Or volant upwards, and the *Motto* "Sic Itur Ad Astra" upon a Compartment suitable to a Burgh Royal and for their Colours Red and White.

(Lyon Register, i, 461: 9 October 1678. Confirmed 28 November 1888)

SIC·ITUR·AD·ASTRA

ELGIN, the cathedral town of the old diocese of Moray, was created a Royal Burgh between 1130 and 1153 by King David I. From 1312 to 1455, it was alienated to the Earls of Moray, from whom it passed to the Douglas family. In 1457, King James II confirmed its status as a Royal Burgh.[1]

The arms resemble the device on the oldest known Burgh seal, believed to have been in use about 1296.[2] They show St. Aegidius or Giles, the patron saint of the Burgh, but the version now in use is a Victorian interpretation of the blazon. Although the Town Council duly matriculated its arms in 1678, no entry was then made in the Lyon Register. The omission was brought to light in 1888 when Mr. Lachlan

Mackintosh, author of *Elgin Past and Present* (1891), discovered in the town's archives a "Double of Discharge and Obleidgement to the Magistrates and Council of Elgin" which had been issued in 1678 by James Skene, merchant in Aberdeen, Lyon Depute in the lands north of the Water of Esk.[3] This document, which had no drawing on it, was accepted as conclusive proof of matriculation by Lord Lyon Burnett, who issued a suitable Interlocutor dated 28 November 1888. The confirmatory Extract included a drawing showing St. Giles as a mitred Abbot in rather Anglican-type vestments; though this was much criticised by local experts at the time, the Council decided to accept it.

St. Giles must be unique among Scottish Burghal patron saints as he was actually elected Provost of Elgin for a year in 1547. The angel supporters are unusual although similar ones were used by Cupar (q.v.) in the eighteenth century and were granted to Rutherglen (q.v.) in 1889. The Latin motto—"This is the way to immortality"—comes from Virgil, *Aeneid*, ix, 641, and seems to refer to the legend that at his death the saint was borne heavenwards by the angels.

Elgin is the earliest known example of the use of a Royal Burgh compartment and is the only case where the colours are specified; red and white seem to have been chosen as they are the old colours of Moray. In the official drawing, the saint's vestments are painted in these colours.

ROYAL BURGH OF FORRES

Argent, on a mount in base between two palm branches slipped Vert, the representation of Saint Lawrence, vested and holding in his dexter hand a book and leaning with his sinister upon a gridiron all Proper; in dexter chief an increscent and in sinister chief a mullet of six points, both Azure.

Above the Shield is placed a coronet suitable to a Royal Burgh and in an Escrol under the same this *Motto* "Jehovah Tu Mihi Deus Quid Deest".

(Lyon Register, xxix, 72: 28 April 1931)

FORRES also was made a Royal Burgh by King David I between 1130 and 1153, and like Elgin came under first the Earls of Moray and then the Douglas family between 1312 and 1455. It received a charter of re-erection from King James IV in 1496, though it may have had its privileges restored about thirty years earlier.[4]

The arms come straight from the Burgh seal, a very fine piece of engraving, of which a fifteenth-century impression is on record.[5] St. Lawrence, the patron saint of the town, is vested in his traditional red and gold (cf. Dunblane's "lowes of flame") and stands in a meadow between two palms of victory. In his right hand he holds the Gospels and he leans upon the gridiron on which he suffered martyrdom. The increscent and the star are probably the moon and the sun and apparently have been coloured blue so as to relate them, as Lord Bute suggested, to recall a traditional saying of St. Lawrence: "The darkness is no darkness to me, but the night is all as clear as the morning that shineth more and more unto the perfect day."[6] The Latin motto, thought to be based on Deuteronomy 2:7, can be translated, "Eternal One, Thou art with me, what can be lacking?"

BURGH OF BURGHEAD

Per fess Argent and Gules, a bar wreathed Or and Azure, between a beacon Sable in flames of the Second upon a hill Vert issuant from the bar, all in chief, and in base a bull passant contournée of the Third.

The Shield ensigned of a coronet proper to a Burgh.

(Lyon Register, xli, 72: 10 August 1957)

BURGHEAD, which became a Police Burgh in 1900, stands on a headland named "Promontorium Taurodunum" in Ptolemy's Map of the British Isles dated A.D. 150 and in 1809, during excavations for harbour improvements, over thirty ancient stone carvings of bulls were found there, as well as remains of what may have been a Mithraic temple.

The arms, which follow closely the device on the Burgh seal, have the old silver and red colours of Moray (as Elgin). The flaming beacon recalls the annual "Burning of the Clavie", an age-old tradition observed each year at Burghead on Old New Year's Eve; the wreath bar in the gold and blue of Orkney, the Norse borg founded there in 880 by Jarl Sigurd of Orkney; the bull, the name given by Ptolemy to the headland on which the town is built; and its gold colour, the Mithraic practice of sacrificing bulls to the sun. The red and gold colours in the base could also allude to the Sutherland family whose stronghold, Duffus Castle, is in the immediate vicinity and was once the home of Freskinus de Moravia, one of the famed warriors of King David I.

BURGH OF GRANTOWN-ON-SPEY

Gules, between three antique crowns Or, a fess undy of five Argent and Azure.

[Above the Shield is placed a Burghal coronet] and in an Escrol below the Shield this *Motto* "Stand Fast".

(Lyon Register, xxix, 26: 24 June 1930)

GRANTOWN-ON-SPEY stems from the Burgh of Barony of Cromdale created in 1609 in favour of John Grant, 5th of Freuchie, and later transferred to Grantown, which in 1694 was erected into a Burgh of Regality for Ludovick Grant, 8th of Freuchie, later Grant of Grant.[7] In 1799, Sir James Grant of Grant began the building of the modern town. Grantown became a Police Burgh in 1898.

The Burgh arms repeat the device on the Burgh seal, which was designed in 1898 by the Marquess of Bute.[8] The arms of Grant are differenced by a silver and blue wavy fess to denote the river Spey, on which the town stands. The motto is that of Grant.

LOSSIEMOUTH & BRANDERBURGH were united as a Police Burgh in 1890. The Burgh has not recorded arms. The device on its seal, which was designed in consultation with the Very Rev. Professor James Cooper of Glasgow University,[9] illustrates the legend of the town's patron saint, St. Gerardine, who is said to have walked along the shore at nights bearing a lantern to warn ships off the dangerous rocks; today the promontory by the harbour is still called Halliman (Holy Man) Point and the rocks to the West, Halliman Skerries. The seal bears the motto "Per noctem lux".

ROTHES, whose Castle was the stronghold of the Leslie Earls of Rothes until they moved to Fife in 1620, became a Police Burgh in 1884.

The arms are based on the Burgh seal and have been made a differenced version

BURGH OF ROTHES

Azure, on a bend Argent three buckles Gules.

[Above the Shield is placed a Burghal coronet.]

(Lyon Register, xxix, 62: 2 February 1931)

of those of Leslie, Earl of Rothes. The blue and silver colours of the field have been interchanged and the buckles made red—a Grant and an Ogilvy colour—since most of the lands in the district passed first into Grant hands and then to the Earls of Findlater, during the eighteenth century. The cost of matriculation was met from the Newlands Legacy.[10]

MORAY COUNTY COUNCIL

Quarterly: 1st and 4th, Azure, three mullets Argent; 2nd and 3rd, Argent, three cushions within a double tressure flory counterflory Gules.

And in an Escrol below the Shield this *Motto* "Sub Spe".

(Lyon Register, xxvii, 48: 20 July 1927)

The County Council of THE COUNTY OF MORAY bears arms which show the silver stars on a blue field for the ancient province of Moray and red cushions within the Royal tressure on a silver field since these were the original arms of Thomas Randolph, the famous Lieutenant of King Robert I, who was created Earl of Moray in 1312. The Latin motto—"In hope"—is that of the family of Dunbar which has long associations with the County and also provides a pleasing punning reference to the river Spey which flows through much of it. Writing in 1927, the Carrick Pursuivant, Mr. Thomas Innes of Learney (later Lord Lyon Innes), stated that, in his view, the combination of the Banner of Moray, with its three stars, and the arms of the celebrated Randolph "is the most beautiful and one of the most historic coats of arms belonging to any County in Scotland".[11] The seal adopted by the County Council in 1890 showed a garb on a shield supported by two lions, with a beehive above; it was chosen partly to recall the seal of the old Commissariat of Moray.

II

COUNTY OF BANFF

The County of BANFF has eleven Burghs, the Royal Burghs of Banff (the County town) and Cullen, and the Police Burghs of Aberchirder, Aberlour, Buckie, Dufftown, Findochty, Keith, Macduff, Portknockie and Portsoy.

ROYAL BURGH OF BANFF

Gules, the Virgin Mary with her Babe in her arms Or.

[And in an Escrol above the Shield] this *Motto* "Omne Bonum Dei Donum".

(Lyon Register, i, 462: 24 November 1673. Motto added 21 June 1897)

BANFF was probably created a Royal Burgh by King William the Lion between 1189 and 1198; there is a charter of confirmation from King Robert II in 1372.[1]

The arms have been in use for many centuries, the Virgin Mary being the patron saint of the Burgh. On the Mercat Cross (restored 1900) there is a carving of the Virgin and Child which may be as old as the sixteenth century and there is also on record a sixteenth-century impression of the Burgh seal bearing such a device. But the arms, as we know them, seem to have been the sacred bearings of the Burgh as there is also on record a 1408 impression of an older seal which bears a boar passant.[2] The Virgin and Child, in gold, stand on a red field; Lord Bute thinks that these colours may have been chosen for Edmondstone of that Ilk whose heiress married an Ogilvy of Findlater from whom the Lords Banff were descended.[3] The Latin motto—"Every good is the gift of God"—was added in 1897 in connection with the presentation of a Chain-of-Office to the Provost. It was suggested by Dr. William Cramond of Cullen, author of *The Town Annals of Banff* (1891–1893), and Mr. John Yeats, Secretary of the Banff Field Club.[4]

ROYAL BURGH OF CULLEN

Per fess Sable and Argent: in chief, on a sedilla Or, cushioned Gules, diapered Or, the Blessed Virgin enthroned Proper, habited Gules, mantled Azure, crowned Or, and holding in her dexter hand a sceptre surmounted of a fleur-de-lys Or, and in her sinister arm the Holy Child enhaloed, also Proper; in base a talbot passant of the First.

Below the Shield, which is ensigned with the Burghal coronet, is placed a Compartment suitable to a Burgh Royal, bearing this *Motto* "In Secula Seculorum", upon which are set for *Supporters* two talbots Sable.

(Lyon Register, xli, 37: 25 July 1956)

CULLEN seems to have been made a Royal Burgh between 1189 and 1198 by King William the Lion.[5] The old town which grew up around the parish church was virtually demolished about 1820 to make way for extensions to Cullen House and a new town was built nearer the sea.

The arms are a slight rearrangement of the device on the Burgh seal, of which a seventeenth-century impression is on record.[6] The black and silver colours allude to Sinclair of Deskford, the early adjacent family. The Virgin and Child recall that the thirteenth-century parish church is dedicated to St. Mary, while the gold and red colours in the faldstool refer to the Burgh's long-standing connection with the Ogilvy family, now represented by the Earl of Seafield, whose seat is Cullen House. The reason for the dog or whelp in base is not certain but it is commonly thought to be a play on the word "Cullen" as the Gaelic "cuilean" means "whelp". The Latin motto—"For ever and ever"—was a local choice. The arms were registered in connection with the presentation of a Chain-of-Office for the Provost by Mrs. Emily Wood in memory of her grandfather, William Duffus, Provost of Cullen, 1881–86.[7]

ABERCHIRDER, a planned town founded in 1746 by General Alexander Gordon of Auchintoul, became a Police Burgh in 1889. The Burgh has not registered arms; its seal bears a device showing a cross patée which could be blue in colour, but which has no special meaning.

ABERLOUR, or Charlestown of Aberlour, was created a Burgh of Barony in 1814 in favour of Charles Grant of Wester Elchies,[8] who laid out the town in 1812. It became a Police Burgh in 1894. The Burgh has not registered arms; its seal bears the arms of its founder, i.e. "Gules, a boar's head couped between three antique crowns Or; for Crest, an oak tree Proper", and also two war-cries of Clan Grant "Craig-a-Chronan" and "Stand Fast".

BURGH OF BUCKIE

Chequy Or and Azure, upon the sea in base undy and of the Second and Argent, a lymphad, sail set of the Last, rigged and pennon Gules; on a chief of the Second between two boars' heads couped of the First, armed Proper and langued of the Fourth, a pale Ermine charged with an escutcheon also of the Fourth.

Below the Shield which is ensigned of a coronet appropriate to a Burgh is placed in an Escrol this *Motto* "Mare Mater".

(Lyon Register, xxxviii, 92: 18 July 1951)

BUCKIE became a Police Burgh in 1888 as a union of the fishing districts of Nether Buckie (Buckpool) and Easter Buckie. In 1901, the hamlets of Gordonsburgh and Ianstown were added and in 1903, the village of Portessie.

The arms show a boat, coloured silver as on the Provost's Chain-of-Office, to denote the importance of the fishing industry to the Burgh. The gold and blue chequy comes from the arms of Gordon of Cluny, recalling the connection with that family and that it was John Gordon of Cluny who conceived and built the present harbour in the 1870's. The same colours are repeated in the chief, where they and the boars' heads recall Gordon of Buckie in the Enzie, and the red shield on the ermine pale, Hay of the Rannes, both prominent local families. The Latin motto—"The Sea our Mother"—is an abbreviated version of one suggested by Mr. W. W. Dickie and Mr. T. J. Laing, who were respectively the Rector and Latin Master of Buckie High School at the time.[9] A secondary version of the arms is shown in the Grant from the

Lyon Office and in this the boat is shown in the old "scaffie" form in which it appears in silver on the Provost's Chain; the Town Council specially asked that this should be embodied in the coat of arms in some way. The fees payable for registration of the arms were a gift to the Burgh from Dr. George Hendry, who was Provost at the time.[10]

BURGH OF DUFFTOWN

Vert, a fess dancetty Ermine between in chief a pale Or, charged of three pallets Sable, surmounted of a tower Argent, port and window Gules, all between, dexter a baton Or, charged of seven roundels Gules, and sinister a barley-ear Or, the barley grains alternately Or and Gules, both bendways all in chief; and in base an escallop Or.

And in an Escrol below the Shield which is surmounted of the coronet proper to a Police Burgh (viz. Azure, masoned Argent) is placed this *Motto* "Lippen".

(Lyon Register, xlv, 158: 10 June 1966)

DUFFTOWN, founded in 1817 by James Duff, 4th Earl Fife, as part of the development of his estates, became a Police Burgh in 1863.

The arms show the green field, ermine fess dancetty and golden shell from those of Duff of Braco, ancestor of the Duff Earls Fife. The red-studded baton is the heraldic symbol of the Bachuil Mor, the famous pastoral staff of St. Moluag of Lismore, who founded a Christian settlement in Mortlach Parish (in which Dufftown lies) in 566; the remains of the Bachuil Mor were returned to its Hereditary Keeper, Baron Alastair Livingstone of Bachuil by the Duke of Argyll in 1952, but for security reasons it has been kept in Inveraray Castle. The black and gold are for the Earls of Atholl who once owned Strathbogie and the Castle of Balvenie which is just outside the town. The tower is the Burgh Tower, a representation of which appears on the Burgh seal; it was paid for by public subscription and built in stages as the money became available. The barley grains represent the whisky industry of which Dufftown is a leading centre. The motto is an old Scots word meaning "Trust".

FINDOCHTY, which was founded in 1716 by a colony of fishermen from Fraserburgh, became a Police Burgh in 1915. The Burgh has not recorded arms; the device on its seal shows a "Zulu" fishing boat, the motto "Just and Honest" and the date 1915.

BURGH OF KEITH

Tierced in pairle reversed: 1st, Azure, semée of fleurs-de-lys Or, an inescutcheon parted per pale, the dexter bendy of six Or and Azure within a bordure Gules, sinister Argent, two open crowns in fess Gules and a martlet in base Azure, on a chief of the Last, a mullet of the field; 2nd, Argent, a lion passant guardant Gules, imperially crowned Or; 3rd, Vert, an escallop Or.

Above the Shield is placed a mural coronet befitting a Burgh and in an Escrol below the Shield is this *Motto* "Fortiter et Suaviter".

(Lyon Register, xxxiv, 80: 10 December 1943)

KEITH is an amalgamation of two communities, Old and New Keith united and enlarged in 1750 by James Ogilvy, 5th Earl of Findlater and 2nd Earl of Seafield, and Fife-Keith founded at the end of the eighteenth century by James Duff, 4th Earl Fife. The Burgh stands on land which was once part of the Regality of Keith and Strathisla which was held by the Cistercian Abbey of Kinloss by grant from King William the Lion (1165–1214). It became a Police Burgh in 1889.

The arms illustrate the three main features in the Burgh's history. In the first part, which recalls the ancient Kirkton of Keith and the tenure of the Lordship of Regality by Kinloss Abbey, are the arms of the Cistercian Order (France differenced Burgundy) but with the sinister half of the inescutcheon showing a star, two crowns, and a martlet from the Abbey seal. The Ogilvy crowned lion on its silver field in the second part is for Keith Town and its founder, the Earl of Findlater, and in the third part is the golden shell of Duff on its green field for Fife-Keith and Earl Fife. The Latin motto "Boldly and Gently" is that of George Ogilvy of Milton, who built the Castle of Milton Keith about 1480. The fees payable on registration of the arms were met from a gift to the Burgh by Sir John Kynoch, the local industrialist and benefactor.[11]

MACDUFF, originally called Doune, was erected into a Burgh of Barony in favour of John Stewart, 3rd Earl of Buchan in 1528. In 1783, it was re-erected as a Burgh of Barony in favour of James Duff, 2nd Earl Fife,[12] and became a Police Burgh in 1853.

The arms show the red lion rampant of Macduff, Earl of Fife, on its gold field surrounded by eight green shells to recall the Duff founder of the Burgh. The crest (a version of which was on the Burgh seal) is based on one of those used by Earl Fife and

BURGH OF MACDUFF

Or, a lion rampant Gules, armed and langued Azure, within an orle of eight escallop shells Vert.

Above the Shield is placed [a Burghal coronet thereon] a Helmet befitting their degree with a Mantling Gules doubled Or, and on a Wreath of their Liveries is set for *Crest* a knight armed at all points on a horse at full speed, in his dexter hand a sword erect, all Proper, his surcoat Argent, on his sinister arm a shield charged with the above-mentioned arms of the Burgh, the visor of his helmet shut, over which issuant from a wreath of his liveries with a mantling Gules doubled Or is set a demi-lion rampant also Gules imperially crowned Gold, the caparisons of the horse of the Second, furnishings of the Third.

(Lyon Register, xxix, 77: 26 May 1931)

now by the Duke of Fife; this was copied from an old seal of Duncan, Earl of Fife, of which there is a 1360 impression on record[13] and which is described by Sir George Mackenzie of Rosehaugh in his *Science of Heraldry* and in Nisbet's *System of Heraldry*.[14] The same seal was used in the design of the arms of Fife County Council (q.v.). In the case of Macduff, the knight's shield bears the Burgh arms. The fees payable on matriculation were met from the Duff House funds.[15] In the official drawing and in the Lyon Register, the shield is shown couché, being, apart from Falkirk, the only example of this among the Burgh arms.

PORTKNOCKIE, which was first settled by some fishermen from Old Cullen in 1677, became a Police Burgh in 1912.

The arms show in the chief the crowned Ogilvy lion on its silver field denoting that the present Superior of the Burgh is the Earl of Seafield. The red and silver colours are repeated in the ships and the fish, which recall the town's long connection with the fishing industry; the green is for the sea and the gold for the sands. The motto echoes the "Toujours" of the Ogilvys of Deskford and Cullen who formerly owned the lands around Portknockie; this family is now represented by the Earl of Seafield.

BURGH OF PORTKNOCKIE

Bendy wavy Vert and Or, two lymphads under full sail Gules, and in base as many fishes paleways naiant counternaiant Argent; on a chief of the Fourth a lion passant guardant of the Third, imperially crowned of the Second.

And in an Escrol below the Shield which is ensigned of a coronet proper to a Police Burgh (videlicet: Azure masoned Argent) this *Motto* "Aye Afloat".

(Lyon Register, xlv, 116: 10 September 1964)

BURGH OF PORTSOY

Argent, a lion rampant guardant Gules, armed and langued Azure, holding between his paws a plumb-rule erect Proper.

[Above the Shield is placed a Burghal coronet.]

(Lyon Register, xxix, 14: 23 April 1930)

PORTSOY was created a Burgh of Barony in 1550 in favour of Sir Walter Ogilvy of Boyne.[16] It became a Police Burgh in 1889.

The arms, which have the silver and red colours of Ogilvy, show a lion with a plumb-rule, which was the crest of Ogilvy, Earl of Findlater, who formerly owned the lands of Portsoy and whose castle, now a ruin, was built on a sea-girt rock, between Cullen and Portsoy, about 1455.

BANFF COUNTY COUNCIL

Quarterly: 1st, Argent, a lion passant guardant Gules, crowned with an antique crown Or; 2nd, Argent, two open crowns in fess Gules and a martlet in base Azure, on a chief of the Last, a mullet of the field; 3rd, paly of six Or and Sable, on a fess Argent two roses Gules, barbed of the Second and seeded of the First; 4th, Or, an open crown Gules, a chief chequy Argent and Azure; over all a pale engrailed, per pale Vert and Sable voided Argent, charged with two chevronels Gules between three boars' heads erased Azure, armed Or and langued Sable.

Below the Shield, which is ensigned of a coronet appropriate to a County Council, is placed in an Escrol this *Motto* "Spe et Spiritu".

(Lyon Register, lv, 13: 6 August 1971)
(Previously matriculated Lyon Register, xxxix, 60: 2 February 1953)

The County Council of THE COUNTY OF BANFF bears arms of a rather elaborate pattern which make references to the various districts of Banffshire and the historic families connected with it. In the first quarter, the Ogilvy lion with its Grant antique crown recalls the Earldom of Seafield and Lower Banffshire. The second quarter shows the same features from the Kinloss Abbey seal as in the arms of the Burgh of Keith, thus referring to the Lordship of the Regality of Strathisla and that region of the County. In the third quarter with its Atholl pallets and the red roses, reference is made to the Lordship of Balvenie which covered the whole County "from Boharm through Glenrinnes to Aberlour". The fourth quarter is for Stewart of Strathavon and thus for that district and for Glenlivet. In the centre, the three boars' heads and the chevronels are for Abercromby and come from the arms of Sir George W. Abercromby, who was Lord Lieutenant and Convener of the County in 1952. This part of the arms is edged with a black engrailed line to recall Sinclair of Deskford, and with a green line, also engrailed for artistic reasons, to allude to Duff of Braco and to the green in the 2nd quarter of the arms of Ogilvy of Banff. The Latin motto—"With Hope and Courage"—was added in 1971; it was suggested by Dr. J. A. Buchanan, the County Medical Officer of Health.[17] It not only reflects the confidence the County feels in its future but also makes a punning reference to the river Spey and the whisky distilling industry. The Spey flows through part of the County and upon its waters most of Banffshire's extensive whisky industry depends. The seal adopted by the County Council in 1890 shows the Virgin and Child.

I 2

COUNTY OF ABERDEEN

The County of ABERDEEN has ten Burghs, the Royal Burghs of Kintore and Inverurie, the Parliamentary Burgh of Peterhead and the Police Burghs of Ballater, Ellon, Fraserburgh, Huntly, Old Meldrum, Rosehearty and Turriff. The County town is the Royal Burgh of Aberdeen which, as mentioned on page 45 above, is itself a County of a City.

ROYAL BURGH OF KINTORE

Or, semée of torteaux, an oak tree eradicated of ten leaves Vert, fructed of two acorns in fess Azure.

The Shield ensigned of a coronet proper to a Burgh Royal and on a Compartment suitable to a Burgh Royal along with this *Motto* "Truth is Strength", are set for *Supporters* two bulls Sable, langued Gules, their horns Argent tipped Sable, each gorged with a chaplet of oak leaves Proper.

(Lyon Register, xli, 105: 23 January 1959)

KINTORE is reputed to have existed since the days of King Kenneth MacAlpin (843–858), and seems to have been made a Royal Burgh between 1187 and 1200 by King William the Lion. But its later history is far from clear until its re-erection as a Royal Burgh by King James IV in 1506–7.[1]

The arms are based on the device on the interesting and attractive old Burgh seal. Tradition has it that when King Kenneth was fighting in the district against the Danes, he was helped by the people of Kintore, who covered themselves with oak branches and drove their cattle towards the enemy. This legend is recalled by the coat of arms. The gold and red colours are those of the Royal House and also appear in the arms of the Keith family; the Forest of Kintore was granted to Robert de Keith, Great Marischal of Scotland, by King Robert I, and the Earldom of Kintore is held by another branch of the Keith family. The acorns have been made blue for artistic reasons and the supporting bulls are Kintore cattle which have black coats and white horns with black tips. The motto is an answer to the Keith motto "Veritas Vincit"—"Truth prevails"—and was suggested by the Rev. J. A. McFadden, who was Minister of Kintore in 1958. The arms were registered in connection with the acquisition of a Chain-of-Office for the Provost, and the Grant of arms was presented to the Burgh by Lord Lyon Innes on an official heraldic visitation to the Burgh, an event which was the first of its kind in Scotland for some two hundred years.

ROYAL BURGH OF INVERURIE

Azure, two castles in fess Or, masoned Sable, windows and portcullis Gules.

Above the Shield is placed a Burghal crown and in an Escrol under the same this *Motto* "Urbs in Rure".

(Lyon Register, xxix, 48: 7 November 1930)

INVERURIE, granted to David, Earl of Huntingdon, by his brother, King William the Lion, between 1178 and 1182, appears to have been a Burgh by 1195 and is counted as a Royal Burgh by Professor Pryde from that date. Subsequently, it seems to have passed to the Earldom of Mar and Lordship of Garioch until the sixteenth century. It was re-erected as a Royal Burgh in 1558 by Mary, Queen of Scots.[2]

The arms show two towers, called castles, as shown on the device on an old Burgh seal.[3] The town has long been recognised as the capital of the Garioch, a district which once had two castles for its protection, the Castle of Inverurie on the Bass and the Castle of Dunnideer, the capital of the Picts. These castles are said to have been also seats of the Mormaers of Mar and Buchan and later of the Regality courts of the Earls of Mar. The blue and gold colours are those of Mar, and the golden and red castles recall the Lords and Earls of Garioch. The Latin motto—"A town in the country"—is said to date from Roman times; there is ample evidence of Roman marching camps in the area, and according to legend some Roman legionaries on a progress through North Britain came upon a settlement on the site of the present Burgh and expressed surprise at finding a town in such remote rural country.

BURGH OF PETERHEAD

Vert, a chief paly of six Or and Gules.

Above the Shield is placed a coronet suitable to a Burgh, thereon a Helmet befitting its degree with a Mantling Vert doubled Or, and on a Wreath of the Liveries is set for *Crest* a roebuck's head erased Proper, attired Gules, and in an Escrol over the same this *Motto* "Veritas Vincit", and on a Compartment below the Shield are set for *Supporters* two roebucks Azure, attired and unguled Or.

(Lyon Register, xxviii, 66: 29 November 1929)

PETERHEAD was licensed as a Burgh of Barony as Peterhead or Keith Inch in 1587 in favour of George Keith, 5th Earl Marischal and Commendator of Deer.[4] It became a Parliamentary Burgh under the 1832 Reform Act.

The arms are a differenced version of those of the Keith Earls Marischal, whose achievement had been used by the Burgh for many years on its seal. The lower part of the shield has been coloured green (instead of the Keith silver) to denote that Peterhead is a seaport and the supporters have been coloured blue with golden antlers, as these are the colours of Buchan, which is the part of Aberdeenshire in which the Burgh is situated, and called roebucks instead of harts. The crest and motto are almost identical to those of the Earls Marischal; the only difference is that the roebucks' (harts') antlers have been coloured red instead of gold. Stonehaven, also a Burgh of the same Earl Marischal, has arms of a similar design.

BURGH OF BALLATER

Quarterly: 1st and 4th, Or, a lion rampant Gules, armed and langued Azure; 2nd, Argent, a fir tree issuant from a mount in base Vert; 3rd, per chevron indented Purpure and Argent, a key fessways, wards upwards Or, garnished Sable, and in base a fountain Azure and Or; surmounting the quarterings a roundel Sable charged of a quatrefoil Or.

And in an Escrol under the Shield, which is ensigned of a Burghal coronet Azure masoned Argent, is placed this *Motto* "Leal and Siccar".

(Lyon Register, xlv, 41: 15 January 1962)

BALLATER was founded in the later part of the eighteenth century by Francis Farquharson, 6th of Monaltrie (the Baron Ban), and a leading Jacobite, as a development associated with the neighbouring medicinal wells of Pannanich. It became a Police Burgh in 1891.

The arms are based on those of Farquharson of Invercauld, of which family Monaltrie was a cadet; these arms were used on the Burgh seal from 1892 to 1929. The Macduff lions in the 1st and 4th quarters and the fir tree in the 2nd quarter are taken straight from the Farquharson coat. The 3rd quarter refers to two important features in the town's history: the golden key on the purple field represents St. Nathalan, the famous Deeside missionary of the seventh century, to whom the nearby church of Tullich is dedicated, and whose legendary symbol is a key;[5] the fountain and the indented chevron are for the Wells of Pannanich which are in appearance rather like the latter. The roundel overall with its quatrefoil recalls the Baron Ban's English wife, Margaret Eyre of Hassop in Derbyshire. The motto, a Scots version of the Farquharson motto "Fide et Fortitudine", was suggested by Mr. J. Fenton Wyness of Aberdeen.

ELLON was the ancient capital of Buchan in Pictish times and in the Middle Ages, under the Comyn Earls of Buchan, the centre of the civil and judicial life of the province. It was created a Burgh of Barony in 1707 in favour of David Erskine, 9th Earl of Buchan,[6] but had previously been accorded Burgh status by the Archbishop of St. Andrews in 1564, and on this it bases its claim to be an "Honest Toun". It became a Police Burgh in 1893.

BURGH OF ELLON

Per fess Azure and Pean, three garbs Or.

Above the Shield is placed a coronet befitting a Burgh and in an Escrol below this *Motto* "Judge Nocht Quhill Ye End".

(Lyon Register, xxxi, 53: 27 May 1935)

The arms are based on the device on the Burgh seal which originally showed the three garbs of the ancient Earldom of Buchan. The three garbs are coloured gold and set on a field, partly blue, for Buchan, and partly pean because it was decided in 1929 to make the background of the seal resemble a stubble field, thus rendering it non-heraldic. The use of a fur can also be said to recall the past glories of the Moot Hill at Ellon, since furs are specially associated with robes of state, and to denote dignity. The motto comes partly from the "Judge Nocht" of the Erskine Earls of Buchan and from a translation of the French "Avise la Fin" used by the Kennedys of Kermucks, Hereditary Constables of Aberdeen, who were the Superiors of the Burgh for a time up to 1668. The Town Council was able to prove "ancient user" of armorial bearings by reference to arms having been displayed on the principal gable of its old Tolbooth, which was known to date from the seventeenth century and possibly earlier. The arms were registered in connection with the gift of a Provost's Chain-of-Office by Sir James G. McDonald, a noted son and benefactor of Ellon.

FRASERBURGH developed from a fishing village called Faithlie and was made a Burgh of Barony in favour of Alexander Fraser, 7th of Philorth, in 1546, and in 1601 raised to a Burgh of Regality in favour of his grandson, Sir Alexander Fraser, 8th of Philorth,[7] who was the real founder of the town and who was granted powers to found a University there; the institution only survived until 1605. Fraserburgh became a Police Burgh in 1840.

The arms, which closely resemble but are not identical to the Burgh seal in use in 1929, are based on those of Fraser of Philorth,[8] with the ostrich in the crest holding in its beak the key of the Burgh instead of a horse-shoe and with the accompaniment of

BURGH OF FRASERBURGH

Quarterly: 1st and 4th, Purpure, three fraises Argent; 2nd and 3rd, Gules, a lion rampant Argent, armed and langued Azure.

Above the Shield is set a coronet suitable to a Burgh, and thereon a Helmet befitting its degree with a Mantling Purpure doubled Argent, and on a Wreath of its Liveries is set for *Crest* an ostrich Proper holding in its beak a key Or, and on a Compartment below the Shield with this *Motto* "Deo Fidens", are set for *Supporters* two angels habited Proper, wings addorsed Or.

(Lyon Register, xxix, 6: 12 March 1930)

angel supporters similar to the cherubim used by Lord Saltoun, the direct descendant of Fraser of Philorth and the Superior of the Burgh. Some change of colours has also been made for difference: the field of the first and fourth quarters has been made purple instead of blue, and in the second and third quarters, the colours of the lion and the field have been interchanged. In addition, the Fraser motto "In God is All" appears in a Latin version. In its Petition to the Lyon Court, the Town Council was able to prove its title to ancient user of arms by reference to the differenced version of the Saltoun arms on its Mercat Cross and to an impression of the Burgh seal dated 1667.[9]

HUNTLY, the capital of Strathbogie, was erected into a Burgh of Barony in 1488 in favour of George, 2nd Earl of Huntly, and was in 1684 raised to a Burgh of Regality in favour of George, 1st Duke of Gordon.[10] It became a Police Burgh in 1834.

The arms show the gold and black paly of the Stewart Earls of Atholl who were Lords of Strathbogie in medieval times. The golden boars' heads on the blue field are for Gordon, since Huntly is the heart of the Gordon country, and the greyhound supporters recall the deerhounds used as his supporters by the Marquess of Huntly. The Latin motto—"By courage and sound judgement"—echoes the Marquess' motto

BURGH OF HUNTLY

Parted per saltire: paly of six Or and Sable and Azure, a boar's head couped of the First, armed Proper and langued Gules, in each flank.

Above the Shield is placed a mural coronet and in an Escrol over the same this *Motto* "Animo et Prudentia"; on a Compartment below the Shield are set for *Supporters* two greyhounds Proper collared Gules.

(Lyon Register, xxxii, 12: 23 April 1936)

"Animo non Astutia". The arms were registered in connection with the presentation of a Provost's Chain-of-Office by Mr. William Will, a distinguished son of Huntly, to commemorate the Provostship (1920–1935) of Mr. Alexander W. Christie.[11]

BURGH OF OLD MELDRUM

Per fess Argent and Or, a demi-otter in chief Sable, crowned of the Second, issuant from a fess of the Third embattled in chief wavy in base, and in base two boars' heads erased Gules, armed Proper and langued Azure, in pale between two pallets of the Third accompanied by as many crescents in the flanks of the Fourth.

Below the Shield, which is ensigned with the coronet proper to a Burgh, is placed in an Escrol this *Motto* "Bene Fac et Bene Dic".

(Lyon Register, xxxix, 130: 31 August 1954)

OLD MELDRUM was created a Burgh of Barony in 1671 in favour of Adam Urquhart, 2nd of Meldrum.[12] It became a Police Burgh in 1893.

The arms, which were registered in connection with the acquisition, by bene-faction, of a Provost's Chain-of-Office, refer to the three notable families, Meldrum,

Seton and Urquhart, who have successively been lairds of the lands of Meldrum. At the top of the shield there is the crowned black otter of Meldrum on its silver field; it issues from an embattled fess to represent the Burgh. Below, on the golden field used by both families, are two red crescents for Seton and two red boars' heads for Urquhart; they are accompanied by two black pallets taken from an ancient seal of Philip de Fedans, an ancestor of Meldrum of Meldrum. The Latin motto—"Do well and speak well"—was suggested by Dr. Margaret le Roux, who was Provost in 1954;[13] it was clearly inspired by the "Mean, speak and do well" used by the Urquharts of Meldrum.

BURGH OF ROSEHEARTY

Azure, two bears combatant Argent, muzzled Gules, supporting between their paws a cinquefoil of the Second.

[Above the Shield is placed a Burghal coronet] and in an Escrol beneath the Shield this *Motto* "Altius Ibunt Qui Ad Summa Nituntur".

(Lyon Register, xxviii, 59: 28 October 1929)

ROSEHEARTY was created a Burgh of Barony in 1681 in favour of Alexander Forbes, 2nd Lord Pitsligo.[14] It became a Police Burgh in 1892.

The arms recall those of Lord Pitsligo; the last holder of the title, a noted Jacobite, was attainted after the '45 when the barony became extinct. The blue and silver colours are those of Forbes and the cinquefoil recalls the fraises (another name for cinquefoils) which appeared in the second and third quarters of the Pitsligo arms. The bears were the Pitsligo supporters and bears' heads appeared in the 1st and 4th quarters of their arms. The Latin motto—"They who strive for the heights will go higher"—is one of those used by Forbes of Pitsligo. In the official drawing and in the Lyon Register the shield was given an eighteenth-century design with pointed ears, by special wish of the Town Council; the Pitsligo arms had been shown on a shield of this kind on the Burgh seal in use before 1929.

TURRIFF became a Burgh of Barony in favour of William Hay, 5th Earl of Erroll in 1511–12,[15] and a Police Burgh in 1858. The Burgh has not registered arms; the device on its seal shows the Mercat Cross and the Hay motto "Serva Jugum"— "Preserve the yoke".

ABERDEEN COUNTY COUNCIL

Quarterly: 1st, Azure, three garbs Or; 2nd, Azure, a bend between six cross-crosslets fitchée Or; 3rd, Or, a fess chequy Argent and Azure between three open crowns Gules; 4th, Azure, three boars' heads couped Or.

(Lyon Register, xii, 35: 11 July 1890)

The County Council of THE COUNTY OF ABERDEEN bears arms which represent the four main historic parts of the County. The 1st quarter has the arms of the ancient Earldom of Buchan, the 2nd those of the Earldom of Mar, the 3rd those of the Lordship of Garioch, and the 4th those of the Chief of Clan Gordon, for Strathbogie and the other Gordon lands in the County.

13

COUNTY OF KINCARDINE

The County of KINCARDINE has four Burghs, the Royal Burgh of Inverbervie and the Police Burghs of Banchory, Laurencekirk and Stonehaven (the County town).

ROYAL BURGH OF INVERBERVIE

Azure, a rose Argent, barbed and seeded Proper.

[Above the Shield is placed a Burghal coronet.]

(Lyon Register, xxviii, 38: 4 June 1929)

INVERBERVIE appears to have been a Royal Burgh since 1341;[1] local tradition has it that King David II conferred this status upon it "on the occasion of his being shipwrecked there and kindly received by the local inhabitants".

The arms are simple and come from a sixteenth- or seventeenth-century Burgh seal. The rose has a long connection with Inverbervie and legend says that King David II bestowed the emblem on the town either in compliment to his English Queen Joan or because the rose was one of his favourite flowers. There may, however, be a connection with the Carmelite Convent of Bervie which was dedicated to the Virgin Mary since a white rose is one of her symbols. The Burgh recorded arms so that they could be displayed on the War Memorial in King's College Chapel in Aberdeen University.[2]

BURGH OF BANCHORY

Argent, the figure of Saint Ternan, vested and mitred Proper, with his crosier in his dexter hand and a book and a bell in his sinister hand, standing between two holly leaves in chief Vert, and in base a hunting horn and an eagle displayed Sable, the former garnished Or and stringed Gules, the latter beaked and membered of the Last.

Above the Shield is placed a mural coronet of befitting degree and in an Escrol under the same this *Motto* "Banchory Bydand".

(Lyon Register, xxxiii, 52: 4 May 1939)

BANCHORY, formerly called Arbeadie, dates from the nineteenth century and is stated by Lord Bute[3] and the Lyon Office to have become a Burgh of Barony in 1805, but this is not confirmed by Professor Pryde. It became a Police Burgh in 1885.

The arms show St. Ternan, patron saint of the parish, who is thought to have founded a Christian settlement in the district in the fifth century and to have been buried there. Vested as a Bishop, he carries his crosier, a book—he is said to have possessed a copy of St. Matthew's Gospel encased in a gold and silver shrine—and his famous bell or "ronnecht", which is still in existence. The holly leaves and the hunting horn come from the arms of Burnett of Leys, the principal local family; the latter represents the famous fourteenth-century horn of Leys, still in the Burnetts' Castle of Crathes, and probably originally their badge of office as Royal Forester of Drum.[4] The eagle comes from the arms of Ramsay of Balmain, another neighbouring family which is related to the Burnetts. The motto has obvious Gordon connections; the Dukes of Gordon owned the estates of Durris close to Banchory in the eighteenth and nineteenth centuries. The fees payable on registration of the arms were paid from a gift to the Burgh by Mr. James Mortimer Burnett, who was Provost of Banchory, 1928–1945.[5]

LAURENCEKIRK was created a Burgh of Barony in favour of Francis Garden, Lord Gardenstone, a Senator of the College of Justice, in 1779.[6] It became a Police Burgh in 1889. The Burgh has not recorded arms: the device on its seal shows the Tower of Johnston which stands on the Hill of Garvock overlooking the town, and the motto "In Justice Secure".

BURGH OF STONEHAVEN

Per fess: in chief paly of six Or and Gules, in base Azure.

Above the Shield is placed a coronet suitable to a Burgh and thereon a Helmet suitable to their degree with a Mantling Gules doubled Or, and thereon is set for *Crest* issuing from a marquess's coronet Gules, a roebuck's head Or, attired Gules, and in an Escrol over the same this *Motto* "Veritas Vincit" and on a Compartment below the Shield are set for *Supporters* two stags Or, attired Gules.

(Lyon Register, xxviii, 57: 18 October 1929)

STONEHAVEN was made a Burgh of Barony in 1587 in favour of George Keith, 5th Earl Marischal of Scotland.[7] It became a Police Burgh in 1889.

The arms are based on those of the founder of the Burgh, a version of which was carved on the Mercat Cross. According to the Petition submitted to the Lyon Court: "The shield is similar to but quite distinct from the arms of the Earl Marischal which show 'Argent, a chief Gules, 3 pallets Or'. The shield on the cross of Stonehaven is at most 'per fess, in chief 3 pallets' and in order that there should be no confusion with the Keith arms, the fess line is well below the fess point." It was, however, known that the arms on the Cross had been recut in the nineteenth century and thus by themselves did not constitute evidence of "ancient user". But then a seal impression was found, showing virtually the same coat of arms and of a date before 1672, and so Stonehaven was not only accepted as "ancient user" but was also allowed to keep the Marquess' coronet in the crest and the supporters. In differencing the arms from those of the Earl Marischal, the lower half of the shield has been made blue to denote that Stonehaven is a seaport while the harts for the crest and supporters have been described as roebucks and rendered in red and gold Keith colours. The Earl Marischal's Latin motto—"Truth Prevails"—has been retained. Peterhead, also a Burgh of the same Earl Marischal, has a similar coat of arms.

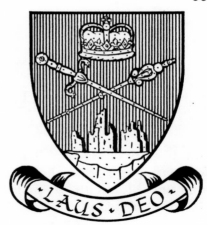

KINCARDINE COUNTY COUNCIL

Gules, the Sword of State and Sceptre of Scotland in saltire, in chief the Crown of Scotland, and in base on a rock a ruined castle all Or.

And in an Escrol below the Shield this *Motto* "Laus Deo".

(Lyon Register, xxvii, 40: 6 June 1927)

The County Council of THE COUNTY OF KINCARDINE bears arms, based on the device on the seal adopted by the Council in 1890, which recall the preservation of the Scottish Regalia after the Coronation of King Charles II at Scone in 1651. Sent for safety to the Earl Marischal's stronghold of Dunnottar Castle, near Stonehaven, they were saved from the besieging Cromwellian troops by the initiative of George Ogilvy of Barras, Governor of the Castle, and Mr. James Grainger, Minister of the adjacent Parish of Kinneff.[8] The crown, sword and sceptre were smuggled out of the Castle and buried under the floor of Kinneff church, where they remained until the Restoration in 1660. The Honours of Scotland thus occupy the centre of the shield, the red and gold colours being those of the Scottish Royal House, and those used in the augmentation granted to John Keith, 1st Earl of Kintore, for his part in saving the Regalia. They are also colours associated with the Keith Earls Marischal whose Castle of Dunnottar appears at the base. The Latin motto—"Praise to God"—is that of the Viscount of Arbuthnott; the 14th Viscount was Lord Lieutenant of the County in 1927.

14

COUNTY OF ANGUS

The County of ANGUS has seven Burghs, the Royal Burghs of Montrose, Brechin, Arbroath and Forfar (the County town), and the Police Burghs of Carnoustie, Kirriemuir and Monifieth. As mentioned on page 45 above, the Royal Burgh of Dundee is a County of a City.

ROYAL BURGH OF MONTROSE

Argent, a rose Gules.

Above the Shield is placed a coronet suitable to a Burgh, thereon a Helmet of befitting degree, with a Mantling Gules doubled Argent, and over a Wreath of the Liveries is set for *Crest* a hand issuing from a cloud and reaching down a garland of roses Proper, and in an Escrol over the same this *Motto* "Mare Ditat Rosa Decorat": and along with a Compartment suitable to a Burgh Royal are placed for *Supporters* two mermaids arising from the sea Proper.

And for a reverse of their seal, Gules, Saint Peter on the cross Proper, with the keys hanging at his girdle Or; which is also to be borne for the sacred flag of the said Royal Burgh and may be impaled with the principal Arms, Argent, a rose Gules.

(Lyon Register, xxxix, 53: 23 January 1953)
(Previously matriculated Lyon Register, i, 457: 16 December 1694)

MONTROSE is thought to have been made a Royal Burgh between 1124 and 1153 by King David I.[1]

Its arms were originally matriculated on 16 December 1694 (Lyon Register, i, 457) and were re-matriculated in 1953 with the addition of a coronet and a Royal Burgh compartment; this followed the discovery by the Town Clerk, Mr. R. O. Barrowman, of documents dated 1553 and 1768, both of which bore seals showing devices very similar to the arms.[2] The rose has nothing whatever to do with the name Montrose which means "mossy headland" (cf. Fortrose) but could be an attempt at canting heraldry. There are on record impressions of the Burgh seal dated 1296 and 1357,[3] and this would seem to strengthen Porteous' suggestion that the rose may be connected with the Dominican priory founded at Montrose in 1230 and dedicated to the Virgin Mary;[4] but the silver and red colours are not easy to explain. The crest of the garland of roses may recall the legend that St. Dominic introduced the rosary after being shown such a garland by the Virgin Mary. The mermaid supporters symbolise the Burgh's situation by the sea. The Latin motto—"The sea enriches, the rose adorns"—aptly sums up the achievement. Montrose is one of the four Royal Burghs with a second coat of arms (or sacred bearings) registered in the Lyon Office; this is similar to one shown on a seal impression dated 1357.[5] But the connection of St. Peter with Montrose is obscure, and even the expert hagiologist Lord Bute could not explain it.[6]

ROYAL BURGH OF BRECHIN

Or, three piles conjoined in base Gules.

[Above the Shield is placed a Burghal coronet.]

(Lyon Register, xxviii, 54: 1 October 1929)

BRECHIN, the cathedral town of the old diocese of that name, is dated as a Burgh of the Bishops of Brechin between 1165 and 1171. Professor Duncan states that it gradually acquired Royal Burgh status and this was ratified by Parliament in 1641 in the reign of King Charles I.[7]

The arms, which make a very beautiful yet simple heraldic composition, appear as part of the device on an old Burgh seal of which a fifteenth-century impression is on

H

record.[8] The Cathedral of Brechin, whose origins go back to the reign of King David I (1124–1153), is dedicated to the Holy Trinity and it seems tenable that the three piles conjoined do represent the Trinity. The field has been coloured gold, as similar arms with a silver field were used by the feudal Lords of Brechin, the first of whom was King David's grandson, David, Earl of Huntingdon, and have since passed into the Wishart family.

ROYAL BURGH OF ARBROATH

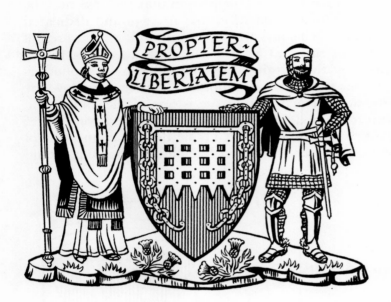

Gules, a portcullis with chains pendant Or.

And in an Escrol over the same this *Motto* "Propter Libertatem", and the following *Supporters* to be placed in a Compartment below the Shield, viz. dexter, Saint Thomas à Becket in his archiepiscopal robes all Proper; sinister, a baron of Scotland, armed cap-à-pie, holding in his exterior hand the letter from the Convention of the Scottish Estates, held at Arbroath in the year 1320, addressed to Pope John XXII, all Proper.

(Lyon Register, xv, 73: 12 January 1900)

ARBROATH became a Burgh dependent on the Abbey of Arbroath between 1178 and 1182 and was accorded the status of a Royal Burgh by King James VI in 1599.[9]

The arms are based on the old Burgh seal. The portcullis which "has for centuries been the heraldic emblem of Arbroath" is said to represent the portcullis of the pend or great gateway close to the west end of Arbroath Abbey which was founded in 1178 by King William the Lion in memory of his martyred friend, Archbishop Thomas à Becket of Canterbury.[10] Because of this connection between the town and the King, the Royal red and gold colours have been used. The supporters are St. Thomas à Becket, a representation of whose martyrdom was apparently used as the sacred bearings of the Burgh, since there is on record a thirteenth-century impression of a seal bearing such a device,[11] and a Scottish Baron holding a copy of the Arbroath Declaration of Scottish Independence (1320). The Latin motto—"For Freedom"—comes from the famous passage in the Declaration which states: "It is not for glory, riches or honour that we fight, but for freedom alone, which no worthy man will lay down save with his life." The arms were matriculated to mark the tercentenary of the Burgh, in honour of which a Provost's Chain-of-Office was presented by the then Town Clerk, Mr. W. K. Macdonald.[12]

ROYAL BURGH OF FORFAR

Azure, a castle Argent, having two tiers of battlements, triple-towered and with two flanking towers, masoned Sable, three windows and port Gules, the tower caps of the Last with balls Or, the central tower having a flag displayed Argent, charged with a lion passant Gules, imperially crowned Proper; on a chief wavy Or, a Scots fir eradicated Proper between a bull's head on the dexter and a stag's head on the sinister, both cabossed Sable, the former armed and the latter attired Gules.

Below the Shield which is ensigned with a Burghal coronet, is placed upon a Compartment suitable to a Burgh Royal this *Motto* "Ut Quocunque Paratus".

(Lyon Register, xxxvi, 138: 31 May 1948)

FORFAR appears to have been a Royal Burgh by some time between 1153 and 1162 and thus probably so created by King Malcolm IV.[13]

The arms are based on those traditionally used and their related seals. The blue and gold colours are those of Gilbert d'Umfraville who acquired the Earldom of Angus by marriage in the thirteenth century. The castle is the old Castle of Forfar, shown triple-towered as on the seals used in the eighteenth and nineteenth centuries (earlier seals had shown the castle in different forms) and from the central tower flies the banner of Gillibride, Earl of Angus about 1135. In the chief, the fir tree recalls the great Forest of Platane which lay to the north of the town and the heads of the bull and the stag, the animals who inhabited it; these animals may also refer to the leather trade of Forfar and its famous sutors (shoemakers) and the bull's head may further allude to the close link between the town and the Earls of Airlie, whose arms have bulls as supporters. The Latin motto—"Ready for any event"—is set on a Royal Burgh compartment; this was the first specific example of such a compartment since the one granted to Elgin in 1678. For various reasons, the Petition took a long time to be approved, but in the end Forfar established its claim to "ancient user" of its arms. There is an interesting monograph on *The Coat of Arms and the Seals of the Royal Burgh of Forfar* by William S. McCulloch (1965).

BURGH OF CARNOUSTIE

Vert, a pale Argent charged with a pallet Azure both wavy between four plates paleways, two in dexter base and as many in sinister chief, all between two flanches Or charged with three bars wavy of the Third, all surmounted of a bend Sable charged with three mascles of the Second; on a chief of the Last a boar's head couped Gules, armed Proper and langued Azure, between two martlets volant of the Fifth.

Below the Shield which is ensigned of a coronet appropriate to a Burgh is placed in an Escrol this *Motto* "Stay the Course".

(Lyon Register, xxxix, 50: 14 January 1953)

CARNOUSTIE is situated partly in Barry parish on land which formerly belonged to Miss Cecilia Kinloch of Kinloch and partly in Panbride parish on land which formed part of the estates of the Earls of Panmure and Dalhousie. It became a Police Burgh in 1889.

The arms follow a rather elaborate pattern and were the subject of some discussion in which Canon W. H. de Voil, Rector of Holy Rood Episcopal Church, Carnoustie, and a member of the Town Council, took a leading part.[14] The mascles recall the Kinloch connection and the black and silver colours on the bend, the link with the Dalhousie family. The barry wavy is for Barry parish, the blue and gold (the Kinloch livery colours) being for the sea and the sands. The green field represents the famous Carnoustie golf courses and the silver roundels, golf balls. The pale wavy is for the Lochty Burn which separates the parishes of Barry and Panbride. In the chief, the boar's head recalls Kinloch and also Elphinstone, Lord and Abbot of Balmerino, who once owned some of Barry parish. The black martlets recall the crows on the device (called the Craws' Nestie) on the Burgh seal, the oyster catcher of St. Bride, and thus Panbride parish, and the Danish raven in allusion to King Malcolm II's defeat of the Danes under Camus at the Battle of Barry in about 1010. The motto is a most appropriate one for a well-known golfing centre and was suggested by Canon de Voil.[15]

KIRRIEMUIR was created a Burgh of Barony in favour of George Douglas, 4th Earl of Angus, in 1458–59 and was, according to the Lyon Office, raised to a Burgh of Barony and Regality in 1510 in favour of his grandson, Archibald Lord Douglas, later 6th Earl of Angus. Raised to a Burgh of Regality in favour of James, 2nd Marquess of Douglas and 12th Earl of Angus in 1670,[16] it became a Police Burgh in 1834.

BURGH OF KIRRIEMUIR

Argent, a man's heart Gules, ensigned with an imperial crown Proper; on a chief Vert, three mullets of the field.

[Above the Shield is placed a Burghal coronet] and in an Escrol under the Shield this *Motto* "Jamais Arrière".

(Lyon Register, xxix, 13: 16 April 1930)

The arms are those of Douglas, and were used on the Burgh seal adopted in 1892 by permission of the 12th Earl of Home, who had succeeded to the estates of Douglas and Angus through his grandmother, the daughter of Lord Douglas (1748–1827), who successfully established his claim to the Douglas estates and the headship of the Douglas family in the very celebrated legal proceedings held between 1762 and 1769 and known as "The Douglas Cause". In token of the Burgh's connections with the Earl of Home, the chief has been given a field of green, the Home colour. The French motto—"Never Behind"—is the Douglas one. The Town Council was able to prove "ancient user" of armorial bearings as the Douglas coat of arms had been carved on the old Town House or Tolbooth associated with the baronial jurisdiction over the Burgh.

BURGH OF MONIFIETH

Barry dancetty of six Argent and Vert, a stag trippant Or, attired Gules.

Below the Shield which is ensigned of a Burghal coronet is placed in an Escrol this *Motto* "Vis Unita Fortior".

(Lyon Register, xli, 53: 8 November 1956)

MONIFIETH, which is said to have been a favourite hunting seat of King David I (1124–1153), became a Police Burgh in 1895.

The arms follow the design of the Burgh seal. The stag denotes the old hunting forest and the green barry dancetty gives the impression of a background of hills; thus together, they recall that Monifieth may mean "hill of the deer". The stag's antlers have been coloured red in reference to Maule, Earl of Panmure, who was the principal landowner in the district. The Latin motto—"United strength is stronger" —comes from the Burgh seal.

ANGUS COUNTY COUNCIL

Quarterly: 1st, Argent, a lion passant guardant Gules, imperially crowned Or; 2nd, Gules, a cinquefoil Or; 3rd, Or, a fess chequy Azure and Argent, surmounted of a bend Gules charged with three buckles of the field; 4th, Argent, a man's heart Gules, imperially crowned Or, on a chief Azure three mullets of the field.

And in an Escrol below the Shield this *Motto* "Lippen on Angus".

(Lyon Register, xxvii, 34: 4 May 1927)

The County Council of THE COUNTY OF ANGUS bears arms which recall the four families who have held the Earldom of Angus. These are Gillibride (from c. 1135), d'Umfraville (from c. 1240), Stuart of Bonkyll (from 1329) and Douglas (from 1389). The coats of arms chosen to represent the first two of these families are those associated with their Earldoms by Lord Lyon Balfour Paul in his work *The Scots Peerage* (1904–1914) and not their own family coats.[17] The Scots motto which means "Trust in Angus" was suggested by Mrs. Lindsay Carnegie of Anniston, Arbroath.[18] The Seal, adopted by the County Council in 1890, had a device showing the arms of the towns of Forfar, Arbroath, Brechin and Dundee.

15

COUNTY OF PERTH

The County of PERTH has twelve Burghs, the Royal Burghs of Perth (the County town) and Auchterarder, and the Police Burghs of Aberfeldy, Abernethy, Alyth, Blairgowrie & Rattray, Callander, Coupar Angus, Crieff, Doune, Dunblane and Pitlochry.

ROYAL BURGH OF PERTH

Gules, a holy lamb passant reguardant staff and cross Argent, with the banner of Saint Andrew Proper, all within a double tressure [flowered and] counterflowered of the Second, the escutcheon being surmounted on the breast of an eagle with two necks displayed Or.

The *Motto* in an Escrol "Pro Rege Lege et Grege".

(Lyon Register, i, 455: c. 1673)

PERTH, a City and former Capital of Scotland, is a Royal Burgh of King David I dating from between 1124 and 1127.[1] It takes precedence over all other Scottish Burghs save Edinburgh.

The arms use the red and silver colours of St. John the Baptist, the patron saint of "the Fair City of Perth". They show the Holy Lamb who is always associated with the Saint (John 1:29) carrying a St. Andrew's flag (cf. Ayr). The arms are set within a Royal tressure, a special mark of Royal favour, probably because Perth was for a time before 1437 the Capital of Scotland. There is on record a 1378 impression of a Burgh seal which shows the arms, with the tressure, virtually as used today.[2] The shield has for bearer a double-headed eagle, which is thought to be a Roman eagle (cf. Lanark) and to recall that there was once an important Roman settlement called "Bertha" in the vicinity of Perth. The Latin motto—"For King, law and people"— is mentioned by R. S. Fittis, a local historian, as being a favourite one of William the Silent, Prince of Orange (1533–1584), and he suggests that, as there were many trading links between Perth and the Netherlands, it may have been adopted by the town in the latter part of the sixteenth century, in admiration of the struggle the Prince was waging to free his country from Spanish occupation.[3]

ROYAL BURGH OF AUCHTERARDER

Chevronny Or and Gules, a falcon displayed Proper, armed beaked and membered Azure, langued of the Second, belled and jessed Argent.

Below the Shield, which is ensigned with a Burghal coronet, on a Compartment along with this *Motto* "Non Potest Civitas Abscondi Supra Montem Posita", are set for *Supporters* two falcons Proper, armed beaked and membered Azure, langued Gules, belled and jessed Argent.

(Lyon Register, xxxvii, 150: 14 March 1950)

AUCHTERARDER appears to have been a Royal Burgh by 1246 (reign of King Alexander II) and in the thirteenth century was the head Burgh of the Sheriffdom of Strathearn. But by 1600 it had declined in status and it does not appear among the list of Royal Burghs mentioned in the 1707 Act of Union. It became a Police Burgh in 1894 and was reinstated as a Royal Burgh on the Roll of the Convention of Royal Burghs in 1951.[4]

The arms show red and gold chevronels to recall the ancient Earldom of Strathearn; similar chevronels had appeared on the nineteenth-century Burgh seal whose use was discontinued in 1929. The falcon comes from an old Burgh seal of which a fourteenth-century impression is on record.[5] The falcon supporters were chosen for the same reason, and it is noteworthy that the old Castle of Auchterarder is said to have been built as a hunting seat by King Malcolm III (1057–1093). The Latin motto—

"A city that is set on a hill cannot be hid"—was on the old Burgh seal and comes from the Sermon on the Mount (Matthew 5:14) and this is most appropriate for a town whose Gaelic name means "the upper high land".

ABERFELDY became a Police Burgh in 1887. The Burgh has not recorded arms; its seal bears a device showing the local Black Watch memorial with General Wade's bridge over the River Tay and the old Ferry of Aberfeldy in the background. There is a Gaelic motto "S Dluth Tric Bat Abairpheallaidh" which means "Swift and often goes the boat of Aberfeldy".

ABERNETHY is said to have been the capital of the ancient Pictish Kings and to have been founded in A.D. 458 by King Nechtan II. Created a Burgh of Barony in 1458–59 in favour of George Douglas, 4th Earl of Angus,[6] it became a Police Burgh in 1877. The Burgh has not recorded arms: its seal bears a representation of the famous Round Tower of Abernethy which dates probably from the tenth century.

BURGH OF ALYTH

Vert, on a cross quadrate Argent, a lion rampant guardant Gules, crowned with an open crown Or.

Above the Shield is placed a coronet appropriate to a Burgh of Barony (that is Gules masoned Argent) and in an Escrol below the Shield this *Motto* "A Licht Abune".

(Lyon Register, xlv, 50: 21 May 1962)
(Previously matriculated with Burghal coronet and without Motto, Lyon Register, xxxvii, 23: 15 October 1948)

ALYTH, by tradition, was created a burgh of Barony in 1488 and is referred to as such in the 1623 retour of James Ogilvy of Clova.[7] It became a Police Burgh in 1834.

The arms, originally registered in 1948, are based on the old seal of the Burgh. The green field is for agriculture, Alyth being in good farming country, and the silver cross quadrate is for the Mercat Cross which was shown on the seal. The fact that the Cross bore the initials JEA (James, 2nd Earl of Airlie) is denoted by the Ogilvy crowned lion on its silver field. The arms were re-matriculated in 1962 so that a motto could be added. "A Licht Abune" was suggested by Dr. W. S. Haldane, a member of the Town Council,[8] because (i) Alicht was the medieval spelling of Alyth; (ii) Alyth stands in the Grampian foothills and is seen as a light above to travellers in Strathmore; (iii) the words have educational and religious meanings. At the same time, the Burghal coronet granted in 1948 was altered to the red and silver coronet of a Burgh of Barony.

BURGH OF BLAIRGOWRIE & RATTRAY

Per pale embattled: dexter, Or, three bars wavy Gules, each charged with an escallop Or, a chief enarched Argent masoned Sable; sinister, Azure, on a fess wavy between three cross-crosslets fitchée Or, a bar wavy Gules.

Which Shield is ensigned with a coronet appropriate to a Burgh.

(Lyon Register, xxxviii, 83: 9 June 1951)

BLAIRGOWRIE & RATTRAY were united as one Burgh in 1929. Blairgowrie was made a Burgh of Barony in favour of George Drummond of Blair in 1634[9] and became a Police Burgh in 1833. Rattray, on the opposite side of the river Ericht, became a Police Burgh in 1873.

The arms signify the fusion of the two Burghs into one by the division by embattled pale. The dexter side, for Blairgowrie, shows a heraldic rendering of the Brig o' Blair, which spans the Ericht between the two towns, with the arms of Drummond of Blair (conveniently wavy and thus like a river) below. On the sinister side, for Rattray, are the Rattray family arms charged with a Drummond golden and red fess wavy recalling that Ann Drummond of Maderty married a seventeenth-century Laird of Craighall-Rattray. The Brig o' Blair appeared on the old Blairgowrie seal and the Rattray arms on the old Rattray seal, both of which went out of use in 1929.

BURGH OF CALLANDER

Argent, a cinquefoil Gules in dexter fess, a dexter hand in base Gules holding a fiery cross in bend sinister Sable inflamed of the Second; and on a chief indented of the Third (showing four serrations of the field) three billets Or.

Below the Shield which is ensigned of a coronet suitable to a Police Burgh (videlicet: Azure masoned Argent) is placed in an Escrol this *Motto* "Beauty is Strength".

(Lyon Register, xlv, 140: 21 September 1965)

CALLANDER stands mostly on the site of the ancient Burgh of Callander or Callendar, the lands of which were granted by King James VI to Alexander, 7th Lord Livingstone, later Earl of Linlithgow, Lord Livingston and Callendar, in 1594. It became a Police Burgh in 1866.

The arms show in the chief, gold billets on a black field from the arms of the family of Callendar of that Ilk whose lands passed into the Livingstone family. The indented under-edge of the chief alludes to Ben Ledi and the other mountain peaks (often snow-capped) in the vicinity of the town. The red cinquefoil on the silver field comes from the Livingstone arms, and the fiery cross, which comes from the Burgh seal, recalls that Callander is set in the heart of the scenes which Sir Walter Scott made famous in his poem "The Lady of the Lake". The motto was a local choice and was selected in preference to the Scott quotation "Ben Ledi saw the Cross of Fire" which was on the Burgh seal.

BURGH OF COUPAR ANGUS

Azure, a dexter arm Proper, clad in a manche Argent, issuant from the sinister and grasping a pastoral staff in pale, between a garb in sinister chief and two fleurs-de-lys in base all Or.

[Above the Shield is placed a Burghal coronet.]

(Lyon Register, xxxviii, 116: 14 November 1951)

COUPAR ANGUS was created a Burgh of Barony in favour of James Elphinstone, Lord Coupar, in 1607.[10] It became a Police Burgh in 1852.

The arms repeat the device on the Burgh seal. This consists of a representation of the seal of Andrew de Buchan,[11] in 1292 Abbot of the Cistercian Abbey of St. Mary at Coupar Angus (founded by King Malcolm IV in 1164), with the addition of a garb to denote the well-known agricultural interests of Strathmore, of which the Burgh is the centre. Appropriately, three garbs appear in the arms of the ancient Earldom of Buchan, whose blue and gold livery colours have been used.

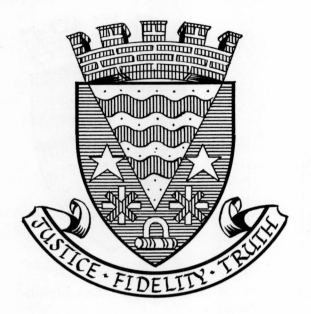

BURGH OF CRIEFF

Azure, on a pile Or three bars wavy Gules, accompanied by two mullets in fess and a fetterlock in base Argent, and in the dexter and sinister of the nombril point two crosses couped of the Last, each surmounted by a saltire couped of the Third.

Below the Shield which is ensigned of a coronet proper to a Burgh of Barony (videlicet: Gules masoned Argent) is placed in an Escrol this *Motto* "Justice Fidelity Truth".

(Lyon Register, xlv, 23: 28 July 1961)

CRIEFF has for centuries been recognised (as successor to Auchterarder) as the capital of Strathearn. It was the seat of jurisdiction of the Earls Palatine until 1483 and of the Seneschal's criminal courts until 1747, when certain hereditary jurisdictions were abolished. According to the Lyon Office, Crieff comprises in large part the Burgh of Barony of Crieff, granted to Anthony Murray of Dollerie in 1674, and the Burgh of Barony of Drummond, granted to James, 3rd Earl of Perth, in 1672; the latter was raised to a Burgh of Regality in 1687 under James, Lord Drummond, later 2nd titular Duke of Perth,[12] who was attainted after the 1715 Jacobite Rising. Crieff became a Police Burgh in 1864.

The arms show the blue field with the silver mullets and red/silver saltire-crosses from the coat of Murray of Ochtertyre-Dollerie. The gold pile with its red wavy bars is for Drummond. The fetterlock symbolises the old baronial powers of justice exercised at Crieff; this was illustrated rather fearsomely, by a baron and scales, on the Burgh seal. The motto was adopted by the Town Council some time before 1961.

DOUNE, anciently Doune of Menteith, was created a Burgh of Barony in favour of James Stewart, 3rd Earl of Moray, in 1611, but may have been a Burgh in 1434–35.[13] It became a Police Burgh in 1890. The Burgh has not recorded arms; its seal shows a representation of the Market Cross with a pair of crossed pistols on either side to recall the celebrated Doune pistol-makers of the seventeenth and eighteenth centuries.

BURGH OF DUNBLANE

Parted per pale: dexter, Vert, on a chevron between a celestial crown in chief Or, and a dexter hand couped in base Argent, the fingers enflamed Proper, two chevronels round-embattled on their upper edges Gules; sinister, Gules, semée of lowes of flame Or, on a fess Argent, two barrulets Azure.

Below the Shield which is ensigned of a coronet appropriate to a Burgh is placed in an Escrol this *Motto* "Renovate Animos Veritate".

(Lyon Register, xxxix, 78: 14 April 1953)

DUNBLANE, the cathedral town of the old diocese of the same name, is said to have been made a City by King James I (1406–1437), but it may have been a Burgh from the middle of the thirteenth century.[14] In 1442, it was erected into a Burgh of Regality in favour of Michael, Bishop of Dunblane.[15] It became a Police Burgh in 1870.

The arms are a heraldic rendering of the old Burgh seal which was, itself, an adaptation of an ancient seal of the Burgh which shows St. Lawrence and St. Blane within a shrine, and of which an impression of the thirteenth or fourteenth century is on record.[16] The dexter side has been accorded to St. Blane. The green field (for Dalriada) recalls the Celtic Church of Dunblane and that the Church of Dunblane is mentioned in the Pictish Chronicle under the reign of King Kenneth MacAlpin (843–858); the crown and the enflamed fingers recall two legends about St. Blane—he is said to have worn a crown and not a mitre in the services of the Church, and on one occasion, to have sparked flames from his fingers to keep monastery fires alight. The hand is coloured silver to show that he was a confessor. The gold chevron and the red chevronels recall the arms of the ancient Earldom of Strathearn, the latter being round-embattled to recall Dunblane Cathedral. The sinister side is for St. Lawrence, who represents the Roman Church at Dunblane; he is symbolised by his traditional red tunic powdered over with "lowes of flame", while the silver and blue fess is for the gridiron on which he suffered martyrdom. The Latin motto—"Renew your courage with truth"—was chosen as a reference to the association of the Hays of Kinnoull with Dunblane: their motto is "Renovate Animos".

MAISE·AGUS·MATHAS

BURGH OF PITLOCHRY

Parted per saltire: in chief Argent, in base Gules, and in flanks paly of six Or and Sable, three hearts two and one of the Second in chief, and in base a dove of the First, around its head a halo of the Third, embellished Vert.

[Above the Shield is placed a Burghal coronet] and in an Escrol below the same this *Motto* "Maise Agus Mathas".

(Lyon Register, xxxix, 61: 5 February 1953)

PITLOCHRY became well known as a health resort after 1845 when Queen Victoria visited nearby Blair Castle and when her physician, Sir James Clarke, began to recommend the village to his patients. It became a Police Burgh in 1947.

The arms, parted per saltire for Scotland, have in chief three red hearts on a silver field for the family of Butter of Pitlochry, which has owned the lands of Pitlochry since 1600. In the flanks, the gold and black paly of the Dukes of Atholl recall that Pitlochry is in the heart of Atholl, said to be the district first mentioned in Scottish history. The enhaloed dove represents St. Colman, a Celtic missionary who is thought to have come from Ireland about A.D. 500 and to have founded the church at Moulin in which parish Pitlochry lies. The Gaelic motto means "Beauty and Beneficence"; the Gaelic words were suggested by a local lady, Mrs. C. M. Hunter, as the most appropriate and most succinct translation of the English words.[17]

The County Council of THE COUNTY OF PERTH bears arms which were designed and presented to the County in 1800 by Robert Auriol Drummond Hay of Kinnoull, 10th Earl of Kinnoull, Lord Lyon King of Arms, 1796–1804, "as a testimony of his respect and affection to the part of the County to which he has the honour and happiness to belong".[18] There seems no doubt that they were closely connected with the Local Militia and Volunteer Forces; Lord Kinnoull, himself, commanded the Perthshire Gentlemen and Yeomanry Cavalry (later Regiment of Light Dragoons) from 1798 to 1803 and they appear on a colour of the Royal Perthshire Militia dated 1812.[19]

Some kind of County arms may have been in use before 1800[20] and it seems reasonable to assume that Lord Kinnoull decided to pull the design together and make

PERTH COUNTY COUNCIL

Or, a lion rampant Gules, armed and langued Azure, standing on a Compartment or mount Proper, and brandishing in his dexter forepaw a scimitar of the Last, all within a double tressure flowered and counterflowered of the Second; on a dexter chief canton of the Third a front view of the Palace of Scone, Argent, ensigned on the top with an imperial crown Proper.

Above the Shield on a Wreath of the Liveries is set for *Crest* a demi Highlander affrontée, bonnet, belted, plaid, dirk, and pistols, brandishing in his right hand a broadsword aloft in a threatening posture, a target on his left arm, all Proper, and on a Compartment

below the Shield on which are *these words* "Pro Lege et Libertate" are placed for *Supporters*, on the dexter, an eagle reguardant, with wings addorsed Proper, and on the sinister, a war horse Argent, furnished Gules.

(Lyon Register, i, 485: 23 January 1800)

it into what he considered a satisfactory heraldic achievement. In this he apparently used the Royal Arms of Scotland as a basis, thus recalling the many connections between the Scottish Royal House and Perthshire and its noble families and that its County town, Perth, was once the Capital of Scotland.

At the same time it should be noted that a Perthshire Militia Troop colour dated 1684 bears a red lion rampant, standing on a mount and brandishing a scimitar[21]— obviously a Scottish lion ready to defend his country. The addition of the Royal tressure could recall that three of the Perthshire local Defence units had been granted the title "Royal";[22] it could also allude to the fact that the Royal tressure appears in the arms of several of the most notable Perthshire families, i.e. Hay, Drummond, Stewart and Murray, as represented by the Earls of Kinnoull, Perth, Moray and Mansfield, and, in the case of the last two, also by the Dukes of Atholl, as well as in those of the City of Perth. The mount on which the lion rampant stands could refer to the Drummond Earls of Perth whose arms stand on a compartment described by Nisbet as "like to a green hill semée of caltraps"; according to Sir George Mackenzie these compartments were only allowed to Sovereign Princes and that besides the Douglases, he knew of no other subject in Britain, except the Earl of Perth, whose arms stood on a compartment.[23]

The likeness of Scone Palace and the Scottish Crown recall that Scone was once the crowning place of Scottish kings. The eagle supporter obviously comes from the arms of the City of Perth, but while the white war-horse is clearly for the cavalry troops, it may also represent the white horse of Hanover and be another mark of Royal favour.

The Highland warrior in the crest stands for the infantry regiments but is also reminiscent of the crest borne (for Murray) by the Dukes of Atholl, a demi-savage brandishing a dagger and a key. The Latin motto—"For Law and Liberty"—echoes that of the City of Perth.

The original parchment was found in the Lyon Office in 1890 and was forwarded to the County Clerk in April of that year.

16

COUNTY OF ARGYLL

The County of ARGYLL has six Burghs, the Royal Burghs of Inveraray and Campbeltown, the Parliamentary Burgh of Oban, and the Police Burghs of Dunoon, Lochgilphead (the County town) and Tobermory.

ROYAL BURGH OF INVERARAY

In the waves of the sea, five herring entering a herring net pendant from the sinister chief, all Proper.

[Above the Shield is placed a Burghal coronet] and in an Escrol below the Shield this *Motto* "Semper Tibi Pendeat Halec".

(Lyon Register, xxvii, 33: 27 April 1927)

INVERARAY, erected into a Burgh or Barony in 1474 in favour of Colin, 1st Earl of Argyll and Lord High Chancellor of Scotland, was made a Royal Burgh in 1648 by King Charles I.[1]

The arms are most unusual in that the blazon is "all Proper". They follow the device on the Burgh seal of which a 1684 impression is on record.[2] The herrings swimming into the net recall the famous herring fishing industry of Loch Fyne on which the town stands. The Latin motto is something of a mystery; one suggestion is that it means "May the fish sauce always be ready for you". Probably Porteous was on the right lines when he said "it seems to refer to the fishing industry being the most important of all industries and the Loch Fyne herrings being the finest of all fish".[3] The arms were registered so that they could appear, to represent Argyll, on the Scottish National War Memorial at Edinburgh Castle.[4]

ROYAL BURGH OF CAMPBELTOWN

Quarterly: 1st, Vert, a castle triple-towered Or, masoned windows and port Gules; 2nd, gyronny of eight Or and Sable; 3rd, Argent, a lymphad Sable, sail furled and oars in action, flagged Gules, at the masthead a beacon in flames Proper; 4th, Argent, a fret Sable.

Above the Shield is placed a coronet suitable to a Royal Burgh, thereon a Helmet befitting their degree, with a Mantling Vert doubled Or, and on a Wreath of their Liveries is set for *Crest* a herring naiant Proper, and in an Escrol below the Shield this *Motto* "Ignavis Precibus Fortuna Repugnat".

(Lyon Register, xxviii, 45: 10 July 1929)

CAMPBELTOWN was created a Burgh of Barony in 1667 in favour of Archibald, 9th Earl of Argyll, and was raised to a Royal Burgh by King William III in 1700.[5]

The quartered arms show (1) the Castle of Kilkerane in Kintyre said to have been built by King James IV; the colours chosen combine the Royal colours with Thistle green which was much used by King James IV as a livery colour; the use of green and gold is doubly appropriate as these are the ancient colours of Dalriada, and Campbeltown is built on the site of its capital Dalruadhain; (2) the gold and black gyronny of the Campbell Earls and Dukes of Argyll, first borne by their forebears, the Campbells of Lochow; (3) the black galley of Lorn, with the flaming beacon at its masthead, the Lordship of Lorn being now held by the Dukes of Argyll; (4) a black fret on a silver field, taken from the arms of Tollemache of Helmingham in Suffolk, to commemorate the long association with the town of Elizabeth Tollemache, wife of Archibald, 1st Duke of Argyll; she lived at Limecraigs House nearby, died there in 1735 and is buried in Campbeltown. The crest of a herring refers to the local fishing industry and also commemorates the time of the Herring Bounty when hundreds of herring "busses" used to assemble at Campbeltown to receive the Bounty. The Latin motto has been freely translated as "Fortune helps those who help themselves".

BURGH OF OBAN

Argent, in the waves of the sea Proper a lymphad Sable, oars in action, with a beacon on the top of the mast Proper, in base a salmon naiant Argent; on a chief parted per pale, dexter, Azure, a lion rampant Argent; sinister, gyronny of eight Or and Sable.

And in Escrol below the Shield this *Motto* "Air Aghart".

(Lyon Register, xvi, 47: 31 May 1901)

OBAN was created a Burgh of Barony in favour of George William, 6th Duke of Argyll, in 1811 but the Charter was set aside by the Court of Session. In 1820, another Charter was issued in favour of the same Duke and Charles Campbell of Combie.[6] Oban became a Parliamentary Burgh under the 1832 Reform Act.

The arms show the black galley of Lorn, flaming beacon at the masthead, to recall the Lordship of Lorn which has been held by the Earls and Dukes of Argyll since the fifteenth century, when Colin, 1st Earl of Argyll, married Isabel Stewart, the Lorn heiress; the galley and the salmon below denote that Oban is an important fishing centre and seaport. In the chief are the silver lion on a blue field of the MacDougalls, ancient Lords of Lorn, the ruins of whose stronghold, Dunollie Castle, still stand on Oban Bay, along with the gold and black gyronny of the Campbell Earls and Dukes of Argyll. The Gaelic motto means "Forward".

BURGH OF DUNOON

Azure, on a rock in base Proper, a castle triple-towered Argent, masoned Sable, windows, port and flags Gules, and flying from the centre tower a banner charged with a gyronny of eight Or and of the Third; on a chief Gold, a galley also of the Third, sail furled Proper, flagged of the Fourth.

Above the Shield is placed a mural crown and in an Escrol below the Shield this *Motto* "Forward".

(Lyon Register, xxx, 14: 23 November 1931)

DUNOON, according to Lord Bute, was created a Burgh of Barony in 1835,[7] but Professor Pryde mentions an earlier creation as Kilmun (the parish of Dunoon) in 1490 in favour of Colin, 1st Earl of Argyll and Lord High Chancellor of Scotland.[8] It became a Police Burgh in 1868.

The arms, based on the device on the Burgh seal, show the ancient Royal Castle of Dunoon with a banner showing the Campbell gyronny, since the Campbells of Lochow and their descendants, the Earls and Dukes of Argyll, have been the Hereditary Keepers of the Castle since 1370. The red windows and doors show that it is a Royal castle and the blue field is for the sea and sky. The Campbell colours are repeated in the chief where the galley recalls the Clyde steamer shown on the Burgh seal, from which the motto also comes.

BURGH OF LOCHGILPHEAD

Sable, an anchor paleways Or, surmounted of a herring fessways Argent, and having a rope reflexed around it Vert and of
the Third.

Below the Shield, which is surmounted of a coronet appropriate to a Burgh, is placed in an Escrol this *Motto* "Dochas".

(Lyon Register, xxxvii, 33: 21 January 1949)

    LOCHGILPHEAD, now the County town of Argyll, grew from a fishing village
and became a Police Burgh in 1858.

    The arms follow closely the device on the Burgh seal. The field has been made
black and the anchor gold as these are the livery colours of the Duke of Argyll, the
principal landowner in the area. The green and silver of the rope refer to the sea and
to Loch Gilp on which the town stands. The whole symbolises the Burgh's close
connection with the fishing industry. The Gaelic motto means "Hope" and comes
from the seal. The arms were registered in connection with the presentation of a
Provost's Chain-of-Office by Mr. John B. Ross, a distinguished son of Lochgilphead.[9]

BURGH OF TOBERMORY

Quarterly: 1st, Gules, a fountain charged with a representation of the Blessed Virgin Mary with the Babe in her arms, Or; 2nd, Argent, on a base undy Azure and of the First, a dolphin hauriant Vert, lipped Gules, spouting forth water of the Second; 3rd, Or, upon the sea in base undy Azure and Argent, a lymphad Proper, oars in action, sails furled and tackling Sable, flagged Gules; 4th, per fess Vert and Azure, a salmon naiant Proper.

Below the Shield which is ensigned with a coronet appropriate to a Burgh is placed in an Escrol this *Motto* "Ceartas".

(Lyon Register, xxxvi, 115: 24 March 1948)

TOBERMORY, on the Island of Mull, was founded in 1788 by the British Society for extending the Fisheries and improving the Sea Coasts of the Kingdom. It became a Police Burgh in 1875.

The arms, which Lord Lyon Innes described as an undoubtedly Highland type of armorial bearing, more or less repeat the device on the Burgh seal, which is said to have been designed by Mr. Colin A. McVean of Kilfinichen, Mull, a former Surveyor-in-Chief of Japan and a native of Iona.[10] In the 1st quarter are the Virgin and Child in gold on a red field but within a fountain to recall that Tobermory means "the well of the Virgin Mary", while the other three quarters reflect the fishing and shipping interests of the town; the galley on the gold field in the 3rd quarter and the salmon in the 4th, come from the arms of Maclean of Duart, since Mull is mostly Maclean country and the use of the colour green in the 4th quarter is a reminder that Mull lay within the ancient Scottish Kingdom of Dalriada, with just a hint of the Mackinnons who once owned the north-western corner of the island. The Gaelic motto means "Justice" or "Equity". The fees payable for registration were met from a special fund collected locally.

ARGYLL COUNTY COUNCIL

Parted per fess and in chief per pale: 1st, gyronny of eight Or and Sable; 2nd, Or, a wing displayed Gules, claw membered Sable, grasping a sword in pale Azure, hilted and pommelled Argent and environed of an antique crown also Gules; in base Argent, a lymphad, oars in action, sails furled Sable, with a beacon enflamed Gules at the masthead; over all a fess wavy Azure charged with a bar wavy Argent, upon the last five fish naiant Gules.

Below the Shield, which is ensigned of a coronet appropriate to a County Council, is set on an Escrol this *Motto* "Seas Ar Coir".

(Lyon Register, xxxix 93: 29 June 1953)

The County Council of THE COUNTY OF ARGYLL bears arms which show in chief (1) the gold and black gyronny of the Campbell Dukes of Argyll; (2) a displayed wing with its claw, a very old heraldic device, alluding to the Macdonald eagle, with a sword and crown for the southern part of the Lordship of the Isles. In the base is the black galley of the Lordship of Lorn, with the flaming beacon at the masthead, while across the middle of the shield the wavy fess and the fish denote the many sea-lochs in the County and its fishing industry; the five fish also hark back to the same number in the arms of Inveraray, which was the original County town. The Gaelic motto means "Maintain our Right" and was a local suggestion. The seal adopted by the County Council in 1890 was a plain one.

17

COUNTY OF BUTE

The County of BUTE has two Burghs, the Royal Burgh of Rothesay, the County town, and the Police Burgh of Millport.

ROYAL BURGH OF ROTHESAY

Party per pale: dexter, Argent, a castle Sable, in the dexter chief a crescent, and in the sinister an estoile of five points, [both] Tenny, and in base a lymphad, sails furled, of the Second, flagged Gules; and on the sinister, Or, a fess chequy Azure and Argent.

[Above the Shield is placed a Burghal coronet.]

(Lyon Register, xxvi, 59: 11 March 1925)

ROTHESAY, on the Island of Bute, was made a Royal Burgh in 1400–1 by King Robert III; its charter uses, for apparently the first time in any Scottish document, the term "Royal Burgh".[1]

The arms, which were matriculated following a private visit to the town by Mr. F. J. Grant, then Albany Herald and later Lord Lyon Grant,[2] show in an impaled form the two sides of what must have been the original Burgh seal since the matrices are dated c. 1401.[3] Lord Bute also states that Blain's *History of Bute* mentions a Town Cross with two shields on it.[4] The dexter side shows Rothesay Castle, rebuilt about the time the Charter was granted. Above are the sun and the moon, both coloured tenny (a dull orange), which Lord Bute said was a livery colour of the House of Stewart[5] but which is very unusual in Scots heraldry; the ship below stands for the fishing and shipping interests of the Burgh. On the sinister side are the arms of the House of Stewart which has a long connection with Rothesay: both King Robert II (1371–1390) and King Robert III (1390–1406) were frequent visitors and in 1398, the latter created his son Duke of Rothesay, which title has ever since been borne by the heir to the Scottish throne.

MILLPORT, on the Island of Great Cumbrae, became a Police Burgh in 1864. The Burgh has not recorded arms; its seal shows a shield bearing a chevron with three stars between three escallops two and one. This is said to have no heraldic significance but merely to refer to the starfish and shells found in Millport Bay. There is a motto— "Altiora Videnda"—meaning "Higher things must be seen", a reference to the light-house near the town.

BUTE COUNTY COUNCIL

Parted per pale: on the dexter, parted per fess Gules and Argent, in chief three cinquefoils two and one Ermine, and in base a lymphad sails furled Sable, flagged of the First; and in the sinister, Or, a fess chequy Azure and Argent.

(Lyon Register, xxvii, 47: 8 July 1927)

The County Council of THE COUNTY OF BUTE bears arms which are based on the seal adopted by the Council in 1890. The dexter side, for Arran, shows three ermine cinquefoils on a red field to recall the long-standing Hamilton connection, while the lymphad is for the Earldom of Arran held in the Hamilton family since 1503. The sinister side, for Bute, shows the arms of the House of Stewart thus referring to its many Royal and other links with Bute; the present Marquess of Bute, whose family name is Crichton-Stuart, is descended from a son of King Robert II.

18

COUNTY OF DUNBARTON

The County of DUNBARTON has eight Burghs, the Royal Burgh of Dumbarton (the County town), and the Police Burghs of Clydebank, Cove & Kilcreggan, Helensburgh, Kirkintilloch, Milngavie, Bearsden and Cumbernauld.

ROYAL BURGH OF DUMBARTON

Azure, an elephant passant Argent, tusked Or, bearing on his back a tower Proper.

The *Motto* in an Escrol is "Fortitudo et Fidelitas".

(Lyon Register, i, 460: c. 1673)

DUMBARTON was created a Royal Burgh in 1222 by King Alexander II.[1]

The arms are similar to the device on the ancient Burgh seal, of which a 1357 impression is on record, and which shows the elephant passant to sinister.[2] This is, however, changed on a later seal. The elephant is said to have been chosen because in shape it is thought to resemble Dumbarton Rock; the castle on its back is Dumbarton Castle. The Latin motto—"Fortitude and Fidelity"—is considered to refer not only to the elephant but also to the fortress of Dumbarton Castle and its loyalty to the Throne.

CLYDEBANK grew up around 1871 when James and George Thomson chose a site by the River Cart for the shipyard they had to move from Govan. It became a Police Burgh in 1886.

BURGH OF CLYDEBANK

Argent, a saltire Gules, in chief a sewing machine Sable, in fess dexter a stag's head cabossed of the Second, in fess sinister a lion rampant of the Third guttée d'Or, and in base upon the waves of the sea a representation of H.M.S. *Ramillies* Proper.

Above the Shield is placed a coronet suitable to a Burgh, thereon a Helmet befitting their degree with a Mantling Gules doubled Argent, and on a Wreath of their Liveries is set for *Crest* a garb Or, and in an Escrol under the Shield this *Motto* "Labore et Scientia".

(Lyon Register, xxviii, 80: 6 February 1930)

The arms follow closely the device on the Burgh seal adopted in 1892. The red saltire on the silver field is for Lennox, in which province Clydebank lies; as it is also a St. Patrick's Cross, it is doubly appropriate since the town is in the parishes of Old and New Kilpatrick. The sewing machine is for the well-known Singer factory at Kilbowie and the depiction of the H.M.S. *Ramillies* (built in 1892 at Thomson's Shipyard and considered to be the most powerful of its time) is for Clyde shipbuilding. The red stag's head comes from the arms of Mr. James Rodger Thomson, the shipbuilder, who was the prime mover in founding the Burgh and its first Provost; the lion guttée d'Or comes from those of Mr. Alexander Dunn Pattison of Dalmuir, whose family were Superiors of the Burgh at its inception and notable benefactors. The garb in the crest recalls the agricultural interests of the area and the farm which once occupied part of the site of the town. The Latin motto—"By Work and by Knowledge"—refers to the skilled craftsmanship of the citizens.

COVE & KILCREGGAN united to form a Police Burgh in 1865.

Using the blue and silver colours of Scotland, and parted per fess wavy to denote water, the arms show a golden Viking ship in chief to indicate that Cove stands on Loch Long, the Skipa Fjord (Ship Firth or Loch of Ships) of the *Hakonar Saga* which tells how the Norwegian King Hakon IV in 1263, before the Battle of Largs, sent sixty ships up Loch Long to be dragged overland to Loch Lomond to raid the province of Lennox. The red cross on the rock is for Kilcreggan, "the church on the crag". The Latin motto—"Who shall separate us"—was chosen to

BURGH OF COVE & KILCREGGAN

Per fess wavy Azure and Argent: in chief a Viking long-ship Or, sail Argent, flagged Gules; in base a cross-crosslet fitchée Gules, issuing from a crag Proper.

Below the Shield, ensigned as a Police Burgh of a Burghal coronet Azure masoned Argent, is set in an Escrol this *Motto* "Quis Separabit".

(Lyon Register, xli, 78: 5 November 1957)

indicate the close ties between the two parts of the Burgh. This is the first instance of a Police Burgh coronet being granted by the Lyon Court. The Town Council were advised on their Petition for arms by Mr. John Stewart of Inchmahome, a well-known Dunbartonshire antiquary.

BURGH OF HELENSBURGH

Per fess Argent and Gules: in chief a saltire engrailed Sable, in base three mullets Or two over one.

Above the Shield is placed a mural coronet with a Helmet befitting their degree with a Mantling Sable doubled Argent, and on a Wreath of their Liveries is set for *Crest* a stag's head Gules, and in an Escrol over the same this *Motto* "Si Je Puis"; on a Compartment with this *Motto* "Cnoc Elachan", are placed for *Supporters*, on the dexter, a greyhound Proper collared Sable, on the sinister, a savage wreathed about the temples and waist with laurel, holding in his exterior hand a club resting on his sinister shoulder, Proper.

(Lyon Register, xxviii, 70: 18 December 1929)

HELENSBURGH grew out of the hamlet of Mulig founded about 1776 by Dame Helen Sutherland, wife of Sir James Colquhoun, 1st Baronet of Luss. It was created a Burgh of Barony in favour of his son, Sir James Colquhoun, 2nd Baronet of Luss, in 1802[3] and became a Police Burgh in 1846.

The arms, which are a variant of the device on the original Burgh seal, fulfil the wish of Sir James Colquhoun that they should include some references to the Colquhoun arms and to those of his mother, who was a daughter of William, Lord Strathnaver and Master of Sutherland. And so the upper part of the shield shows the black engrailed saltire of Colquhoun on its silver field and the lower part, the three golden stars of Sutherland on their red field. The red stag's head crest and the greyhound supporter recall similar features in the Colquhoun arms, and the savage the almost identical supporter in the Sutherland arms. The French motto—"If I can"—is that of Colquhoun and the Gaelic one—"The willow hill"—is their war-cry.

BURGH OF KIRKINTILLOCH

Azure, a wall towered and embattled Argent, port Sable, standing upon a mount Proper; in chief three stars of five points Or, and in base in a stream a fish naiant Proper.

Above the Shield is placed a mural coronet and under the same this *Motto* "Ca' Canny But Ca' Awa' ".

(Lyon Register, xxxiii, 27: 21 June 1938)

KIRKINTILLOCH grew up originally around one of the forts on the Roman Wall built by Antonine about A.D. 142. It was granted as a Burgh to William de Comyn, Baron of Lenzie and Lord of Cumbernauld, about 1214, and in the fourteenth century, the Barony was granted first to a Fleming, then to a Kennedy and for a time thereafter the Burgh may have lapsed; in 1526 it was created a Burgh of Barony in favour of Malcolm, 3rd Lord Fleming.[4] It became a Police Burgh in 1836.

The arms which resemble the device on the Burgh seal show a towered wall to represent the Roman fort (on Antonine's Wall) which formerly stood on Peel Hill at Kirkintilloch. The water represents the Luggie and Kelvin rivers which pass through the town, and the fish a trout in them. In the upper part of the shield, the blue and gold colours of the Comyns are used; the three stars are said to refer to the ancient ecclesiastical affairs of the Burgh and to the symbolism of the triad (connected with the Holy Trinity) and the pentalpha (five-pointed stars which refer to the wounds of Christ); these are symbolic of health and strength.[5] The Scots motto refers to the former weaving industry and is mentioned in *Kirkintilloch Town and Parish*, by T. Watson (1894).

BURGH OF MILNGAVIE

Gyronny of eight Argent and Sable, charged with four roses Gules, barbed and seeded Proper, and as many escallops alternately Or, over all a cross moline square pierced of the field and divided per cross of the Third and the Last.

Above the Shield is placed a mural coronet, thereon a Helmet of befitting degree with a Mantling Sable doubled Argent, and on a Wreath of their Liveries is set for *Crest* a mill water-wheel Proper between two garbs Or, and in an Escrol over the same this *Motto* "Salubritas et Industria".

(Lyon Register, xxxiii, 38: 21 October 1938)

MILNGAVIE, which probably took its name from the old meal mill of Gavie on the Allander Burn, became a Police Burgh in 1875.

The arms, as far as the shield is concerned, follow closely the second design suggested by Lord Bute.[6] The red roses on their silver field recall the Earls of Lennox to whom the lands of Milngavie belonged before they passed to the Grahams, later Earls and Dukes of Montrose. It was the Grahams who founded Gavie's Mill, and they are recalled by the four golden shells on the black field. The square-pierced cross-moline represents a mill-rind, since it is somewhat similar in form to the iron fitting set in the netherstone of a mill; in addition, the gyronny background gives a rotatory effect and could easily be taken to refer to the mill-wheel. The crest of the mill-wheel (specially chosen as an overshot wheel)[7] and the sheaves show that Gavie's Mill was a meal mill and also refer to the agricultural interests of the district. The Latin motto—"Healthiness and Hard Work"—is conventional.

BURGH OF BEARSDEN

Per fess enarched Or and in base per bend Gules and Sable, a bend engrailed of the Third, in dexter chief charged with a buckle Argent and in sinister chief a rose of the Third, barbed and seeded of the Second, and in base a bear's head couped of the Fourth, muzzled Azure.

Below the Shield which is ensigned of the coronet proper to a Police Burgh, videlicet: Azure masoned Argent, is placed in an Escrol this *Motto* "Bear the Gree".

(Lyon Register, xli, 122: 29 June 1959)

BEARSDEN, which originated in a village called New Kirk, is a town which developed in the present century. It became a Police Burgh in 1958.

The arms were the subject of some discussion in which the Dunbartonshire antiquary, Mr. John Stewart of Inchmahome, was involved.[8] The upper part of the shield has a black engrailed bend and gold buckle to recall the Colquhouns of Garscadden and Killermont, Superiors from the fourteenth century of the land on which the Burgh stands, while the Campbells of Succoth, who owned the adjacent estate of Garscube from 1687, are remembered by the black and gold colours; these two families are now represented by the Campbell-Colquhouns of Killermont and Garscadden. The rose, strangely coloured black (for artistic reasons), is the Lennox rose. In the lower part of the shield, the red colour recalls Lennox and St. Patrick (Bearsden is in New Kilpatrick parish), while the bear is supposed to be looking into his "den", thus making a direct reference to the Burgh's name: there is also a hint of a Galbraith connection here as Sir Andrew de Galbraith, who once owned the estate of Gartconnel (now part of the Burgh), is said to have borne a shield with a single bear and the Lennox saltire in chief. The Scots motto which includes the word "bear" comes from Robert Burns' song "A Man's a Man for a' that" and means "Have the first place"; it was suggested by Mr. John Stewart of Inchmahome.[9]

CUMBERNAULD, according to the *Ordnance Gazetteer* (1882), was made a Burgh of Barony in 1649.[10] After the Second World War, it became one of Scotland's new towns, and was granted Police Burgh status in 1968. The arms show the silver chevron on a red field of the famous family of Fleming, Earls of Wigtown and Lords of Cumbernauld; in base is the hunting-horn of the Burns family of Kilmahew, one of whose seats was Cumbernauld House. The blue and silver chequered lozenge on the chevron recalls the weaving industry, which was prominent in the district in the early

K

BURGH OF CUMBERNAULD

Gules, upon a chevron Argent a lozenge chequy of twenty-five panes Azure and of the Second, and in base a hunting-horn also of the Second, stringed Vert.

Above the Shield is placed a coronet proper to a Police Burgh, viz. Azure masoned Argent, and in an Escrol below the same this *Motto* "Daur and Prosper".

(Lyon Register, 1, 77: 2 July 1969)

nineteenth century and also depicts the pedestrian underpasses which are a feature of the new town; the line of blue squares rising from the base of the chevron represents its situation on the watersheds of the rivers Forth and Clyde. The Scots motto was chosen as "symbolic of the attitude of the Town Council and of the concept of the new town".

DUNBARTON COUNTY COUNCIL

Argent, a saltire cantoned with four roses Gules, barbed and seeded Vert.

And in an Escrol below the same this *Motto* "Levenax".

(Lyon Register, xxvii, 52: 20 July 1927)

The County Council of THE COUNTY OF DUNBARTON bears the arms of the "Erles of Lennox of Auld" as given in the Armorial dated 1542 of Sir David Lindsay of the Mount, the famous Scottish satirical poet, who was Lord Lyon King of Arms from 1530 to 1555. The County covers much of the ancient province of Lennox of which name the motto "Levenax" is an older version. The seal adopted by the County Council in 1890 showed a sexfoil or rose charged with the Lennox arms; it was designed by Mr. Francis C. Buchanan, a member of the Council.[11]

19

COUNTY OF STIRLING

The County of STIRLING has six Burghs, the Royal Burgh of Stirling (the County town), the Parliamentary Burgh of Falkirk, and the Police Burghs of Bridge of Allan, Denny & Dunipace, Grangemouth and Kilsyth.

STIRLING was made a Royal Burgh between 1124 and 1127 by King David I[1] and was one of the original members of the Curia Quattuor Burgorum (Berwick, Edinburgh, Roxburgh and Stirling) out of which the Convention of Royal Burghs developed.

The arms replaced the version recorded in the Lyon Register in 1849; this was almost identical to what is shown in the 1st and 4th quarters of the new coat of arms. Stirling has a most interesting collection of old seals, and in 1960 the Town Council, prompted by Mr. Walter H. Gillespie, the Burgh Architect and Planning Officer, decided to record all its seals; this led to a new grant of arms with supporters and a Royal Burgh compartment. The 1st and 4th quarters show the device on the reverse of the Great Seal of the Burgh and the 3rd quarter, the obverse: there is on record an impression of this seal dated 1296.[2] The 2nd quarter shows the device on another Common Seal used by the Burgh of which a seventeenth-century impression is on record.[3]

In the 1st and 4th quarters are the Royal Castle and Forest of Stirling; the 2nd quarter shows the wolf on the crag, recalling the rocky crag called the Craigs or the Wolf's Crag, in whose vicinity there is a spring of water which from ancient times was used as the public washing area. There is a legend that during a Danish invasion in the ninth century, the garrison was warned of the enemy's approach by the barking of a wolf on this crag and was consequently able to repel the attack. In a Town Council Minute of 15 June 1624, the Burgh arms are described as "the wolf upon ane craig".[4] The 3rd quarter shows what are really the sacred bearings of the town. The bridge with its warriors and the cross above it are said to recall the stone bridge and cross built across the river Forth in c. 860 by King Oswald of Northumbria who captured the Scottish King Donald I, and after marching on Stirling was able to secure the cession of all the lands south of the Forth and Clyde. The warriors on the bridge are apparently an English bowman and a Scottish pikeman.

The soldier supporters, as well as alluding to the fighting men in the 3rd quarter, appropriately refer to Stirling's long history as a garrison town. The pikeman with the Scottish saltire on his jacket comes from the time of the War of Independence and the

ROYAL BURGH OF
STIRLING

Quarterly: 1st and 4th, Azure, on a mount in base Vert, a castle triple-towered without windows Argent, masoned Sable, the gate closed Gules, surrounded with four oak trees disposed in orle Proper, the field semée of stars of six rays of the Third; 2nd, Argent, issuant from a base undy Azure and of the First, a rock Proper, thereon a wolf couchant Or in front of a thicket of bushes Vert; 3rd, per fess, in chief Azure, in base undy Argent and of the First, upon an enarched bridge of seven arches Argent, a cross patée fitchée Or issuant from the bridge, accompanied in the dexter and sinister by two men-at-arms respectant Argent, that on the dexter holding a drawn bow Gules, that on the sinister a javelin fessways also Gules, and in dexter chief a star of six rays, and in sinister chief a crescent, both Argent.

Above the Shield which is ensigned of a coronet of a Royal Burgh (videlicet: Proper masoned Sable) is, in an Escrol, this *Motto* "Continet Hoc In Se Nemus et Castrum Strivelinse", and below the Shield on a Compartment suitable to a Royal Burgh, inscribed of this *Motto* "Hic Armis Bruti Scoti Stant Hic Cruce Tuti", are set for *Supporters*, dexter, a pikeman armed cap-à-pie, having a leather jacket charged of a roundel Azure, a saltire Argent, and sustaining in his dexter hand a pike, the shaft Azure; sinister, an archer, his legs and arms naked, his feet in brogues, attired in a jupon per pale Vert and Gules, charged on the breast of a cinquefoil Ermine, about his waist a belt and quiver Or, and in his exterior hand a bow also Or.

(Lyon Register, xlv, 48: 3 May 1962)
(Previously registered Lyon Register, i, 455: 25 April 1849)

Battles of Stirling Bridge (1297) and Bannockburn (1314). The archer comes from earlier days, possibly from the period of the first Battle of Stirling (c. 860), and he represents the Highland and Lowland Kingdoms of Scotland, Alba and Strathclyde. His golden arrow and the green half of his tunic are for Alba, the red half and the ermine cinquefoil for Strathclyde.

The Latin mottoes, which come from the oldest known Burgh seal, have been the subject of a good deal of discussion. That shown above refers to the 1st and 4th quarters and has been happily translated in a couplet by Sir Robert Sibbald:[5]

> The Castle and the Wood of Stirling Town
> Are in the compass of this Seal set down.

The motto below refers to the 3rd quarter but is difficult of translation owing to doubts as to the meaning of the word "Bruti". Some say it means "Britons" and that the motto could mean, "Here stand the Britons protected by arms, here the Scots protected by the Cross". But "Bruti" may refer to a Welsh tribe which possessed much of the Scottish Lowlands in early times.

BURGH OF FALKIRK

Sable, on a bend bretessed, accompanied by six billets Or, three in chief and three in base, the Church of Falkirk, between two swords and two Highland claymores both in saltire, the former surmounted of a shield of 1298, the latter of a target of 1746, all Proper.

On a Compartment below the Shield with the *Motto* "Better Meddle wi' the Deil than the Bairns o' Fa'kirk", is placed behind the Shield for *Supporter* a lion rampant affrontée Gules, armed and langued Azure, crowned with a mural crown Argent masoned Sable, and in an Escrol over the same this *Motto* "Touch ane Touch A' ".

(Lyon Register, xviii, 66: 20 April 1906)

FALKIRK stands on land which, in medieval times, lay partly within the Thanedom of Callendar and partly within the Lordship of Kerse owned by Holyrood Abbey; in course of time most, if not all, of these lands passed into the Livingstone family. It was created a Burgh of Barony in 1600 in favour of Alexander, 7th Lord

Livingstone, later Earl of Linlithgow, Lord Livingston and Callendar, and in 1646 was raised to a Burgh of Regality for his kinsman, James, 1st Earl of Callendar.[6] It became a Parliamentary Burgh under the 1832 Reform Act.

The arms with their black field and gold billets closely resemble those of Callendar, the historic family associated with the district from early times and whose estates passed into the Livingstone family after the War of Independence in the fourteenth century. The bend has been made embattled to denote the Roman Wall of Antonine which passed close to the town and on it is a representation of the parish church—"the Fa' Kirk"—which may mean "the speckled church" or the "church by the wall". On either side of it are swords and shields to commemorate the two Battles of Falkirk: one in 1298 when King Edward I of England defeated the Scots patriot, Sir William Wallace, and the second in 1746 when the retreating Jacobite army of Prince Charles had a pyrrhic victory over the Hanoverian troops of General Hawley. The idea (cf. Perth) of having a bearer, instead of supporters, comes from the carving on the Cross Well of the Burgh, which shows a lion wearing a kind of mural crown and holding a shield with the arms of Alexander, 2nd Earl of Callendar.[7] The two mottoes are well-known local sayings. Up to 1906, the Burgh used a seal with a device showing a Highland warrior but the Town Council decided that something more impressive and more relevant was required as the civic insignia of the Burgh.

BRIDGE OF ALLAN became a Police Burgh in 1870. The Burgh has not registered arms; its seal bears a representation of the bridge over the Allan river from which the town takes its name.

BURGH OF DENNY & DUNIPACE

Per fess Azure and Vert: an arched bridge Argent, masoned Sable, charged in fess with a barrulet of the Last, engrailed on its lower edge, all between an angel Proper, attired of the Third, the wings displayed Or, and celestially crowned of the Last, holding in either hand a palm branch of the Second, issuant from the bridge in chief; and in base a pale wavy of the Third, charged with a pallet wavy of the First.

And in an Escrol below the Shield which is ensigned of a Burgh coronet this *Motto* "For God and the People".

(Lyon Register, xli, 39: 23 April 1956)

DENNY & DUNIPACE became a Police Burgh in 1877. Denny has associations with the Roman occupation and later with the Knights Templar, while Dunipace takes its name from two ancient mounds—the Hills of Dunipace—in the neighbour-hood which George Buchanan calls "Duni Pacis" or "hills of peace".[8]

By request of the Town Council, the arms closely resemble the device on the 1892 Burgh seal, for whose design Mr. W. W. Hunter (Provost of the Burgh 1888–1896 and 1902–1908) was mainly responsible.[9] The angel of peace is very appropriate since the district is said to have been the setting for three important treaties in Scottish history: that between the Caledonii and the Roman Emperor Severus in the third century A.D.; a parley between Sir William Wallace and Robert the Bruce after the Battle of Falkirk in 1298; the signing in 1301 by King Edward I of England of a warrant authorising a truce with Scotland. The angel is placed above the bridge over the River Carron which flows between Denny and Dunipace; the bridge is charged with a black engrailed barrulet to recall the connection of the Sinclair (or St. Clair) Earls of Orkney, with the neighbouring Barony and Castle of Herbertshire. The blue and green background is for the sky and the land, while the motto comes from the Burgh seal.

BURGH OF GRANGEMOUTH

Parted per pale Argent and Gules: in the dexter on a base undy Azure and of the First a representation of the *Charlotte Dundas* steamship Proper; and in the sinister a stag's head erased with a cross-crosslet fitchée between her attires Or.

Above the Shield is placed a Burghal crown and a Helmet befitting their degree with a Mantling Azure doubled Argent, and on a Wreath of their Liveries is set for *Crest* a steamship on the waves of the sea all Proper, and in an Escrol over the same this *Motto* "Ingenium Vincit Omnia".

(Lyon Register, xxix, 34: 1 August 1930)

GRANGEMOUTH was founded in about 1777 by Sir Laurence Dundas of Kerse, grandfather of the 1st Earl of Zetland, in connection with the opening of the Forth and Clyde Canal. It became a Police Burgh in 1872.

The arms partly reflect the device on the Burgh seal adopted in 1888. The shield is parted in the silver and red colours of Dundas. On the dexter, there is a representa-tion of the first practical steamboat, built for Thomas, 1st Lord Dundas (son of Sir Laurence Dundas), at Grangemouth in 1802, and designed for towing vessels up the

River Carron and along the Forth and Clyde Canal. On the sinister, the stag's head with the cross-crosslet recalls the town's connection through Abbots Kerse with Holyrood Abbey, which once held the Lordship of Kerse, and with the Bellenden family who were granted it as part of the Barony of Broughton after the Reformation; such a feature appears on old Abbey seals and in the Bellenden arms. The steamship in the crest indicates Grangemouth's importance as a seaport. The Latin motto— "Skill conquers all"—came from the Burgh seal. An interesting commentary on the Burgh's arms appears in *Grangemouth's Modern History* by Robert Porteous (1970).

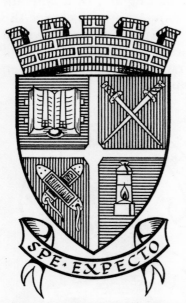

BURGH OF KILSYTH

Quarterly, Azure and Gules: 1st, an open Bible Proper; 2nd, two swords in saltire Argent, hilts uppermost Or; 3rd, two shuttles in saltire Or, garnished with thread Argent; 4th, a miner's lamp Argent, inflamed Proper; over all a cross fillet nowy lozengy Argent.

Above the Shield is placed a coronet appropriate to a Burgh of Barony (videlicet: Gules masoned Argent) and in an Escrol below the same this *Motto* "Spe Expecto".

(Lyon Register, lv, 42: 1 November 1972)

KILSYTH was licensed as a Burgh of Barony in 1620 in favour of Sir William Livingstone of Kilsyth,[10] whose brother Sir James Livingstone was created Viscount Kilsyth in 1661. It became a Police Burgh in 1878.

The arms of the Burgh follow closely the design of the non-armorial Burgh seal adopted in 1929 to the design of Mr. A. G. Law Samson, then Herald Painter to the Court of the Lord Lyon. The four quarters show (1) an open Bible on a blue field to recall Kilsyth's connections with the Covenanters and the two important Scottish religious revivals which started in the town in 1742 and 1838; (2) crossed swords on a red field in allusion to the Battle of Kilsyth (1645) fought between the Marquess of Montrose and a Covenanting army under General William Baillie; (3) crossed shuttles for the weaving industry which was so important in the early nineteenth century; (4) a miner's lamp for coal and ironstone mining. The colours used for the fields in these last two quarters were chosen for artistic reasons to balance up those in the first two quarters; this is as suggested by Lord Bute.[11] Overall the graceful cross not only reflects the similar motif on the Burgh seal but also appropriately recalls the town's many religious connections. The Latin motto—"I look forward with hope"— is that of Livingstone, Viscount Kilsyth.

STIRLING COUNTY COUNCIL

Azure, on a saltire between two caltraps in chief and base and as many spur rowels in the flanks Argent, a lion rampant Gules, armed and langued of the First.

(Lyon Register, xii, 38: 29 September 1890)

The County Council of THE COUNTY OF STIRLING bears arms which use the shield and saltire of Scotland as a base and to it have been added two caltraps (cheval traps) and two spur rowels to recall the famous Scottish victory at the Battle of Bannockburn, which occurred near Stirling in 1314; in that battle, King Robert I successfully used caltraps to prevent the approach of the English cavalry. The Scottish Royal lion has been added at the centre of the saltire to indicate the close connection between the County and the Royal Family of Scotland.

20

COUNTY OF CLACKMANNAN

The County of CLACKMANNAN has four Burghs, the Police Burghs of Alloa (the County town), Alva, Dollar and Tillicoultry.

BURGH OF ALLOA

Argent, on the waves of the sea Proper, an ancient galley Sable in full sail, the sail charged with the arms of the Earls of Mar & Kellie, pennon Gules, flag of the field charged with a pale of the Second; on a chief Vert, in the dexter a garland, the dexter half hops and the sinister barley, all Or, and in the sinister a golden fleece.

Above the Shield is placed a Helmet befitting their degree with a Mantling Sable doubled Argent, and on a Wreath of their Liveries is set for *Crest* a griffin Gules winged, armed and beaked Or, langued Azure, and on an Escrol over the same this *Motto* "In the Forefront".

(Lyon Register, xvii, 2: 11 June 1902)

ALLOA, as Alway, was confirmed as a Burgh of Regality in 1497 in favour of Alexander, 3rd Lord Erskine, and later in 1620, was erected into a Burgh of Regality in favour of John, 7th Lord Erskine and 2nd Earl of Mar, Lord High Treasurer of Scotland.[1] It became a Police Burgh in 1854.

The arms show a ship which bears on its sail the arms of the Earls of Mar & Kellie and the Erskine banner at its stern. These allude to the long-standing shipping and shipbuilding interests of the town and the close connections with the Erskine family, of which the Earl of Mar & Kellie is the Head. The green chief represents agriculture and on it are two symbols of other local industries; the golden garland of barley and hops is for whisky distilling and brewing and the golden fleece for woollen manufacturing. The griffin crest is taken from the supporters of the Earls of Mar & Kellie and the same colours are used; a griffin had been used on the Burgh seal and was carved on the seventeenth-century Town Cross. The arms were registered in honour of the Coronation of King Edward VII, the fees being paid, as a gift to the Burgh, by Walter, 12th Earl of Mar and 14th Earl of Kellie, who also suggested the motto adopted.[2]

ALVA became a Police Burgh in 1876. The Burgh has not recorded arms; its seal has on it representations of a bag of wool, a shuttle, a distaff and a water wheel with the motto "Industria et Labore"; all this refers to the spinning and weaving industries of the town.

DOLLAR, which was created a Burgh of Regality in 1702 in favour of Archibald, 10th Earl and 1st Duke of Argyll,[3] became a Police Burgh in 1891. The Burgh has not recorded arms; its seal shows a representation of the ruins of Castle Campbell, which stands high above the town and was once a seat of the Earls and Dukes of Argyll. There is a motto "Litterarum sedex amoenae"—"A place of learning and of pleasantness"; this refers to Dollar's famous Academy founded in 1818, and to the fair countryside in which the Burgh lies.

TILLICOULTRY was made a Burgh of Barony in 1634 for William Alexander of Menstrie, 1st Earl of Stirling.[4] It became a Police Burgh in 1871. The Burgh has not registered arms; its seal shows a view of the town with the Ochil Hills behind and the River Devon in the foreground, with the name "Tullich Cul Tir" (the Gaelic version of Tillicoultry) which means "the hill at the back of the land".

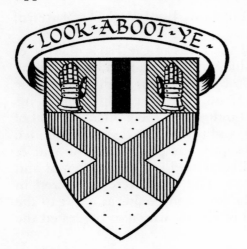

CLACKMANNAN COUNTY COUNCIL

Or, a saltire Gules; a chief tierced per pale, in the 1st Vert, a sinister gauntlet and in the 3rd [also Vert] a dexter gauntlet, both Proper, and in the 2nd, Argent, a pale Sable.

And in an Escrol over the same this *Motto* "Look Aboot Ye".

(Lyon Register, xxvii, 32: 22 April 1927)

The County Council of the COUNTY OF CLACKMANNAN bears arms which show the red saltire on a gold field used by Bruce of Annandale and by Bruce of Clackmannan. This, the gauntlets and the motto recall a legend which tells how King Robert I, when on a visit to Clackmannan, left his glove (mannan) on a stone (clack), and how, when he sent his squire to fetch it, the latter said, "Look aboot ye here till I return"; ever since, the place has been known as "Look-Aboot-ye Brae". The green field in the chief is for agriculture and the black pale on the silver ground recalls the long connection with the County of the family of Erskine, as represented by the Earls of Mar & Kellie. The fees involved in registering the arms were met by Walter, 12th Earl of Mar and 14th Earl of Kellie, who was Lord Lieutenant and County Convener at the time, and also Chancellor of the Order of the Thistle and Lord Clerk Register.[5] The seal adopted by the Council in 1890 had shown on it a representation of the old Tower on Clackmannan Hill, Clackmannan being then the County town.

21

COUNTY OF KINROSS

The County of **KINROSS** has one Burgh, the Police Burgh of Kinross, also the County town.

BURGH OF KINROSS

Argent, between two piles Gules, a representation of the Market Cross of the Burgh therefrom pendant the jougs all Proper; on a chief of the Second, two mullets of the field.

Above the Shield is placed a mural coronet suitable to a Burgh and in an Escrol under the same this *Motto* "Siccar".

(Lyon Register, xxxi, 18: 23 July 1934)

KINROSS was created a Burgh of Barony in 1540–41 in favour of Robert Douglas of Loch Leven, and was raised to a Burgh of Regality in favour of Sir William Bruce of Kinross in 1685.[1] It became a Police Burgh in 1864.

The arms are closely related to those of Douglas of Loch Leven, the major difference being that the third pile in the Douglas arms has been replaced by a representation of the Town Cross, with its iron "jougs", an old instrument of punishment by which defaulters could be secured to the Cross. The Town Cross was shown on the Burgh seal and also the motto "Siccar" which, while obviously referring to the "jougs", has clearly a connection with the "Lock Sicker" of the Earls of Morton; this Earldom was inherited by Sir William Douglas of Loch Leven in 1588 and until the early eighteenth century the Earls of Morton lived at Kinross.

KINROSS COUNTY COUNCIL

Argent, on an island Proper, in a loch undy Azure and of the field, a castle also Proper.

And in an Escrol under the Shield this *Motto* "For All Time".

(Lyon Register, xxvii, 35: 18 May 1927)

The County Council of THE COUNTY OF KINROSS bears arms which are based on the device on the seal adopted by the Council in 1890. They show a representation of the tower of Loch Leven Castle which stands in the Loch of the same name beside Kinross Burgh. This was the stronghold of the Douglases of Loch Leven from 1353 and it was there that Mary, Queen of Scots, was imprisoned and forced to abdicate in favour of her infant son, King James VI, in 1567, and thence she made her famous escape in the following year. The motto "For All Time" was chosen in 1927 and its selection was apparently influenced by the struggle the Council was then having to retain its separate identity in the negotiations prior to the passing of the Local Government (Scotland) Act, 1929.[2]

22

COUNTY OF FIFE

The County of FIFE has twenty-five Burghs, the Royal Burghs of St. Andrews, Kirkcaldy, Cupar (the County town), Kilrenny, Anstruther Easter & Anstruther Wester, Burntisland, Inverkeithing, Kinghorn, Pittenweem, Dunfermline, Crail, Culross, Auchtermuchty, Elie & Earlsferry, Falkland and Newburgh, and the Police Burghs of Buckhaven & Methil, Cowdenbeath, Ladybank, Leslie, Leven, Lochgelly, Markinch, Newport-on-Tay, St. Monance and Tayport.

ROYAL BURGH OF ST. ANDREWS

Parted per pale Azure and Argent: in the dexter, on a mount in base the figure of Saint Andrew Proper, bearing his cross in front of him Argent; in the sinister, growing out of a mount in base an oak tree Proper, fructed Or, in front of the trunk a boar passant Sable, langued Gules, armed Or.

Above the Shield is placed a mural crown and in an Escrol below the Shield this *Motto* "Dum Spiro Spero".

(Lyon Register, xxi, 57: 29 May 1912)

ST. ANDREWS, the cathedral town of the old diocese of the same name which was the Metropolitan see of Scotland, was founded as a Bishop's Burgh by leave of King David I between 1124 and 1144. In 1614, it was made a Burgh of Regality under the Archbishop of St. Andrews, and King James VI made it a Royal Burgh in 1620. It was, however, recognised as a *de facto* Royal Burgh from much earlier times.[1]

The arms consist of a rearrangement of the device on the reverse of the old Burgh seal of which a 1357 impression is on record.[2] The shield is parted in the blue and silver colours of St. Andrew and Scotland. The figure of the Saint with his cross needs no explanation. The boar and the oak tree which were, before 1912, sometimes regarded as the Burgh arms, recall the ancient name of the Burgh, which was Muckross, "the headland of the boars"; in olden times, the swamps near the town were inhabited by wild boars and the seal impression mentioned above bears the legend "Cursus Apri Regalis"—"Course of the Royal Boar". The Latin motto— "While I breathe, I hope"—comes from a seal of fairly modern origin. The arms were matriculated so that they could be displayed on the restored roof of Glasgow Cathedral.[3]

ROYAL BURGH OF KIRKCALDY

Azure, an abbey of three pyramids Argent each ensigned with a cross patée Or.

And on the reverse of the seal is insculped in a field Azure, the figure of Saint Bryce with long garments, on his head a mitre, in the dexter hand a fleur-de-lys, the sinister laid upon his breast, all Proper, standing in the porch of the church or abbey ensigned on the top as before, all betwixt a decrescent and a star in fess Or.

The *Motto* is "Vigilando Munio".

(Lyon Register, i, 457: c. 1673)

KIRKCALDY appears as a Burgh of the Abbot of Dunfermline in a Royal Charter dated between 1315 and 1328 and was set in feu to the bailies and the community in 1451. Though represented in the Convention from 1574, it was not until 1644 that it was created a Royal Burgh by King Charles I.[4] In 1930, the Royal Burgh of Dysart was joined to Kirkcaldy.

The Burgh is one of the four in Scotland which has two coats of arms. In the first coat, the abbey may refer to the church of Kirkcaldy dedicated in 1242 to St. Bryce, a disciple of St. Martin of Tours,[5] or it may have some connection with the west gable of Dunfermline Abbey. We may discount the suggestion made in 1927 by Mr. W. L. Macindoe, then Town Clerk, that it may have been copied from a similar feature on a medal of the Emperor Charlemagne.[6] It is a pity that the blazon says nothing about a gate in the Abbey wall, as in one version of the seal there is a man (? St. Bryce or a watchman) standing by a gate or door and this would seem to relate directly to the Latin motto—"I guard by watching".[7] The second coat shows St. Bryce standing in front of the Church, with the sun and moon above; he holds a fleur-de-lys, which may recall that he came to Scotland from France. In 1901, the possibility of showing the two coats on an impaled shield was discussed with the Lyon Office but the matter was never finalised.

ROYAL BURGH OF CUPAR

Gules, three crowns of myrtle Or.

Above the Shield is placed a coronet suitable to a Royal Burgh, thereon a Helmet befitting their degree with a Mantling Gules doubled Or, and on a Wreath of their Liveries is set for *Crest* a lion rampant Gules, armed and langued Azure, and in an Escrol under the Shield this *Motto* "Unitas".

(Lyon Register, xxviii, 50: 14 September 1929)

CUPAR is dated by Professor Pryde as a Royal Burgh of 1327 and thus of King Robert I.[8] It appears, however, that it may have been a Royal Burgh a considerable time before that as it seems to have been a place of some importance by the time of King Alexander III, whose wife Queen Margaret died there in 1275.

The arms are based on a post-Reformation seal used by the Burgh, though when the change was made is not clear, since there is on record an impression, dated as late as 1780, and similar to that on the pre-Reformation seal, which shows the Holy

Trinity on the obverse and a lion rampant on the reverse.[9] Despite this, tradition has it that the three wreaths of myrtle were substituted to commemorate the bloodless victory of the Protestant Lords of the Congregation over Queen Mary of Guise at Cupar Moor in 1559. The colours used are the red and gold of Macduff, Earl of Fife, and the crest is the Macduff lion; in the Middle Ages, Cupar was the seat of this powerful Earldom. The Latin motto—"Unity"—may refer to the Holy Trinity. An offer by Lord Lyon Grant to allow the Burgh to have two angels as supporters (as shown on one of its former (probably eighteenth century) seals) was not accepted by the Town Council.[10]

ROYAL BURGH OF KILRENNY, ANSTRUTHER EASTER & ANSTRUTHER WESTER

Tierced in pairle reversed: 1st, Sable, an anchor Argent; 2nd, Gules, three fish fretted in triangle Proper; 3rd, Argent, on the waves of the sea in base Azure and of the field, an open boat rowed by four mariners, the steersman at the helm, a hook suspended by a chain dependant from the side near the stern, in chief the rays of the sun issuant from a cloud, all Proper.

Above the Shield is set a Burghal crown and in an Escrol over the same this *Motto* "Virtute Res Parvae Crescunt" and in another below the Shield this *Motto* "Semper Tibi Pendeat Hamus".

(Lyon Register, xxix, 31: 12 July 1930)

KILRENNY, ANSTRUTHER EASTER & ANSTRUTHER WESTER were united in 1929. Kilrenny was created a Burgh of Regality in favour of John Betoun of Balfour in 1578 and was, by accident, included in the roll of Royal Burghs in 1592; there it stayed despite an attempt to resign in 1672.[11] Anstruther Easter was made a Burgh of Barony in favour of John Anstruther of that Ilk in 1571–72 and raised by King James VI to a Royal Burgh in 1583.[12] Anstruther Wester was erected into a Burgh of Barony in favour of the Prior of Pittenweem in 1540–41 and was raised to a Royal Burgh by King James VI in 1587.[13]

The arms of the united Burgh conjoin the devices on the seals of the three former Burghs; though there are only eighteenth-century impressions on record, the seals themselves are obviously older.[14] The anchor is for Anstruther Easter and denotes that it is a seaport; the black and silver colours are those of Anstruther of that Ilk, whose fortress, Dreel Castle, is now a ruin at the mouth of the Dreel Burn. The three fish are for Anstruther Wester, and are thought to refer to the salmon in the Dreel Burn which is the boundary between the two Anstruthers; the colours follow tradition. The Kilrenny arms show a typical fishing scene (cf. Crail); again, the colouring is traditional. The mottoes caused some discussion as Anstruther Wester had no motto on its seal. Eventually, it was decided to place the Anstruther Easter one—"By well-doing poverty is enriched"—above the shield, and the Kilrenny one—"May the hook ever hang in your favour"—below; the latter refers directly to the hook shown in the arms.

ROYAL BURGH OF BURNTISLAND

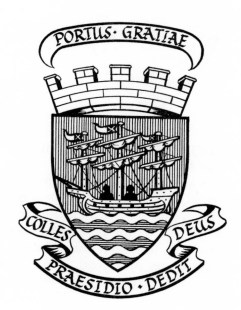

Gules, on the sea in base undy Argent and Azure, a three-masted galiot Or, on deck two mariners, her sails furled and pennants flying Proper.

Above the Shield is placed a mural coronet and in Escrols over and below the Shield these *Mottoes* "Portus Gratiae" and "Colles Praesidio Dedit Deus".

(Lyon Register, xxxiii, 13: 6 April 1938)

BURNTISLAND town and harbour belonged from ancient times to Dunfermline Abbey. It was created a Royal Burgh by King James V in 1541.[15]

The arms repeat the device on the Burgh seal, a device said to have been used by Burntisland for centuries. The ship refers to the town's long history as a seaport and its connection in more modern times with shipbuilding. The red and gold colours of Fife are used; they are also the colours of Wemyss, a family which once owned all the lands in the neighbourhood. Two mottoes were allowed: "Portus Gratiae" (or "Portus Salutis") was the name given to the place by the Romans because of its safe harbour; the other motto (also in Latin)—"God gave the hills for protection"—was suggested by Mr. A. Wishart, W.S., of Edinburgh, who was a native of Burntisland parish and an authority on its history. The hills referred to in the motto are Dunearn and The Binn, which guard the town to the North.[16]

INVERKEITHING seems to have been created a Royal Burgh by King Malcolm IV between 1153 and 1162 but to have been granted by King William the Lion

ROYAL BURGH OF INVERKEITHING

Parted per pale Gules and Azure: in the dexter on a base undy Argent and of the Second, a ship with crenellated prow and stern Or, sail furled Argent, the mast surmounted with a cross Gold; and in the sinister the figure of Saint Peter vested and crowned standing in front of a bench, and holding in his dexter hand a church, and in his sinister two keys all Proper.

[Above the Shield is placed a Burghal coronet.]

(Lyon Register, xxix, 57: 29 December 1930)

to his illegitimate son, Sir Ralph de Londoniis, before 1195. By 1223, it was again held of the Crown.[17]

The arms are taken from the obverse and reverse of the oldest known Burgh seal of which impressions dated 1296 and 1357 are on record.[18] On the suggestion of the parish minister and local historian, the Rev. William Stephen, the Town Council specially asked for both sides of the seal to be included in the coat of arms.[19] The dexter side in the red and gold colours of Fife shows a ship, with crenellated prow and a cross at its masthead, described by the Lyon Clerk in 1930 as "most unique in heraldry", thus recalling "the passage and ship of Inverkeithing" granted by King David I to the monks of Dunfermline in 1129; the red, gold and silver colours also allude to Scrymgeour, Lord Inverkeithing and Earl of Dundee. The sinister side shows St. Peter, patron saint of the Burgh, holding his keys and a model of the parish church. The blue field and the gold of the Saint's halo could refer to the special connection the town had, through its ferry, with the shrine of St. Margaret at Dunfermline.

KINGHORN appears to have been a Royal Burgh of King William the Lion between 1165 and 1172 and was so recognised by King Alexander III in 1285.[20]

The arms follow the device on the obverse of the Burgh seal of which a sixteenth-century impression is on record.[21] They show the Castle of Kinghorn, a favourite residence and hunting seat of early Scottish Kings, and specially connected with King Alexander III (1249–1286) who was accidentally killed near the town. The blue and silver colours recall that the Castle was granted to Sir John Lyon of Glamis about 1375 as part of the dowry of his bride Jean, daughter of King Robert II, and that his descendant Patrick, 9th Lord Glamis, was created Earl of Kinghorne by King James VI in 1606. This is the family of H.M. Queen Elizabeth, the Queen Mother. The red

ROYAL BURGH OF KINGHORN

Azure, on a mount Proper, a castle triple-towered Argent, masoned Vert, windows, portcullis and fans Gules, the middle tower ensigned with a cross patée fitchée Or, between two mullets in fess of the Second.

[Above the Shield is placed a Burghal coronet] and in an Escrol under the same this *Motto* "Sanctus Leonardus De Kinghorn".

(Lyon Register, xxviii, 43: 3 July 1929)

windows show that it was a Royal castle and the green masoning seems to be for St. Leonard, patron saint of the Burgh, since green is a colour specially associated with him.[22] The Latin motto—"St. Leonard of Kinghorn"—comes from the reverse of the old seal referred to above and which showed St. Leonard giving a blessing.

ROYAL BURGH OF PITTENWEEM

Azure, in the sea a galley with her oars in action Argent, and therein standing the figure of Saint Adrian with long garments close girt, and a mitre on his head Proper, holding in his sinister hand a crosier Or; on the stern a flag disveloped Argent, charged with the Royal Arms of Scotland.

With this *Word* "Deo Duce".

(Lyon Register, i, 460: 2 August 1673)

PITTENWEEM was created *de novo* a Burgh of Barony of the Prior of Pittenweem in 1526 and was made a Royal Burgh by King James V in 1541.[23]

The arms repeat the device on an old seal of the Burgh of which a sixteenth-century impression is on record.[24] They show St. Adrian, the martyr of the May, on his hazardous sea journey to Scotland from Pannonia in Hungary. He established a community on the Isle of May, off the Fife coast, became a missionary to the Picts and is said to have been slain on the May about 870 during a Danish invasion. St. Adrian is connected with Pittenweem, as a convent there was joined to the May community, and about the twelfth century monks from the May moved to Pittenweem to be nearer their property on the mainland. They built a priory and the town grew up around it. The Latin motto—"With God as leader"—seems to refer to the Saint's journeyings and his missionary enterprises.

ROYAL BURGH OF DUNFERMLINE

Azure, on a rock Proper two lions supporting a tower with four steps Argent, masoned Sable, windows and portcullis Gules.

And in an Escrol over the same this *Motto* "Esto Rupes Inaccessa".

(Lyon Register, xx, 35: 12 May 1909)

DUNFERMLINE, the ancient Capital of Scotland's Celtic Kings, was created a Royal Burgh by King David I between 1124 and 1127. Later it was dependent on the Abbey of Dunfermline and in 1395 was set in feu to the provost, bailies and community. After the Reformation, it was created a Burgh of Regality in favour of George, 6th Earl (and later 1st Marquess) of Huntly, in 1588–89 but five years afterwards was conveyed in regality to the Queen, Anne of Denmark. From then on, it was regarded as a Royal Burgh.[25]

The arms are clearly based on the old Burgh seal but only eighteenth-century impressions are on record.[26] The tower is Malcolm's Tower, the fortress of King Malcolm III (1057–1093), husband of Queen Margaret; some remains of it can still be seen in Pittencrieff Glen. The red windows and portcullis denote its Royal ownership and the lions supporting it are considered to be Royal lions. The Latin motto—"May the rock be inaccessible"—appears to recall that Malcolm's Tower was built on a site "strikingly adapted for a stronghold".[27] The arms were matriculated in 1909 after the Lord Advocate had directed the prosecution of the Town Council for illegal use of arms; this arose after the Council had presented an unauthorised version of its arms for display at the Royal Caledonian School at Bushey, Hertfordshire.[28]

ROYAL BURGH OF CRAIL

Sable, on the waves of the sea in base undy Argent and Azure, a ship with one mast Or, sail furled, pennoned of Scotland, and manned by seven mariners full-faced Proper; in the dexter chief four stars of the Fourth, and in the sinister as many like stars, accompanied by a crescent of the Second.

Above the Shield is placed a mural coronet and in an Escrol under the Shield this *Motto* "In Verbo Tuo Laxabo Rete".

(Lyon Register, xxxiii, 28: 25 August 1938)

CRAIL appears about 1170 as a Burgh of Ada, Countess of Northumberland, mother of King William the Lion and King Malcolm IV. On her death in 1178, it fell to the Crown and became a Royal Burgh. It subsequently received a Charter from King Robert I between 1314 and 1329.[29]

The arms show what Lord Bute calls "the very beautiful conventionalising of a realistic subject"—a night fishing scene.[30] The seal on which they are based is very old—there is an impression almost exactly the same attached to the 1357 Document relating to the Ransom of King David II, Crail being one of the Burghs which attested that Document.[31] An old sealing instrument, of pre-1550 date, which bore an identical sealing device, was found in 1902 during the demolition of a house in Castle Street in Crail.[32] The Latin motto—"At Thy Word I will let down the net"—was chosen in 1938 on the suggestion of the Rev. Professor J. H. Baxter of St. Andrews University.[33] The cost of matriculation of the arms was met from a gift made to the Burgh by Mrs. Torrance, Croft Bank, Crail, to mark the Coronation of King George VI.[34]

ROYAL BURGH OF CULROSS

Azure, on a mount, a representation of the Abbey of Culross Proper, in front thereof the figure of Saint Servanus, vested Argent, his hands raised in prayer Proper.

Above the Shield is placed a mural coronet.

(Lyon Register, xxxiii, 22: 26 May 1938)

CULROSS was created a Burgh of Barony for the Abbot of Culross in 1490 and was made a Royal Burgh by King James VI in 1592.[35]

The arms are based on the device on the Burgh seal and show St. Servanus or Serf standing in prayer in front of the Abbey of Culross founded by Malcolm, Earl of Fife, in 1217. St. Serf is said to have sheltered Thenew, Princess of Lothian and mother of St. Kentigern or Mungo, at Culross, and to have baptised and educated St. Kentigern there, before the latter went on to the West to become the great missionary to the Clyde Valley and the founder of Glasgow Cathedral. The blue and silver colours probably recall that Culross Abbey was dedicated to the Virgin Mary and St. Andrew as well as to St. Serf. The three birds on the roof are traditionally associated with the Abbey and St. Serf, and this appears to be the reason why they are not specifically mentioned in the blazon.

The group of four Royal Burghs which follows is quite special since none of them was ever represented in Parliament, or in the Convention of Royal Burghs until modern times; they are known to historians as the four inactive Royal Burghs of Fife.

ROYAL BURGH OF AUCHTERMUCHTY

Per pale: dexter, per chevron Gules and Or, a boar passant Or in chief and in base a crescent of the First accompanied by two barrulets wavy Sable; sinister, per fess indented Vert and barry of six indented Argent and Sable, three barley heads paleways Or and Gules in chief.

Below the Shield, which is ensigned of a coronet proper to a Royal Burgh, upon a Compartment with this *Motto* "Dum Sero Spero" are set for *Supporters* dexter, a boar Or, langued and bristled Gules, and armed and hooved Proper; sinister, a countryman attired in doublet and breeches Gules, stockings Argent and shoes Sable, upon his head a blue bonnet, and with his left hand sowing from a seed-basket, both supporters sustaining over their exterior shoulders respectively a thistle and a rose stem, leaved Vert and flowered Proper.

(Lyon Register, l, 1: 25 July 1966)

AUCHTERMUCHTY was made a Royal Burgh by King James V in 1517.[36] The arms show on the dexter side a boar above a chevron to recall that Auchtermuchty means "upland of the boars"; the boar is a royal boar, as indicated by the gold and red colours, from Falkland Forest, of which the site of the town once formed part; below, there is a red Seton crescent in reference to George Seytoun, a near kinsman of George, 5th Lord Seton, the faithful adherent of Mary, Queen of Scots; in 1542 he obtained part of the south quarter of Auchtermuchty; the black wavy lines allude to the swampy ground of the district and to Myres Castle near the town. The sinister side shows the barley grown in the fertile fields of Auchtermuchty and used for whisky distilling, and, in the lower part, the ground where the sower (the sinister supporter) casts his seed. The supporters are a Royal boar from Falkland Forest and a countryman sowing seed; the latter comes from the Burgh seal which showed a sower at his work in a field. The thistle and the rose also come from the seal and respectively recall the Charter of King James V in 1517 and the confirmation by King Charles I in 1631 of a Charter granted by King James VI in 1591. The Latin motto—"While I sow, I hope"—was on the Burgh seal.

ROYAL BURGH OF ELIE & EARLSFERRY

Quarterly: 1st and 4th, Gules, on the waves of the sea in base undy Argent and Azure, an ancient one-masted ship in full sail Or, flying the Scottish pennon, and the mainsail charged with (the arms of Macduff, Earl of Fife) a lion rampant of the field, armed and langued of the Third; 2nd and 3rd, Vert, an ancient one-masted ship in full sail, oars in action, Or, flying the Scottish pennon, and on the mainsail the arms of Scott of Grangemuir, viz.: Or, on a bend Azure, between two crescents of the field, a mullet Argent, a bordure engrailed Gules.

[Above the Shield is placed a Burghal coronet] and in an Escrol below the Shield this *Motto* "Unitas Alit Comitatem" (1589 & 1598)

(Lyon Register, xxix, 32: 22 July 1930)

ELIE & EARLSFERRY united to form a single Burgh in 1929. Elie was created a Burgh of Barony in favour of William Scott of Grangemuir in 1598–99,[37] while Earlsferry received from King James VI in 1589 a Charter which confirmed that it had been a free Burgh "beyond the memory of man".[38] The united Burgh has been accepted as a Royal Burgh.

The arms recall in the 1st and 4th quarters Earlsferry, the older Burgh: the red and gold colours of Fife are used and the ship with Macduff's arms on its sail alludes to "The Earl's Ferry" ("Passagium Comitis") between the town and North Berwick which was for a time one of the main routes from the Lothians to Fife.[39] The name of the Burgh and of the Ferry is traditionally associated with the assistance given to Macduff, Earl of Fife, by local fishermen who ferried him over to East Lothian when he was fleeing from Macbeth, the Mormaer of Moray, who succeeded Duncan I as King of Scotland (1040–1057). The 2nd and 3rd quarters are for Elie, also by the sea, and repeat the ship motif; in this case the ship's sail bears the arms of Scott of Grangemuir. The Latin motto—"Unity fosters courtesy"—is followed by the foundation dates of the two Burghs.

ROYAL BURGH OF FALKLAND

Azure, on a mount a stag lodged reguardant at the foot of an oak tree, all Proper.

Above the Shield is placed a mural coronet and in an Escrol below the same this *Motto* "Discite Justitiam Moniti Non Temnere Christum".

(Lyon Register, xxxiii, 18: 29 April 1938)

FALKLAND was created a Royal Burgh by King James II in 1458.[40] The arms repeat the device on the Burgh seal of which a seventeenth-century impression is on record.[41] The stag resting under the blue sky in the shade of a great oak tree refers to the Royal hunting Forest of Falkland, which was cut down by Cromwellian forces in 1652 to supply wood for the construction of a fort at Dundee; the Castle and later the Palace of Falkland were favourite holiday residences of Scottish Kings from James I to James VI. The Latin motto means "Learn righteousness and take heed not to despise Christ" and is an adaptation of Virgil, *Aeneid*, vi, 620, "Discite justitiam moniti et non temnere divos" and is most appropriate for a town which was the birthplace of the famous Covenanter, Richard Cameron.

NEWBURGH was granted as a Burgh to the Abbot of Lindores by King Alexander III in 1266 and was, in 1600, raised to a Burgh of Regality in favour of Patrick Leslie, later Lord Lindores, son of the 5th Earl of Rothes. In 1631, King Charles I created the town a Royal Burgh.[42a] The arms repeat several of the features on the old Burgh seal. They use the red and gold colours of Macduff, Earl of Fife. The couped cross quadrate with its lion rampant represents the famous and ancient Cross Macduff, situated near to the Burgh, and of which the base still remains; the Cross formed the sanctuary of the Clan Macduff. The blue colour of the thistles and the buckle in the chief recall the Leslie connection, the thistle being part of an augmentation granted by King Charles I to Alexander Leslie, 1st Earl of Leven, the noted Covenanting General. The battlements refer to the castle in the arms of the Lordship of Lindores. The Latin motto—"By the Cross of St. Andrew were the people taught"—is intended to be a shortened version of the motto of Lindores Abbey which was "Biduo Pendens in

ROYAL BURGH OF NEWBURGH

Gules, on a cross quadrate [couped] Or, a lion rampant of the field, armed and langued Azure; on a chief embattled of the Second a round buckle between two thistles of the Third, flowered of the First.

Above the Shield is placed a coronet appropriate to a Burgh, and in an Escrol below the same this *Motto* "Cruce Sancti Andreas Docebatur Populum".

(Lyon Register, xxxix, 54: 23 January 1953)

Cruce Beatus Andreas Docebat Populum". Unfortunately something went wrong with the Latin in the process and the motto granted contains two grammatical errors, "Andreas" should be "Andreae" and "Populum" should be "Populus". These errors were brought to the notice of the present Lord Lyon (Sir James Monteith Grant) in 1970 by Professors A. A. M. Duncan and E. L. G. Stones of Glasgow University, but, after some consideration and discussion, he decided to leave things as they were.

BUCKHAVEN & METHIL was formed in 1891 when the three towns of Buckhaven, Innerleven and Methil united to form a Police Burgh. Methil is said to have been created a Burgh of Barony in favour of David, 2nd Earl of Wemyss, by Archbishop James Sharp of St. Andrews in 1662.[42b] The Burgh has not recorded arms; the device on its seal shows a steamship with sails on the sea and a fish in a net below with the motto—"Carbone Carbasoque", which could be translated "By coal and by sail".

BURGH OF COWDENBEATH

Per fess Argent and Or: a bar dehanced Vert, in chief two birch trees issuant from the bar Proper, fructed of the Second, and in base two barrulets wavy Sable; over all a chevron of the Last charged with a wheel of the Second.

Below the Shield which is ensigned with a coronet appropriate to a Burgh is placed in an Escrol this *Motto* "Stent Nae Stent".

(Lyon Register, xxxix, 25: 29 July 1952)

COWDENBEATH grew up around the extensive coalfields of the area and became a Police Burgh in 1890.

The arms are partly a conventionalising of the device on the seal adopted by the Burgh in 1892 which showed a pit-head scene. The silver field and black chevron recall that this was once country owned by the Balfour family, but with its golden wheel the chevron also symbolises the pit-head hoist just as the black barrulets denote the coal underground. It is also intended to indicate that the days of feudalism are long past and that coal-mining (now nationalised) is the major interest of the town. The birch trees are for Beath (the name of the parish) which is a Gaelic word meaning "birch tree". The Scots motto which means "Effort always effort" or "Don't stint, always give of your best", is of special interest as the word "stent" refers to the amount of work allocated to a miner during a shift and has the same meaning as the English word "stint". It was suggested by Mr. A. K. M. Reid of Dunfermline.[43]

LADYBANK became a Police Burgh in 1877. The Burgh has not recorded arms; its seal bears a device showing a decorative capital letter "L", with a mural crown above.

BURGH OF LESLIE

Party per chevron Azure and Argent: in chief two garbs Or, in base, on a bend of the First, three buckles Gold.

Above the Shield is placed a Burghal crown and thereon a Helmet befitting their degree with a Mantling Azure doubled Argent, and on a Wreath of their Liveries is set for *Crest* a demi-griffin Proper, armed and winged Or, and in an Escrol over the same this *Motto* "Grip Fast".

(Lyon Register, xxix, 29: 4 July 1930)

LESLIE was (as Leslie Green) created a Burgh of Barony in favour of George Leslie, 1st Earl of Rothes, in 1457–58.[44] It became a Police Burgh in 1865.

The arms are to some extent a conventionalising of the device on the Burgh seal in use in 1929. The Leslie blue and silver colours are used and the Leslie arms are shown in base. The two garbs are for the agricultural and manufacturing industries (especially flax-spinning) of the town. The demi-griffin crest and the motto are those of the Leslie Earls of Rothes who were closely associated with the town until after the 1914–18 war.

LEVEN was created a Burgh of Barony in 1609 by George Gladstanes, Archbishop of St. Andrews, in favour of George Lauder of Bass.[45] It became a Police Burgh in 1867.

The arms retain the saltire pattern of the device on the old Burgh seal which was designed by a local clergyman, the Rev. A. T. Grant.[46] The gold field and black bend sinister recall the family of Christie of Durie and the golden crescents thereon Durie of that Ilk; both these families have a long association with the town. The blue bend dexter with its golden buckles comes from the Leslie arms and refers to the Burgh's connection with that family and in particular with Alexander Leslie, the famous

BURGH OF LEVEN

Or, a bend sinister Sable, charged with two crescents of the First, surmounted of a bend dexter Azure, charged with a mitre in pale betwixt two buckles also of the First; in chief a lymphad Gules, sails furled Argent, oars in action Sable, flagged of Scotland, viz.: Azure, a saltire Argent, and in base, a griffin's head erased Gules.

Below the Shield which is ensigned of a Burghal coronet is placed in an Escrol this *Motto* "Grip Fame".

(Lyon Register, xli, 14: 1 December 1955)

Covenanting General, who was created Earl of Leven in 1641. The mitre is for the archi-episcopal founder of the Burgh, the red griffin's head for Lauder of Bass, and the galley for Leven's importance as a seaport. The motto is a variant of the Leslie "Grip Fast".

BURGH OF LOCHGELLY

Quarterly wavy: 1st, Argent, three lozenges Sable; 2nd, per bend Azure and Gules, on a bend engrailed Or, between a mullet in chief and a fleur-de-lys in base Argent, a baton of the First; 3rd, Sable, a plate charged with a lowe of flame Gules; 4th, Argent, a miner's pick Sable, the head in chief and the haft Proper, surmounted of a fess of the Second, charged with three cinquefoils of the field.

Below the Shield which is ensigned with a coronet appropriate to a Burgh is placed in an Escrol this *Motto* "By Industry we Flourish".

(Lyon Register, xxxvii, 20: 21 September 1948)

LOCHGELLY grew from a village into a thriving coal-mining town in the second half of the nineteenth century. It became a Police Burgh in 1876.

The quartered arms show (1) three black lozenges for coal and the coal-mining industry; (2) three features from the arms of the Earls of Minto, who formerly owned Lochgelly House, and whose ancestor, Sir Gilbert Elliot, first exploited the Lochgelly coalfield; these are a blue baton and golden engrailed bar on a red field (for Elliot), a silver star on blue (for Murray), and a fleur-de-lys (for Kynynmound); the wavy in the base also recalls Loch Gelly; (3) a representation of a lamp, both for a miner's safety lamp and for the old tallow lamp of which the town was the main centre of manufacture; (4) a miner's pick, which is another reference to coal-mining, with three silver cinquefoils on a black fess for Boswell of Balmuto, a family closely connected with the district. The motto comes from the seal adopted by the Burgh in 1892. Mr Alexander Westwater, Editor of *The Lochgelly Times*, advised the Town Council regarding its Petition to the Lyon Court.

BURGH OF MARKINCH

Gules, on a cross nowy-quadrat Argent a cock of the First.

Above the Shield is placed a coronet appropriate to a Burgh of Barony (videlicet: Gules masoned Argent) and in an Escrol below the same this *Motto* "Constans In Fide".

(Lyon Register, lv, 35: 29 June 1972)

MARKINCH, which was created a Burgh of Barony in favour of James Law of Brunton in 1673,[47] became a Police Burgh in 1891.

The arms show a cross nowy quadrat (similar to a cross quadrate, cf. Alyth) in allusion to the ancient parish church, a representation of which appeared on the 1892 Burgh Seal and whose Norman tower is one of the finest in Scotland; as the church was dedicated in 1243 to St. John the Baptist, silver and red colours have been used. The cock, also coloured red, comes from the arms of Law of Brunton. The Latin motto—"Constant in the Faith"—has been used for many years by the Burgh; it is obviously a reference to the long history of the parish church and probably also recalls the strong attachment of the men of Markinch to the Covenanting cause "in defence of which they spent lives, land and gear".[48]

NEWPORT-ON-TAY, which owes its existence to the ancient ferries which plied from there to Dundee, became a Police Burgh in 1887.

BURGH OF NEWPORT-ON-TAY

Gules, upon a base undy Argent and Azure, a lymphad Or, its mast flagged of Scotland, and in the stern a demi-lion rampant issuant of the Second, armed and langued and sustaining in his paws a cross-crosslet fitchée Azure, the sail emblazoned of the arms of Nairne of Sandfoord (videlicet: per pale Argent and Sable, on a chaplet four mullets, all counterchanged).

Below the Shield which is ensigned of a coronet appropriate to a Burgh is placed in an Escrol this *Motto* "Dei Flumen Nobis Lumen".

(Lyon Register, xl, 156: 3 August 1956)

The arms resemble the device on the 1892 Burgh seal but most of the detail has been altered. The ship and the sea recall that Newport was at the southern end of the ferry of Seamylnes, a ferry which ran for centuries until the opening of the Tay Road Bridge in 1966. The ship bears on its sail the arms of Nairne of Sandford (now St. Fort) while the lion with the cross in the stern comes from the arms of Berry of Tayfield; these two families have very close associations with the town. The red and gold colours are those of Fife and are a reminder that on the former Burgh seal, the ship's sail bore the Macduff lion rampant. The Latin motto—"The river of God is a light to us"—was suggested by the parish minister, the Rev. R. A. Howieson; based on Psalm 46:4; its thought is this: "Though we dwell by the banks of the noble Tay and admire its beauties and appreciate its benefits, yet it is the river of God which is our guiding light."

ST. MONANCE, formerly called Abercrombie, was created a Burgh of Barony in 1596 in favour of Sir William Sandilands of St. Monance.[49] In 1649, the superiority of the Burgh passed to General David Leslie, 1st Lord Newark, the able Scottish Covenanting general, and thereafter in 1696 by marriage to Sir Alexander Anstruther. It became a Police Burgh in 1933.

The arms show the silver dog from the crest of Sandilands, Lord Abercrombie, the gold buckle of Leslie and also the griffin's head from the crest of the Bairds of Elie who became the Superiors of the Burgh in modern times. The griffin's head also recalls the Leslies, as they have a demi-griffin as their crest. The two features of the Leslie arms implement the desire of the Town Council that General David Leslie's special connection should be clearly shown in the arms. The cross represents the famous Church of St. Monance, built by King David II between 1363 and 1367, and a great landmark above the sea; the fishing scene comes from the seventeenth-century seal of the Burgh[50] and the fish could refer to the fish "reddendo" payable annually

M

BURGH OF ST. MONANCE

Per chevron Azure and Or: a buckle of the Second between a talbot's head couped Argent and a griffin's head of the Last, both langued Gules and respectant, all in chief; and in base an open boat contournée, manned of four fishermen Sable, and issuant therefrom a cross-crosslet fitchée of the Fourth, and on a base undy of the First and Third a fish naiant of the Second, surmounted of a pile of two points reversed issuant from the base masculé-pierced fretwise Gules.

Below the Shield which is ensigned of the proper mural coronet of a Burgh of Barony (videlicet: Gules masoned Argent) is placed in an Escrol this *Motto*, "Mare Vivimus".

(Lyon Register, xlv, 64: 7 November 1962)

by the Burgh to its Sandilands superior. The Latin motto—"From the sea we have life"—comes from the old seal. Mr. R. G. Cant of St. Andrews University advised the Town Council in connection with their Petition for a Grant of arms.[51]

BURGH OF TAYPORT

Per fess wavy Or and in base undy Azure and Argent: a pile chequy of the Last and Sable [issuant from base] ensigned of a mullet of six points Gules in the honour point, accompanied on the dexter by a lymphad of the Second, flagged of Scotland, her sail charged with the arms of Durie of that Ilk, viz.: Azure, a chevron Argent between three crescents Or, and on the sinister by an anchor also Azure.

Below the Shield which is ensigned of a coronet appropriate to a Burgh is set in an Escrol this *Motto* "Te Oportet Alte Ferri".

(Lyon Register, xxxix, 89: 12 June 1953)

TAYPORT, also called Ferryport-on-Craig or South Ferry, was created a Burgh of Barony for Robert Durie of that Ilk in 1598–99 and was raised to a Burgh of Regality in 1725 in favour of Robert Douglas of Glenbervie.[52] It became a Police Burgh under its present name in 1887.

The arms, which were registered in honour of the Coronation of Queen Elizabeth

II are really a heraldic version of the non-armorial Burgh seal adopted in 1892. The silver and black chequered pile with the red star recall the lighthouse; silver and black are also the Young colours and thus allude to the first Provost of the Burgh, Mr. James Stephen Young. The star could also refer to the Douglas connection and also to the Scott family who had the lands of Scotscraig nearby. The anchor is for the port and the ship for the ferry which went across the Firth to Broughty Ferry in Angus and is said to have been the oldest in Scotland; on its sails are the Durie arms. The Latin motto, which was composed by the distinguished Scottish poet and scholar, Professor Douglas Young, grandson of the first Provost, puns on the fact that the town was both a Tay port and a Tay ferry. Its meaning is "It behoves thee to bear thyself loftily" and is thus appropriate both for the lighthouse and for the citizens of the Burgh.

FIFE COUNTY COUNCIL

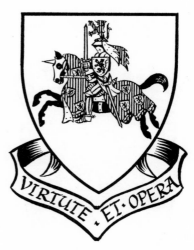

Argent, a knight armed at all points on a horse at full speed, in his dexter hand a sword erect all Proper, his surcoat Argent, on his sinister arm a shield Or, charged with a lion rampant Gules, the visor of his helmet shut, over which on a wreath of his liveries with a Mantling of the Fourth doubled of the Third, is set a lion rampant, issuing out of the wreath, of the Fourth, the caparisons of the horse of the Last, fimbriated of the Third, and thereon six shields of the Last, each charged with a lion rampant of the Fourth.

And in an Escrol below the Shield this *Motto* "Virtute Et Opera".

(Lyon Register, xxvii, 39: 31 May 1927)

The County Council of THE COUNTY OF FIFE bears arms which are virtually the same as the device on the seal adopted by the Council in 1890. They are based on a seal of Duncan, Earl of Fife, of which a 1360 impression is on record and described as "an armed knight on horseback at full speed, a sword in his right hand, and on his left arm a shield charged with a lion rampant which is repeated on the caparisons of the horse".[53] This representation of "The Thane of Fife" has long been recognised as the County emblem. It appears on a colour of the Fife Fencible Cavalry (disbanded 1797) and was used during the nineteenth century by the County Yeomanry.[54] Something very similar was granted as a crest to William Duff of Dipple, who was created Earl Fife and Baron Braco in 1759, and passed down to his descendants the Dukes of Fife (cr. 1889); in 1931, it was granted with suitable differencing to the Burgh of Macduff (q.v.). The Latin motto—"By virtue and energy"—was that of Duff of Braco and is now used by the Dukes of Fife. The fees connected with the grant of arms were met from a gift to the Council by Sir Ralph Anstruther and Dr. William Low of Blebo, respectively Convener and Vice-Convener of the County in 1927, and H.R.H. the Duchess of Fife gave her approval to the use of her family crest as the basis of the coat of arms.[55]

23

COUNTY OF EAST LOTHIAN

The County of EAST LOTHIAN has seven Burghs, the Royal Burghs of Haddington (the County town), Dunbar and North Berwick, and the Police Burghs of Cockenzie & Port Seton, East Linton, Prestonpans and Tranent.

ROYAL BURGH OF HADDINGTON

Azure, on a mount in base Proper, a goat rampant contournée Argent, attired and unguled Or, browsing upon a vine also Proper.

[Above the Shield is placed a Burghal coronet.]

(Lyon Register, xxvii, 44: 8 July 1927)

HADDINGTON, which appears to have been created a Royal Burgh by King David I between 1124 and 1153, may also for a short time have been a Burgh of Ada, Countess of Northumberland, and mother of King William the Lion and King Malcolm IV, reverting to the Crown on her death in 1178.[1]

The arms are based on the device on the oldest known Burgh seals of which impressions dated 1296 and 1357 are on record.[2] The significance of the goat browsing on the tree is not very clear. It may be merely a classical design adopted by the engraver, since these were common enough in medieval times, or it may have some local significance, as the names Goat Burn and Goatfield still survive in Haddington today. The blue field merely provides a suitable background for a day-time scene. The arms were matriculated so that they could appear on the Scottish National War Memorial at Edinburgh Castle.[3]

ROYAL BURGH OF DUNBAR

Gules, on a rock Proper a castle triple-towered Argent, masoned Sable, windows and portcullis closed of the field.

Above the Shield is placed a mural coronet as befitting a Royal Burgh.

(Lyon Register, xxxiv, 60: 20 November 1942)

DUNBAR, a thirteenth-century Burgh of the Earls of Dunbar, was granted in 1370 to the Earl of March but reverted to the Crown on the forfeiture of George, Earl of March and 11th Earl of Dunbar, in 1434. It was created a Royal Burgh in 1445 by King James II.[4]

The arms come straight from the oldest known Burgh seal, of which an impression dated 1357 is on record.[5] The red and silver colours are those of the ancient Earldom of Dunbar and the castle is the Castle of Dunbar whose most famous defender (1338) was Agnes, Countess of March and Dunbar and Countess of Moray (in her own right), daughter of the renowned Thomas Randolph, Earl of Moray (d. 1332). The Castle was destroyed by Act of Parliament in 1567. The arms were registered so that the Burgh could present a plaque bearing them to H.M.S. *Dunbar*.[6]

NORTH BERWICK was a Burgh dependent on the Earls of Douglas in the fourteenth century. By 1425, it had been created a Royal Burgh,[7] but it is not certain by which King; there is a local tradition, not authenticated, that the Charter was granted by King Robert III (1390–1406).

The arms are closely modelled on the device on the Burgh seal, of which a seventeenth century impression is on record.[8] They show a day-time scene with a ship, with four rowers, and the Earl of Fife on board. The Earl is being taken across the "Earl's Ferry" which went from North Berwick in East Lothian to Earlsferry in Fife (cf. Elie & Earlsferry).[9] The ship's figurehead is the red lion of Fife. The lands of North Berwick formerly belonged to the old Earls of Fife, and Malcolm, the 5th Earl, founded a Benedictine nunnery near the town early in the thirteenth century.

ROYAL BURGH OF NORTH BERWICK

Azure, upon a sea in base undy Argent and of the First semée of fish Sable and Or respectively, a lymphad of the Second, her jib set and mainsail furled, within her four rowers with oars in action, and seated in the stern an Earl robed and coroneted all Proper, for figurehead a demi-lion rampant Gules, and at the masthead a pennon of the Last charged of Scotland (viz.: Azure, a Saint Andrew's cross Argent) in the hoist; in the sinister chief is set the sun in his splendour Or.

Above the Shield is placed a coronet suitable to a Burgh Royal and in an Escrol under the same this *Motto* "Victoriae Gloria Merces".

(Lyon Register, i, 464: 12 November 1947)

The sun and the fish denote the well-being and industry of the Burgh; the gold and black colours of the latter were chosen purely for artistic reasons. The Latin motto (cf. Berwick-upon-Tweed)—"Glory is the reward of victory"—comes from the seal.

BURGH OF COCKENZIE & PORT SETON

Gules, on the waves of the sea undy Argent and Azure, a one-masted ship in full sail Proper; on a chief Or, three crescents of the field.

Above the Shield is placed a coronet suitable to a Burgh of Barony (videlicet: Gules masoned Argent) and in an Escrol below the same this *Motto* "Hazard Yet Forward".

(Lyon Register, xxxiv, 66: 9 February 1943)
(On 7 February 1958, the coronet in the Lyon Register was changed to a Burgh of Barony coronet on instructions from the Lord Lyon.)

COCKENZIE & PORT SETON grew from the villa of Seton granted by King Robert I in 1321 to Sir Alexander Seton, the famous Governor of Berwick. In 1591,

Cockenzie was created a Burgh of Barony in favour of Robert, 6th Lord Seton, later 1st Earl of Winton, and in 1686, the Burgh of Cockenzie alias Port Seton was raised to a Burgh of Regality (to be called Winton) in favour of George, 4th Earl of Winton.[10] It became a Police Burgh in 1885.

Using the Seton colours of gold and red, the arms show Seton crescents in the chief to denote the Burgh's connection with the Seton family and the Earls of Winton. The ship stands for the port and the shipping interests of the town. The motto is one of those used by the Earls of Winton. The decision to seek a grant of arms arose from the discovery by a member of the Town Council of a likeness of the old seal of the Burgh adopted in 1892 and surrendered to the Lyon Court in 1929.

EAST LINTON became a Police Burgh in 1863. The Burgh has not recorded arms; its seal shows a view of a Roman bridge over the river Tyne on which the town stands. The seal was designed by Robert Noble, R.S.A.[11]

PRESTONPANS was famous as early as the twelfth century for the manu-facture of salt from the sea by means of salt pans. In 1552 it was created a Burgh of Barony in favour of the Abbot of Holyrood.[12] It became a Police Burgh in 1862. The Burgh has not recorded arms; its seal shows the ancient Cross of Preston, with an anchor entwined with a miner's pick and spade on one side and a sheaf with two sickles on the other; at the base is a shell. These symbolise the town's connections with coal-mining, agriculture and the sea.

TRANENT, which claims to be the oldest mining community in Scotland, was created a Burgh of Barony in favour of George, 4th Lord Seton, in 1541–42.[13] It became a Police Burgh in 1860. The Burgh has not recorded arms; its seal shows, on the dexter side, a harvester with his hand on a sheaf of corn, and on the sinister side, a miner holding a pick and lamp beside a pit-head with a bright star above; over all, the sun's rays shine down. These represent the agricultural and mining interests of the district.

EAST LOTHIAN COUNTY COUNCIL

Gules, three bars Ermine, over all a lion rampant Or, armed and langued Azure.

(Lyon Register, xxvii, 38: 1 June 1927)

The County Council of THE COUNTY OF EAST LOTHIAN bears arms of great beauty and simplicity. The red and ermine field comes from the arms of the Giffords of Yester, a family granted lands in East Lothian by King William the Lion (1165–1214) and now represented by the Marquess of Tweeddale. While the lion could recall the King, since the County Buildings occupy a site said to be that of his palace at Haddington, it was chosen in reference to the ancient Earldom of Dunbar, the celebrated East Lothian family of Maitland of Lethington, the Earl of Wemyss and March (then Lord Lieutenant) and Sir Archibald Buchan Hepburn (then County Convener), since a lion rampant appears in all of their coats of arms. The seal adopted by the County Council in 1890 bore the monogram HCC with a goat on a mount above it, all within the legend MDCCCXC; when the County name was changed to East Lothian in 1921, a new seal was adopted bearing the monogram ELCC with a similar goat above.

24

COUNTY OF MIDLOTHIAN

The County of MIDLOTHIAN has five Burghs, the Parliamentary Burgh of Mussel-burgh, and the Police Burghs of Bonnyrigg & Lasswade, Dalkeith, Loanhead and Penicuik. The County town is Edinburgh, which as mentioned on page 45 above, is itself a County of a City.

BURGH OF MUSSELBURGH

Azure, three anchors in pale, one in chief and two in the flanks, Or, accompanied with as many mussels, two in the dexter and sinister chief points and the third in base Proper.

In an Escrol above the Shield this *Motto* "Honesty".

(Lyon Register, i, 468: 2 October 1771)

MUSSELBURGH, "the Honest Toun", first seems to have been a Burgh dependent on the Abbey of Dunfermline early in the fourteenth century. It was made a Burgh of Regality in 1562 in favour of Robert Pitcairn, Archdeacon of St. Andrews, as Commendator of Dunfermline,[1] and became a Parliamentary Burgh under the 1832 Reform Act.

The arms are an eighteenth-century attempt at canting heraldry. The anchors indicate that the town is a seaport and the mussels refer to the large mussel bed at the mouth of the river Esk on which the Burgh stands; the blue field is for the sea and the river. The motto is very appropriate for "The Honest Toun of Musselburgh" and is, according to one tradition, derived from the tribute—"Sure you are honest men"—paid to the citizens by Donald, Earl of Mar, Regent of Scotland (1332), for their care of his famous predecessor in the Regency, Thomas Randolph, Earl of Moray, who died at Musselburgh on 20 July 1332.[2]

BURGH OF BONNYRIGG & LASSWADE

Parted per pale wavy: dexter, Argent, a fess Pean between two martlets respectant in chief and a lion rampant in base Gules; sinister, barry dancetty Sable and Argent, a pale raguly Vert charged with five cinquefoils of the Second; and en surtout of the whole shield a pallet wavy Azure.

Above the Shield is placed a coronet appropriate to a Burgh and in an Escrol below the same this *Motto* "Floreat".

(Lyon Register, xxxix, 19: 27 June 1952)

BONNYRIGG & LASSWADE were united as one Burgh in 1929. Bonnyrigg had become a Police Burgh in 1865 and Lasswade in 1881.

The arms are parted by a blue wavy line representing the river North Esk, which separates the two parts of the Burgh. The dexter side is for Bonnyrigg: the pean (fur) fess and the lion allude to Dundas of Arniston, the main family of the district. Their silver and red colours have been used and are continued in the chief where the birds denote the wooded character of the countryside. In addition, the use in the fess of pean (instead of the Dundas ermine) recalls the "bonny rig" and the similar use of pean to represent a stubble field in the arms of Ellon (q.v.). The sinister side, for Lasswade, shows an heraldic version of the hawthorn tree which appeared on that Burgh's seal; in olden times the slopes of the surrounding valley were covered with white hawthorns. The Latin motto "May it flourish" comes originally from the old Lasswade seal and was adopted and shown on its seal by the united Burgh in 1929.

DALKEITH grew up within the Manor of Dalkeith, which was granted to William de Graham by King David I (1124–1153) and in 1341 passed by marriage to Sir William Douglas of Liddesdale, one of whose nephews, James, succeeded him in the Lordship of Dalkeith and his other extensive estates—and another Henry, became Douglas of Lugton and Lochleven. The Dalkeith Douglases became Earls of Morton

BURGH OF DALKEITH

Quarterly: 1st, Or, on a chief Sable, three escallops of the field; 2nd, Argent, three piles Gules, on a chief of the Last, three mullets of the First; 3rd, Or, on a bend Azure, a mullet of six points between two crescents of the field; 4th, Vert, a castle of two towers Or, masoned Sable, port and windows Gules, in chief two open crowns Or.

Above the Shield is set a coronet suitable to a Burgh, and on a Compartment below the Shield with this *Motto* "Olim Custodes Semper Defensores" are set for *Supporters* two men in complete armour each holding in his exterior hand a halbert Proper.

(Lyon Register xxix, 5: 28 February 1930)

(1457–1458), but the Earldom passed into the Loch Leven family as heirs of entail in 1588. Dalkeith was created a Burgh of Barony in favour of Sir James Douglas, 1st Lord Dalkeith, in 1401, and was raised in 1540 to a Burgh of Regality in favour of Robert Douglas of Loch Leven.[3] In 1642, his descendant, William, 7th Earl of Morton, disposed of his estates at Dalkeith to the Scotts of Buccleuch. Dalkeith became a Police Burgh in 1878.

The arms are related to the device on the Burgh seal which is reputed to have been originally designed (by competition) as a badge for the Town Volunteers and was later adopted by the Town Trustees and inherited by the Burgh Commissioners and Town Council.[4] The first three quarters recall the three famous families which have been so closely connected with Dalkeith, and show the arms of Graham, Douglas (represented by the arms of Douglas of Dalkeith and Lochleven as conjoined by the Earls of Morton, but with three stars in chief instead of two) and Scott; on the seal Douglas had been wrongly represented by the more familiar Douglas arms showing the crowned heart below a chief with three stars. The 4th quarter is for the Burgh itself; it shows a castle to recall the old Castle of Dalkeith and the later Dalkeith Palace, built in the eighteenth century by Anne, Duchess of Buccleuch and Monmouth. The two crowns above, the supporters and the motto are in reference to the occasion in 1637–38 when the Scottish Privy Council removed from Linlithgow to Dalkeith, taking the Scottish Regalia with them for safety. The Latin motto means "Once the keepers, always the defenders" and comes from the old seal.

BURGH OF LOANHEAD

Or, on a fess raguly Vert, between an eagle volant Gules in chief, and a boar's head erased Sable, armed and langued Proper, accompanied by two crescents of the Third in base, three cinquefoils Argent.

Above the Shield is placed a coronet appropriate to a Burgh.

(Lyon Register, xxxviii, 127: 7 March 1952)

LOANHEAD, as Clerkington or Nicolson, was created a Burgh of Barony in 1669 in favour of Sir John Nicolson, 2nd of that Ilk and Lesswaid.[5] It became a Police Burgh in 1884.

The arms have the gold and red colours of Nicolson and the eagle recalls that Nicolson of that Ilk has eagles as supporters. The black boar's head and the red crescents in the base refer to the family of Clerk of Penicuik, the present Superiors of the Burgh. The fess raguly represents a branch of white hawthorn, the traditional emblem of the parish of Lasswade, and its associations with the nearby estate of Hawthornden and its owners, the Drummonds.

BURGH OF PENICUIK

Or, a fess chequy Azure and Argent between in chief two bugle-horns stringed Sable, and in base the figure of Saint Kentigern from the waist, mitred and vested, his right hand raised in the act of benediction and having his crosier in his left hand, all Proper.

Above the Shield is placed a mural coronet suitable to a Burgh and in an Escrol under the Shield this *Motto* "Pen-y-Coc".

(Lyon Register, xxxiii, 11: 24 March 1938)

PENICUIK, the Barony of which was sold by Dr. Alexander Pennicuik to John Clerk in 1646, became a Police Burgh in 1866.

The arms show the gold field and blue/silver chequy from the arms of Clerk of Penicuik, with two black bugle-horns from the arms of the Penicuik family, as represented by Penicuik of New Hall. In base is St. Kentigern (or Mungo), the patron saint of the town; at one time the parish was known as St. Mungo. The saint is depicted (as in Glasgow) without a halo. The motto is the Welsh phrase meaning "Hill of the Cuckoo" which gives the Burgh its name. A cuckoo was shown on the seal adopted by the Burgh in 1900, but Lord Lyon Grant did not consider it as suitable for inclusion in the coat of arms.

MIDLOTHIAN COUNTY COUNCIL

Or, a lion rampant Vert, armed and langued Gules, surmounted of a fess Azure charged with three suns in their splendour of the field.

Which Shield is ensigned of a coronet appropriate to a County Council.

(Lyon Register, xxxviii, 82: 25 June 1951)

The County Council of THE COUNTY OF MIDLOTHIAN obtained in June 1956 a Brieve of Precedency from Lord Lyon Innes recognising it as the Premier County of the thirty-three Counties of Scotland.

In the coat of arms, the green lion on the gold field refers to the old arms of the Viscountcy of Primrose, now held by the Earls of Rosebery and Midlothian. "Vert, a lion rampant Or", was a coat of augmentation granted to Sir Archibald Primrose of Carrington (grandfather of the 1st Viscount Primrose) by King Charles II as a mark of favour for his loyalty.[6] The gold suns on the blue fess allude to the 1st and 3rd quarters of the arms of the Earldom of Lothian, now held by the Marquis of Lothian; this was a coat of augmentation assumed by Sir William Kerr, son of the 1st Earl of Ancrum, when he was created Earl of Lothian in 1631.[7] The seal, adopted by the County Council in 1890, bore a device showing the Royal Arms of Scotland.

25

COUNTY OF WEST LOTHIAN

The County of WEST LOTHIAN has six Burghs, the Royal Burghs of Linlithgow (the County town) and Queensferry, and the Police Burghs of Armadale, Bathgate, Bo'ness and Whitburn.

ROYAL BURGH OF LINLITHGOW

Azure, the figure of the Archangel Michael with wings expanded, treading on the belly of a serpent lying with its tail nowed fessways in base, all Argent, the head of which he is piercing through with a spear in his dexter hand and grasping with his sinister an escutcheon charged with the Royal Arms of Scotland.

The *Motto* being "Collocet In Coelis Nos Omnes Vis Michaelis".

The reverse is Or, a greyhound bitch Sable, chained to an oak tree within a loch Proper.

[With the *Motto* "My Fruit is Fidelity to God and the King"]

(Lyon Register, i, 456: 16 July 1673)

LINLITHGOW is a Royal Burgh of King David I created about 1138.[1] With Lanark, it was chosen to make up the Court of the Four Burghs when the loss of Berwick and Roxburgh was formally recognised in 1369.

The Burgh is one of the four in Scotland with two coats of arms matriculated in the Lyon Register. They are based on the oldest known Burgh seals, of which impressions dated 1296 and 1357 are on record.[2] The coat now commonly used is the second one, which shows the celebrated black bitch of Linlithgow chained to an oak tree standing on a mound in Linlithgow Loch. The tree represents the former Royal Forest and the black bitch may also be connected with the chase; it may also recall one of the possible meanings of Linlithgow, "the lake of the grey dog". Associated with this coat of arms, by long tradition, is the motto "My fruit is fidelity to God and the King"; although this is not recorded in the Lyon Office, it can be accepted as authentic. The first coat shows the sacred bearings, St. Michael the Archangel killing the dragon; he holds a shield bearing the Scottish Royal Arms because the Burgh has had many links with the Royal Family, of which Linlithgow Palace was a favourite residence from the fourteenth century. The Latin motto means "Michael's strength sets us all in heaven". The Burgh uses both coats of arms with burghal coronets; these were added by the Lyon Office Herald Painter in specially-commissioned drawings in 1938.

ROYAL BURGH OF QUEENSFERRY

Argent, in the sea Azure a galley with her sails trussed up Sable, on the middle part thereof Queen Margaret of Scotland standing richly apparelled and crowned Proper, holding in her dexter hand a sceptre ensigned with a fleur-de-lys Or, and in her sinister lying on her breast a book folded Purpure.

With these *Words* in an Escrol underneath "Insignia Burgi Passagii Reginae".

(Lyon Register, i, 466: c. 1673)

QUEENSFERRY was a Burgh dependent on the Abbey of Dunfermline by about 1328, and as South Queensferry was created a Burgh of Regality in favour of Robert Pitcairn, Archdeacon of St. Andrews, as Commendator of Dunfermline, in 1576–77. It was made a Royal Burgh by King Charles I in 1636.[3]

The arms, which are sometimes used with a Burghal coronet added to them, are the same as the device on the oldest known seal of the Burgh, of which an impression dated 1529 is on record.[4] They show Queen Margaret, who gave the place its name, standing in a boat on the sea. She is said to have landed here after her flight from England about 1067, and it was here that she usually crossed the Firth of Forth when going to and from Edinburgh between 1068–69 and 1093. She and her husband, King Malcolm III (1057–1093), granted the Dunfermline monks the right to ferry pilgrims to St. Andrews across the Firth free of charge and from this franchise descended the Ferry, which continued until the opening of the Forth Road Bridge in 1965. The Queen carries her famous copy of the Gospels, coloured purple for Royalty. The Latin motto means "The insignia of the Burgh of the Queen's Ferry". The Burgh has also used for a long time a second coat of arms which is not recorded in the Lyon Register but appears on a seal impression dated 1676.[5] This can be blazoned as "Argent, a cross patonce Azure between four martlets and ensigned of a fifth"; it is obviously based on Queen Margaret's family arms, those of King Edward the Confessor.

BURGH OF ARMADALE

Argent, on a chevron engrailed Gules, voided of the field, three bears' heads couped Azure, muzzled Or, in base an oak tree eradicated Proper, fructed Or.

Above the Shield is placed a mural crown and in an Escrol below the Shield this *Motto* "Ferveant Opera".

(Lyon Register, xxiii, 48: 28 May 1918)

ARMADALE was founded by Sir William Honeyman of Graemsay (c. 1760–1825), a Lord of Session who took the title of Lord Armadale from the Sutherland property he had inherited from his mother, Margaret, daughter of John Mackay of Strathtay in Sutherland. He also gave the name to his new town, which became a Police Burgh in 1864.

The arms granted were considerably influenced by the design suggested by Lord Bute.[6] The silver and red colours and the engrailed voided chevron of Honeyman recall the founder of the Burgh, and the Mackay bears' heads his mother, and thus the connection with Armadale in Sutherland. The oak tree was included in reference to Mr. James Wood of Wallhouse, a generous benefactor of the town, who took some part in obtaining the Grant of arms and met the cost of the fees involved.[7] The Latin motto—"May the works glow"—was stated at the time to have both a classical and a modern signification; no doubt the latter would refer to the chemical and paraffin works in the vicinity.

BURGH OF BATHGATE

Azure, on a mount between two oak trees, a castle triple-towered Proper, an open gate Gules, the main tower flagged with the arms of Fitzalan (videlicet: Gules, a lion rampant Or, armed and langued Argent) and the other two towers with a banner of Scotland (videlicet: Azure, a saltire Argent), in base a loch undy Argent and of the field.

Above the Shield is placed a mural coronet and in an Escrol under the same this *Motto* "Commune Bonum Intra Muros".

(Lyon Register, xxxiii, 20: 17 May 1938)

BATHGATE was well known by the fourteenth century as its Castle was the residence of Walter Fitzalan, 6th High Steward of Scotland, who married in 1315 Marjorie, daughter of King Robert I, and from whom is descended the Royal House of Stewart. It was created a Burgh of Barony in 1663 in favour of Sir Thomas Hamilton of Bathgate[8] and was made autonomous by Act of Parliament in 1824. It became a Police Burgh in 1865.

The arms are based on the device on the Burgh seal adopted in 1892 to the design of Mr. George F. Shanks, Crosshill, Glasgow, who also designed Whitburn's seal. They show the Castle of Bathgate under a blue sky with Walter Fitzalan's banner flying over it. The open gate, the loch and the wooded mound are supposed to refer to "the bath gate" where horses and cattle were watered; the loch also recalls the marshy ground on which the Castle was built. The oak trees could just have a Hamilton reference. The Latin motto—"The common good within the walls"—comes from the seal. The cost involved in obtaining the Grant of arms was met by public subscription.[9]

BO'NESS (properly BORROWSTOUNNESS) was erected into a Burgh of Regality in 1668 in favour of Anne, Duchess of Hamilton.[10] It became a Police Burgh in 1883.

The arms are based on the device on an old Town Crier's Bell dated 1647, which is reputed to have belonged to the United General Sea Box Society of Borrowstounness.

N

BURGH OF BO'NESS

Per pale Gules and Sable: in a sea in base undy Azure and Argent, a three-masted ship of the seventeenth century Or, in full sail Proper, flagged Gold, at the stern a banner of Scotland of the First, cantoned of the Third, charged with a saltire of the Fourth; in chief a lion passant also Gold, armed and langued of the Third.

Above the Shield is placed a Burghal Crown and in an Escrol under the Shield this *Motto* "Sine Metu".

(Lyon Register, xxviii, 74: 10 January 1930)

The red and black colours of the field are respectively for Hamilton and the coal-mining industry associated with the town. The ship, in full sail to denote prosperity, refers to its shipping interests and recalls that in the eighteenth century Bo'ness was the third seaport in Scotland. The meaning of the lion is not clear; it could be the Scottish lion, as the lion on the seal of the Sea Box Society was shown as rampant and not passant. But it seems just possible that it has a connection with the former Castle Lyon which stood near the sea and was probably the jointure house of Lady Margaret Lyon, daughter of the 7th Lord Glamis, and widow of John, 1st Marquess of Hamilton, whom she had married about 1577.[11] The Latin motto—"Without Fear"—comes, as does the ship, from the seal.

WHITBURN, until 1760 merely a hamlet, developed in the early nineteenth century into a prosperous weaving town. This trade, however, gradually decayed, and coal-mining and general trading took its place as the town's main interests. It became a Police Burgh in 1861.

The arms have the blue and silver colours of Scotland and the silver wavy bar is for the White Burn which gives the town its name. The two estoiles very probably recall the Baillies of Polkemmet, who have been closely connected with the district since the sixteenth century and have been generous benefactors of the Burgh. The golden sheaf represents the agricultural interests of this part of West Lothian; the *Imperial Gazetteer* (1854) records that the low-lying part of Whitburn parish "has been brought to a fine state of cultivation" and the *Ordnance Gazetteer* (1885) confirms this.[12] The unusual crest of a stage coach comes from the Burgh seal adopted in 1892 to the design of Mr. George F. Shanks, Crosshill, Glasgow, a native of Whitburn, who also designed Bathgate's seal. This device was chosen because the old

BURGH OF WHITBURN

Azure, a bend wavy between two estoiles in chief Argent and a garb in base Or.

Above the Shield is placed a mural coronet thereon a Helmet of befitting degree with a Mantling Azure doubled Argent, and on a Wreath of their Liveries is set for *Crest* the representation of a stage coach and four all Proper,† and in an Escrol over the same this *Motto* "Onward".

(Lyon Register, xxxiii, 37: 30 September 1938)

halfway house of the Edinburgh-Glasgow turnpike road was about half-a-mile west of the town, and Whitburn itself was the principal station on the coach route between the two cities, the first service being started in 1678. Mr. Shanks was still alive in 1938 and his interest in the arms was a contributory factor in having the stage coach retained. The motto also comes from the seal. The cost of obtaining the Grant of arms was met by public subscription.[13]

† This is drawn "contournée" as in the Lyon Register.

WEST LOTHIAN COUNTY COUNCIL

Azure, issuant from a mount in base, an oak tree fructed all Or, a bordure Argent charged with four gillyflowers Gules, alternately with as many laurel leaves slipped Vert.

Which Shield is ensigned of a coronet appropriate to a County Council, videlicet: Issuant from a circlet Vert, five paling piles also Vert, alternately with four garbs Or, banded Sable.

(Lyon Register, xxxviii, 139: 6 May 1952)

The County Council of THE COUNTY OF WEST LOTHIAN bears arms which show the coat borne, for their Earldom, by the Livingstone Earls of Linlithgow, on an escutcheon en surtout of their shield, but four of the red gillyflowers on the bordure have been replaced by green laurel leaves in reference to the Hope Earls of Hopetoun and Marquesses of Linlithgow who have a green bay leaf in the centre of their arms. The seal adopted by the Council (as Linlithgowshire) in 1890 showed the Scottish Royal Arms, environed of the collar of the Order of the Thistle and ensigned with the Imperial Crown; a similar seal was used after the County name was changed to West Lothian in 1921.

26

COUNTY OF LANARK

The County of LANARK has nine Burghs, the Royal Burghs of Lanark and Ruther-glen, the Parliamentary Burghs of Airdrie, Coatbridge and Hamilton (the County town), and the Police Burghs of Biggar, Motherwell & Wishaw, East Kilbride and Bishopbriggs. As mentioned on page 45 above, the Royal Burgh of Glasgow is a County of a City.

ROYAL BURGH OF LANARK

Or, an eagle with two heads displayed Sable, armed and mem-bered Gules, holding in his dexter claw an ancient handbell Proper, in the flanches two hounds paleways confrontée Proper, collared of the Third and belled Proper, in the two base points as many fish hauriant addorsed, that in the dexter in bend and that on the sinister in bend sinister, both Proper, holding in their mouths an annulet of the Third.

[Above the Shield is placed a Burghal coronet.]

(Lyon Register, xxviii, 33: 4 April 1929)

LANARK was a Royal Burgh by between 1153 and 1159 in the reign of King Malcolm IV, but the date of its foundation may be slightly earlier.[1] Along with Linlithgow, it was chosen to make up the Court of the Four Burghs with Edinburgh and Stirling when the loss of Berwick and Roxburgh was formally recognised in 1369.

The arms are based on the old seals of the Burgh, the oldest known impression being dated 1357.[2] There are on record seven different seals which have been used in the six succeeding centuries, and that introduced at the beginning of the present century has a mural crown above the shield with the arms. The double-headed eagle appears on each seal but other details vary. The eagle is thought to be the Roman eagle (cf. Perth); there were several Roman camp sites near Lanark. The two hounds recall that Lanark was a favourite hunting seat of King Alexander I (1107–1124) and other early Scottish Kings. The fish with the rings in their mouths and the ancient handbell are for St. Kentigern or Mungo (cf. Glasgow); the ancient parish church of Lanark, where the famous Scottish patriot, William Wallace, was married to Marian Braidfute, was dedicated to St. Kentigern. According to Lord Bute, there is evidence of a gold background in the etching on some of the older seals.[3]

ROYAL BURGH OF RUTHERGLEN

Argent, in a sea Proper, an ancient galley Sable, flagged Gules, therein two men Proper, one rowing, the other furling the sail.

Above the Shield is placed a suitable Helmet with a Mantling Gules doubled Argent, and on a Wreath of the proper Liveries is set for *Crest* a demi-figure of the Virgin Mary with the infant Saviour in her arms Proper, and on a Compartment below the Shield on which is an Escrol containing this *Motto* "Ex Fumo Fama" are placed for *Supporters* two angels Proper, winged Or.

(Lyon Register, xii, 14: 4 April 1889)

RUTHERGLEN was created a Royal Burgh by King David I between 1124 and 1153 and its privileges were confirmed by King William the Lion between 1179 and 1189.[4]

The arms are based on the devices on the oldest known seal of the Burgh; impressions dated 1357 and 1493 are on record.[5] It has been said that they show three things characteristic of Rutherglen: her ships, her seamen and her church. The ship and mariners, from the obverse of the seal, recall that for a long period, the town was the chief trading and commercial centre on the lower part of the river Clyde. The Virgin and Child and the angel supporters come from the reverse of the seal; the twelfth-century parish church, of which only a stone tower of later date remains, was dedicated to St. Mary the Virgin. The motto is a free Latin rendering by Professor G. G. Ramsay of Glasgow University of the local saying "Ru'glen's roon red lums reek briskly". The compartment on which the supporters stand may be intended to be a Royal Burgh compartment, as it is of a more solid character than the metal-work grille type granted to Glasgow twenty-three years previously. In an article in its issue of 16 November 1888, *The Rutherglen Reformer* states: "To our worthy Town Clerk, Mr. George Gray, will ever be the credit of giving to our ancient Burgh a coat of arms."

BURGH OF AIRDRIE

Or, a double-headed eagle displayed Sable, beaked and membered Gules, in chief a crescent between two spur rowels Vert.

Above the Shield is set a Burghal crown and a Helmet befitting their degree with a Mantling Sable doubled Or, and on a Wreath of their Liveries is set for *Crest* a cock Or, and in an Escrol under the Shield this *Motto* "Vigilantibus".

(Lyon Register, xxix, 23: 11 June 1930)

AIRDRIE was made a Market Town by Parliament in 1695; by 1820, its population had grown to over 5,000 and in response to public desire, funds were collected for the promotion of private legislation to create the town a Burgh of Barony. The necessary Act was passed in 1821, the right of an annual appointment to the office of Town Clerk being reserved to the proprietor of the estate of Rochsolloch and Airdrie, then Miss Margaret Aitcheson.[6] Airdrie was made a Parliamentary Burgh under the 1832 Reform Act.

The arms follow the device on the Burgh seal, which shows a shield with the charges, but not the chief, in the arms of Aitcheson of Rochsolloch and Airdrie and with their crest of a cock above. This family were the Superiors of the town from 1769 until 1824. In granting the arms, Lord Lyon Grant made the field gold instead of silver and made the spur rowels and crescent green; in the arms of the Aitchesons they had been respectively gold and silver on a green chief. The Latin motto—"Being Watchful"—comes from the seal and is that of Aitcheson of Rochsolloch and Airdrie.

BURGH OF COATBRIDGE

Sable, a tower Argent, masoned of the First, window and port Gules, from the battlements flames issuant Proper.

Above the Shield is placed a Burghal coronet and a Helmet befitting their degree, with a Mantling Sable doubled Argent, and on a Wreath of their Liveries is set for *Crest* a demi-monk habited Proper, holding on his sinister shoulder a stone also Proper, and in an Escrol over the same this *Motto* "Laborare Est Orare".

(Lyon Register, xxix, 53: 2 December 1930)

COATBRIDGE, although a large town with a population of 25,000 or more, was unable to become a Police Burgh under the 1862 Act because, owing to its iron trade, it could not meet the smoke abatement requirements of the Public Health (Scotland) Act, 1867. In 1885, it was given Burgh status (with all the powers of a Royal Burgh) by a private Act and it is thus unique among the Burghs of Scotland. In the Convention of Royal Burghs, it takes its place among the Parliamentary Burghs.

The arms, which incorporate some features from the seal adopted by the Burgh in 1892, have a black field and on it a flaming tower to represent a blast furnace, and thus the iron and steel industry. The crest of the monk with the stone recalls Monkland, the ancient barony and parish, now divided into two, in which Coatbridge lies, and the legend of the "Aul' Kirk Stane". This relates that the first Christian church in the area was built by a monk who, as a penance, had been ordered to carry on his shoulder a heavy stone until an angel told him where to lay it down; on that spot he was to build a church and that is how Old Monkland Church came into being. The Latin motto—"To work is to pray"—is a phrase from the writings of St. Benedict, which became specially connected with the Cistercian Order. Its use here is appropriate, as the lands of Monkland were once owned by the Cistercian Abbey of Newbattle in East Lothian. The arms were recorded so that they could be included in an armorial window in the Lanarkshire County Council Offices in Glasgow.

BURGH OF HAMILTON

Gules, three cinquefoils pierced Argent.

Above the Shield is placed a suitable Helmet with a Mantling Gules doubled Argent, and on a Wreath of the proper Liveries is set for *Crest* a cinquefoil pierced as in the arms, and in an Escrol over the same this *Motto* "Sola Nobilitat Virtus".

(Lyon Register, xi, 86: 20 July 1886)

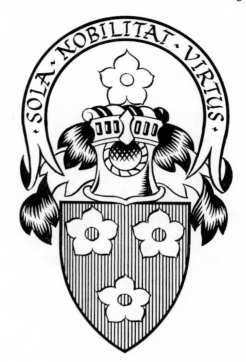

HAMILTON appears in 1475 as an existing Burgh of Barony of James, 1st Lord Hamilton, and was made a Royal Burgh in 1548–49 under his grandson, James, 2nd Earl of Arran, Regent of Scotland (1542–1554), but the Charter proved ineffective. In 1669, it was created a Burgh of Regality in favour of Anne, Duchess of Hamilton.[7] It became a Parliamentary Burgh under the 1832 Reform Act.

The arms are based on the version of the Hamilton family arms which are reputed to have been given to the Burgh by Duchess Anne. They have the pierced cinquefoils in silver instead of ermine. The cinquefoil crest has obvious Hamilton connections while the Latin motto—"Virtue alone ennobles"—is that of Hamilton, Earl of Arran. The matriculation of the arms arose in connection with the purchase of insignia of office for the Provost and Magistrates; the cost of the fees payable for matriculation was met, as a gift to the Burgh, by Mr. Edward P. Dykes, then Town Clerk.[8]

BIGGAR has a long connection with the Fleming family, Lords Fleming from c. 1451 and Earls of Wigtown, 1606–1747. Created a Burgh of Barony in 1451, in favour of Robert Fleming of Biggar who became 1st Lord Fleming,[9] it became a Police Burgh in 1863.

The arms follow the device shown on the seal adopted by the Burgh in 1892. The plough and the sheaf stand for the agricultural interests of the district; the latter may possibly refer to the Norse word for a barley field from which the name Biggar may

BURGH OF BIGGAR

Tierced in pairle reversed: 1st, Azure, on a meadow Proper, a plough contournée Argent; 2nd, Azure, on a meadow Proper, a garb Or; 3rd, Gules, a goat's head erased Argent, armed Or.

[Above the Shield is placed a Burghal coronet] and in an Escrol below the Shield this *Motto* "Let the Deed Shaw".

(Lyon Register, xxix, 41: 1 October 1930)

be derived. The goat's head is the Fleming crest and the Fleming red and silver colours have been used in this part of the shield. The motto is that of Fleming; according to tradition, the words "Let the deed shaw" were uttered by Sir Robert Fleming to Robert Bruce (later King Robert I) after the latter had killed the Red Comyn in Greyfriars Church in Dumfries in 1306.

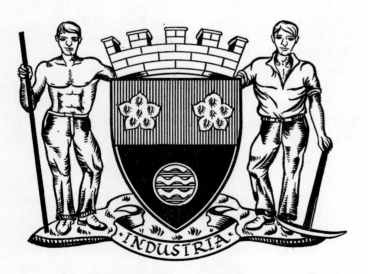

BURGH OF MOTHERWELL & WISHAW

Per fess Gules and Sable, in chief two cinquefoils Ermine, in base a well Proper.

[Above the Shield is placed a Burghal coronet and] on a Compartment below the Shield along with this *Motto* "Industria" are set for *Supporters* on the dexter, a puddler naked to the waist and holding in his exterior hand a pole, on the sinister, a miner holding in his exterior hand a pick-axe, both Proper.

(Lyon Register, xxix, 38: 18 September 1930)

MOTHERWELL & WISHAW were united as one Burgh in 1920. Motherwell had become a Police Burgh in 1865 and Wishaw in 1855.

The arms show two ermine cinquefoils on a red field to denote the close connection with the Burgh of the Lords Hamilton of Dalzell. The black field in base is for coal-mining, while the fountain recalls the ancient Lady's Well (dedicated to the Virgin Mary) from which Motherwell may have got its name. The supporters come from the seal adopted by the Burgh in 1921, and are in imitation of the savage, with a club on his shoulder, which is one of the supporters of the arms of Hamilton of Dalzell.[10] They represent Motherwell iron and Wishaw coal. The Latin motto "Industry" came from the old Wishaw seal. It is of interest that Motherwell had previously made enquiries about a Grant of arms in 1902–3.

BURGH OF EAST KILBRIDE

Per fess, in chief Gules and in base per pale Or and Vert, a cross flory of the Second between two mullets Argent in chief and an oyster catcher bird Proper in base; a chief chequy per pale, dexter, Argent and Azure, sinister, Argent and Sable.

Above the Shield is placed a Burghal coronet Azure masoned Argent, and in an Escrol [below the Shield] this *Motto* "Prosper but Dreid".

(Lyon Register, xlv, 81: 23 September 1963)

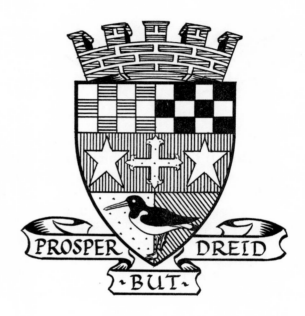

EAST KILBRIDE became a Police Burgh in 1963. A place of considerable antiquity, it is now one of Scotland's new towns.

The arms are a very interesting composition. At the top of the shield is the Stewart silver/blue chequy, to recall Stewart of Torrance, balanced by a chequy in the silver and black Maxwell colours to recall Maxwell of Calderwood; both these families have a long connection with the district. The cross flory is for the Church (of St. Bride), which gives the town its Gaelic name, while the silver stars on the red field refer to the Lindsays of Dunrod who lived at Mains Castle and were Superiors of most of the surrounding country until the seventeenth century. In base is the oyster-catcher bird, always associated with St. Bride, standing on a background of gold for the industry and wealth of the new Burgh, and green, for the rural surroundings of the old village. The motto is derived from the "Live but Dreid" used by the Lindsays, as now represented by the Earls of Lindsay.

BURGH OF BISHOPBRIGGS

Per fess, in chief Sable and in base bendy Or and Vert, a fess wavy Argent charged with a barrulet wavy Azure, and in chief an episcopal mitra pretiosa of the Second, stoned and jewelled Proper.

Below the Shield which is ensigned of a coronet suitable to a Police Burgh (viz.: Azure masoned Argent) is placed in an Escrol this *Motto* "God Gie the Gain".

(Lyon Register, xlv, 117: 16 September 1964)

BISHOPBRIGGS, which is situated on land which belonged to the Bishops and Archbishops of Glasgow for many centuries before the Reformation, became a Police Burgh in 1964.

The arms show a richly-jewelled mitre for the Bishops and Archbishops of Glasgow, and the gold/green pattern in the base denote the "riggs" which once belonged to them. The mitre is set on a black field to recall the local connection with the Stirlings of Cadder (now represented by Stirling of Keir); the silver/blue fess is for the river Kelvin and the Forth and Clyde Canal, both of which are nearby. The Scots motto was based on a suggestion by Mr. David Blane, the Town Clerk.[11]

LANARK COUNTY COUNCIL

Parted per chevron Gules and Argent, two cinquefoils pierced in chief, and a man's heart in base counter-changed.

Above the Shield is placed an Esquire's Helmet with a Mantling Gules doubled Argent, and on a Wreath of the proper Liveries is set for *Crest* a demi-eagle displayed with two heads Sable, beaked Gules, and in an Escrol over the same this *Motto* "Vigilantia".

(Lyon Register, xi, 97: 24 December 1886)

The County Council of THE COUNTY OF LANARK bears arms which were originally granted to the Commissioners of Supply for Lanarkshire. They recall simply and directly the two families, Hamilton and Douglas, who have played such a large part in the history of the County. The eagle crest resembles the badge used by the Lanarkshire Yeomanry from 1826[12] and by the Clerk of Supply, but is obviously taken from the seal of the Royal Burgh of Lanark. It could also allude to the family of Aitcheson of Rochsolloch and Airdrie, a variation of whose Latin motto "Vigilantibus" has been used; it means "Watchfulness".

27

COUNTY OF RENFREW

The County of **RENFREW** has seven Burghs, the Royal Burgh of Renfrew, the Parliamentary Burghs of Greenock, Paisley (the County town) and Port Glasgow, and the Police Burghs of Barrhead, Gourock and Johnstone.

ROYAL BURGH OF RENFREW

Gules, in the sea Proper, a ship with her sails trussed up and mast and tackling, the prow ensigned with the sun and the stern with the moon crescent all Argent, betwixt two escutcheons in the honour point Or, that on the dexter charged with a lion rampant with a double tressure [flowered and] counterflowered Gules, being the Royal coat, that on the sinister with a fess chequy Azure and Argent as the coat of Stewart, and betwixt also as many cross-crosslets fitched of the Second.

The *Motto* "Deus Gubernat Navem".

(Lyon Register, i, 460: 7 July 1676)
(Coronet added in Extract of Matriculation dated 24 November 1932)

RENFREW was created a Royal Burgh by King David I between 1124 and 1147 but was before 1153 granted by him to Walter Fitzalan, the High Steward of Scotland. It remained in Stewart hands until they attained the throne, and in 1397 King Robert III confirmed its status as a Royal Burgh.[1]

Before 1932, the arms were blazoned differently in the Lyon Register and in the Extract from it issued to the Burgh; in particular, the initial word "Gules" was omitted in the Register. The entry therein was suitably amended and a drawing added when an Extract of Matriculation, the cost of which was met by Mr. D. K.

Michie, the then Provost,[2] was issued on 24 November 1932. In his drawing, the Lyon Office Herald Painter interpreted the blazon as Lord Bute had done.[3]

The arms are similar to the device on the oldest known Burgh seal, of which an impression dated 1555–56 is on record.[4] The ship recalls that Renfrew was once an important port on the river Clyde, though it has not been so since the course of the river was changed in the seventeenth century. The Royal arms recall the long connection between the Burgh and the Crown; in 1404, the title of Baron Renfrew was conferred upon the heir to the Scottish throne and is still borne by him. The Stewart arms are a reminder that Renfrew was the first abode in Scotland of the Fitzalans, who became High Stewards and later succeeded to the Throne as the House of Stewart. The sun and moon are common enough features in municipal heraldry, though Porteous makes the interesting suggestion that they may have been included to indicate that out of obscurity (the moon being night) the Stewarts rose to the brilliance of Royalty (the sun being day).[5] The two cross-crosslets may refer to the Latin motto "God steers the ship"; it is of interest to note that in his *History of Port Glasgow* Dr. W. F. Macarthur refers to the ancient ceremony of blessing a ship and to a Protestant Gaelic liturgy (dated 1566) for doing this.[6]

BURGH OF GREENOCK

Or, a three-masted ship of the year 1641, in full sail Proper, flagged at each masthead and at the jack-staff with the banner of Scotland, viz.: Azure, a Saint Andrew's cross Argent, and at the stern with an ensign Gules, cantoned with the Arms of Scotland as above, in a sea in base undy of the Second and Third, two herrings counternaiant Proper; on a chief of the Second, three covered cups of the First.

[Above the Shield is placed a Burghal coronet and] below the Shield this *Motto* "God Speed Greenock".

(Lyon Register, xxvi, 12: 2 December 1923)

GREENOCK was created a Burgh of Barony in favour of John Shaw of Wester Greenock in 1635.[7] It became a Parliamentary Burgh under the 1832 Reform Act.

The arms, which were matriculated as a result of representations by Lord Lyon Balfour Paul some five years previously about the Burgh's irregular use of a coat of arms, have as their main feature, a ship of date 1641 (the date of the confirmation of Greenock's Charter as a Burgh of Barony). The ship, whose four St. Andrew's flags were specially requested, and the herring in base denote the town's importance as a seaport and its connection with the fishing industry; the herrings also recall the quayside barrels on the old Burgh seal. The golden cups on the blue field come from the arms of Shaw of Greenock. The motto, which has been in use since about 1832, needs no comment.

BURGH OF PAISLEY

Or, a fess chequy Azure and Argent between two cinquefoils Gules in chief, and in base two covered cups of the Second, over all the figure of a mitred abbot, vested Proper, his dexter hand in the act of benediction and his sinister holding a crosier also Proper.

Above the Shield is placed a mural crown and on an Escrol below the Shield this *Motto* "Lord, Let Paisley Flourish by the Preaching of Thy Word".

(Lyon Register, xxi, 52: 4 April 1912)

PAISLEY, the largest Burgh (other than a Royal Burgh) in Scotland, was created a Burgh of Barony in favour of George Shaw, Abbot of Paisley, in 1488 and was raised to a Burgh of Regality in favour of Lord Claud Hamilton, Commendator of Paisley and 1st Lord Paisley, in 1587.[8] It was made a Parliamentary Burgh under the 1832 Reform Act.

The arms repeat several of the features on the Burgh seal in use in 1912. The gold field and Stewart chequy recall Walter Fitzalan, High Steward of Scotland, who founded in 1163 the monastery, which later became Paisley Abbey, and also the long connection of the Stewart family with the town and its Abbey. The mitred abbot represents the great Abbey of St. James and St. Mirren which, in pre-Reformation times, had a Charter of Regality "which made Paisley the centre of a little kingdom".[9] The two red cinquefoils refer to the close relationship of the Hamiltons with the Abbey—at one time the abbacy had become almost hereditary in that family. The covered cups come from the arms of Shaw and commemorate Abbot George Shaw. The motto is similar to that of Glasgow. The arms were matriculated so that they could be displayed on the restored roof of Glasgow Cathedral.[10] This is the first example of a Burgh's arms being ensigned with a mural coronet.

BURGH OF PORT GLASGOW

Or, on the waves of the sea a three-masted ship in full sail both Proper, having for figure-head a lion rampant Gules, armed and langued Azure, flying from the foremast and mizzen-mast streamers Gules, from the mainmast the Union Jack as borne previous to the Union with Ireland, viz.: Azure, a saltire Argent surmounted by a cross Gules fimbriated of the Second, and at the stern the national flag of Scotland, viz.: Azure, a saltire Argent; on the mainsail a representation of the arms of the City of Glasgow, viz.: Argent, on a mount in base Vert, an oak tree Proper, the stem at the base thereof surmounted by a salmon on its back, also Proper, with a signet ring in its mouth Or, on the top of the tree a red-breast, and in the sinister fess-point an ancient hand-bell, both also Proper.

Above the Shield is placed a coronet suitable to a Burgh, and in an Escrol below the Shield this *Motto* "Ter Et Quater Anno Revisens Aequor Atlanticum Impune".

(Lyon Register, xxviii, 62: 14 November 1929)

PORT GLASGOW was created a Burgh of Barony in favour of the City of Glasgow in 1668[11] when the Magistrates of Glasgow feued some land in the vicinity of Newark in Renfrewshire and established a harbour and a community there known as the New Port of Glasgow. Previously, the Glasgow merchants had used Ayrshire ports. In 1775, Port Glasgow and the Barony of Newark were united for municipal purposes and, under the 1832 Reform Act, Port Glasgow became a Parliamentary Burgh.

The arms are based on the device on the seal presented to the municipality of Port Glasgow and Newark by the Magistrates of Glasgow in 1791–92. The ship was the obvious choice for a thriving seaport, its figurehead is the Scottish lion, and it flies the Union Flag in use in 1791–92. The arms of Glasgow on the mainsail are those which were used by the City in 1791, i.e. without the salmon supporters and the crest of St. Kentigern. In 1929, the City Council of Glasgow confirmed to the Burgh of Port Glasgow the use of these arms only to the extent used in 1791; the modern arms of Glasgow were matriculated in 1866 and Port Glasgow had wrongly used them on the seal it adopted in 1891. The Latin motto—"Three and four times a year revisiting the Atlantic with impunity"—comes from the 1791–92 seal and refers to the frequent Atlantic crossings made from Port Glasgow. It should be noted that the waves of the sea are blazoned "Proper" but the drawing in the Lyon Register shows them as "barry undy Azure and Argent".

BARRHEAD dates from about 1770 and is closely connected with the beginning of the cotton industry in the Levern valley, the cotton mill at nearby Arthurlie being the second in Scotland. Barrhead became a Police Burgh in 1894.

o

BURGH OF BARRHEAD

·VIRTUTE·ET·LABORE·

Quarterly: 1st and 4th, Vert, on a saltire Or within an orle Argent, three fleurs-de-lys one and two Azure; 2nd and 3rd, Or, three hearts Gules, each charged with a cross Argent, on a bordure of the Second eight fountains; over all at the centre of the quarterings, a rose Gules, barbed and seeded Vert.

Above the Shield is placed a coronet suitable to a Burgh and on a Compartment below the Shield along with this *Motto* "Virtute Et Labore" are set for *Supporters* two wolves Sable.

(Lyon Register, xxxvii, 21: 21 September 1948)

The arms follow closely the device on the Burgh seal adopted in 1894. This shows what are supposed to be the arms of Stewart of Darnley and Lennox which the Town Council decided to use, as Sir William Stewart of Arthurlie was of that family. But for some unexplained reason, the 2nd and 3rd quarters engraved on the seal show not the Stewart fess chequy but three hearts, each surmounted by a cross. The seal was prepared by a local printer who was given as his brief an excerpt from Crawford's *History of Renfrewshire* about the arms of Darnley,[12] a brief which he seems to have chosen to interpret with some artistic licence. After some discussion Lord Lyon Innes agreed to grant a modified version of the device on the seal as the Burgh arms. In the 1st and 4th quarters, the green field and gold saltire of Pollock of Pollock have been used since that family once owned the lands around Barrhead; the d'Aubigny fleurs-de-lys have been retained but coloured blue, while the engrailed bordure has been replaced by a silver orle. In the 2nd and 3rd quarters, the hearts with the crosses remain but the red bordure has been charged with eight fountains (one concealed by the rose in the centre of the shield) "to denote that Barrhead is famous for casting baths and water fittings". Instead of the escutcheon overall, a red Lennox rose has been used. The wolves of Stewart of Lennox have been kept and have been coloured black to match the colour of the Pollock supporters. The Latin motto—"By Virtue and by Industry"—came from the Burgh seal.

GOUROCK was created a Burgh of Barony in favour of Sir William Stewart of Castlemilk in 1694.[13] It became a Police Burgh in 1858.

The arms retain many of the features of the device on the seal adopted by the

BURGH OF GOUROCK

Per pale: dexter, Or, a point dexter and a point base Gules, surmounted of a fess chequy Azure and Argent, and in sinister chief a dexter hand couped Gules grasping a skean Azure; sinister, per fess wavy, in chief Argent, a three-masted ship issuant Sable, sails Proper, flagged Azure, accompanied by two oak trees eradicated Vert, in base undy Azure and Argent, a demi-man Sable holding in his dexter hand a skean Or.

Above the Shield is placed a Burghal coronet and in an Escrol below the Shield this *Motto* "Avant and Be Watchful".

(Lyon Register, xl, 46: 1 December 1954)

Burgh in 1892. The dexter side, with its unusual "points" shows a version of the arms of Stewart of Castlemilk with their crest of a red hand clasping a skean incorporated in the chief. The sinister side incorporates the main features of the arms of Darroch of Gourock, who purchased the lands of Gourock in 1784, with their crest of a negro holding a golden skean added in the base. The motto is "Avant" (for Stewart) and "Be Watchful" for Darroch.

BURGH OF JOHNSTONE

Or, on a cross chequy Azure and Argent, cantoned between two martlets Sable in the 1st and 4th quarters, and two bendlets wreathed Argent and Sable in the 2nd and 3rd Quarters, a cinquefoil Gules at the fess-point.

Below the Shield which is ensigned of a Burghal coronet is placed in an Escrol this *Motto* "Gang Forward".

(Lyon Register, xli, 16: 13 June 1955)

JOHNSTONE, founded in 1781 by George Houston of Houston and Johnstone on the site of a hamlet called Brig o' Johnstone, became a Police Burgh in 1857.

The arms retain, by special request of the Town Council, the cross pattern used on the Burgh seal adopted in 1892. The gold field, the black martlets and the silver/blue chequy come from the arms of Houston of Johnstone. The silver/black bendlets represent twisted threads and thus the weaving industry once so important to the Burgh. The red cinquefoil in the centre of the shield recalls the town's connection with Paisley Abbey; originally it was in the Abbey parish. The Scots motto comes from the Burgh seal.

RENFREW COUNTY COUNCIL

Azure, a lymphad sails furled Argent, on a shield Or pendant therefrom, a fess chequy of the First and Second.

Above the Shield is placed an Esquire's Helmet with a Mantling Gules doubled Argent, and issuing out of a Wreath of the proper Liveries is set for *Crest* a demi-lion rampant Gules, armed and langued Azure, and in an Escrol over the same this *Motto* "Avito Viret Honore".

(Lyon Register, xii, 13: 11 March 1889)

The County Council of THE COUNTY OF RENFREW bears arms which were originally granted to the Commissioners of Supply for Renfrewshire. The design was obviously influenced by the arms of the Royal Burgh of Renfrew (q.v.). The silver/blue fess on the gold shield and the ship combine the coat of the Stewards of Scotland, and thus the House of Stewart, with the galley of the West of Scotland and the Burgh of Renfrew in particular. The demi-lion was the crest of Robert Stewart before he ascended the throne as King Robert II. The Latin motto—"He flourishes through the honour of his ancestors"—is one of those used by the Stewarts, and is still used by some of their descendants, including the Marquess of Bute.

28

COUNTY OF AYR

The County of AYR has seventeen Burghs, the Royal Burghs of Ayr (the County town) and Irvine, the Parliamentary Burgh of Kilmarnock, and the Police Burghs of Ardrossan, Cumnock & Holmhead, Darvel, Galston, Girvan, Kilwinning, Largs, Maybole, Newmilns & Greenholm, Prestwick, Saltcoats, Stewarton, Troon and Stevenston.

ROYAL BURGH OF AYR

Gules, a castle triple-towered Argent betwixt a Holy Lamb, cross staff and banner of Saint Andrew, on the dexter, and on the sinister the head of John the Baptist in a charger Proper, in the base the sea Azure.

(Lyon Register, i, 456: 5 September 1673)

AYR became a Royal Burgh between 1203 and 1206 in the reign of King William the Lion. It possesses the oldest surviving Charter of any Royal Burgh.[1]

The arms are based on the earliest known seal of the Burgh, of which a thirteenth-century impression is on record.[2] They use the red and silver colours of St. John the Baptist and show the Castle of Ayr, built between the Doon and Ayr rivers by King William the Lion in 1197, standing by the sea. St. John the Baptist, the patron saint of the Burgh, is recalled by the Holy Lamb, who carries a St. Andrew's flag (as in Perth) and by the charger containing his head, the latter referring to his beheading by Herod at the request of Herodias and Salome (Matthew 14). The sea in base denotes that Ayr is a seaport.

ROYAL BURGH OF IRVINE

Argent, on an imperial crown Or, a lion sejant affrontée Azure, imperially crowned Gold, holding in his dexter paw a sword and in his sinister a sceptre both Proper.

[Above the Shield is placed a Burghal coronet] and in an Escrol below the Shield this *Motto* "Tandem Bona Causa Triumphat".

(Lyon Register, xxvii, 37: 20 May 1927)

IRVINE, an early Baronial Burgh dating from between 1214 and 1249, was created a Royal Burgh by King Robert II in 1372.[3]

The arms show the crest of the Kings of Scotland, a crowned lion sitting on a crown and holding the sword and the sceptre. There is an impression dated 1680 of the reverse of one of the oldest known Burgh seals which shows a similar device.[4] The right to use the Royal crest is said to have been granted to the citizens by King Robert I in return for special services they had rendered to him. Lord Lyon Swinton was unable to grant the arms in the gold and red Royal colours but the choice of silver and blue is a happy one as these were the livery colours of the Bruce family before they assumed the arms of the Lords of Annandale. The Latin motto—"A good cause triumphs in the end"—is thought to date from and to refer to the Restoration of King Charles II in 1660; it could also be an appropriate reference to King Robert I and his long but successful struggle for Scottish independence.

BURGH OF KILMARNOCK

Purpure, a fess chequy Or and Vert.

Above the Shield is placed a coronet suitable to a Burgh and thereon a Helmet befitting their degree with a Mantling Purpure doubled Or, and on a Wreath of their Liveries is set for *Crest* a dexter hand couped Proper, the third and fourth fingers closed, and in an Escrol over the same this *Motto* "Confido", and on a Compartment below the Shield are set for *Supporters* two squirrels sejant Proper, and in an Escrol beneath this *Motto* "Virtute Et Industria".

(Lyon Register, xxviii, 51: 18 September 1929)

KILMARNOCK was created a Burgh of Barony in 1591–92 in favour of Thomas Boyd, 6th Lord Boyd of Kilmarnock, who lived in Dean Castle nearby.[5] It became a Parliamentary Burgh under the 1832 Reform Act.

The arms are based on the device on the Burgh seal, which shows the arms of Boyd, Earl of Kilmarnock. The main changes are in colour: the field has been made purple instead of blue and the fess chequy gold/green instead of silver/red. The unique sejant squirrel supporters of Boyd[6] have been retained. The second motto "Virtute et Industria" has been taken from one of the Burgh seals and replaces "Goldberry", a motto used by the Boyds to commemorate a victory by Robert Boyd over the Norsemen in 1263 at Goldberry Hill near Largs. It is fairly certain, however, that the gold and green colours in the fess, which were a local suggestion, are intended as a direct allusion to the name "Goldberry". The Latin mottoes mean "I trust" and "By virtue and by industry".

ARDROSSAN was founded in 1805 by Hugh, 12th Earl of Eglinton (1739–1819), who planned to build a harbour there and provide a seaport for the Glasgow trade and connect it by canal to Glasgow. The scheme, however, took forty years to complete, and by that time the town had a population of over 5,000. It was created a

BURGH OF ARDROSSAN

Per pale Azure and Gules, a castle triple-towered Or, windows and ports Sable, the towers capped Vert with balls of the Third, between three crosses patée Argent.

Beneath the Shield which is surmounted of a Burghal coronet Proper is set in an Escrol this *Motto* "Takand Care".

(Lyon Register, xxxvi, 79: 24 July 1947)

Burgh of Barony in 1846,[7] the last example of this kind of Burgh in Scotland, and became a Police Burgh in 1865.

    The arms show the old Castle of Ardrossan which had been shown on the Burgh seal adopted in 1892. The silver crosses and the blue half of the field are for the Barclays of Ardrossan who founded the Castle, while the blue/red field and the gold in the castle towers recall the families of Eglinton and Montgomerie to whom it passed by marriage. The Scots motto which means "Taking care" echoes the Earl of Eglinton's motto "Gardez Bien". The arms were recorded in connection with the Burgh's centenary in 1946 and, by request of the Town Council, were allowed to follow the design suggested by Lord Bute.[8]

BURGH OF CUMNOCK & HOLMHEAD

Per chevron: in chief per pale Gules and Argent, a demi-lion rampant issuant counterchanged Argent and Azure; in base Or, a cushion Gules; all within a bordure per pale Argent and Gules charged with eight roses counterchanged barbed and seeded Vert.

And in an Escrol below the Shield which is ensigned of a mural coronet Gules masoned Argent as befitting a Burgh of Barony this *Motto* "Prompt in Progress".

(Lyon Register, xli, 127: 18 August 1959)

CUMNOCK & HOLMHEAD united to form a Police Burgh in 1866. Cumnock was created a Burgh of Barony in favour of James Dunbar of Cumnock in 1509[9] and was raised to a Burgh of Regality in favour of Charles, Lord Crichton, in 1680;[10] the Cumnock Dunbars had married into the Crichton family in the seventeenth century.

The arms refer to the Dunbar and Crichton connections. Surrounded by a bordure of eight roses, recalling a similar feature in the Dunbar arms, they show a demi-lion rampant which is half silver on a red field (for Dunbar) and half blue on a silver field (for Crichton). In base is the red cushion of Thomas Randolph, Earl of Moray and Lieutenant of King Robert I, which was quartered on a gold field by the Dunbars of Cumnock and by their present representatives, the Dunbars of Westfield in Moray. Agnes, Randolph's daughter, married Patrick, Earl of March and Dunbar, and brought the Earldom of Moray into the Dunbar family. The motto echoes the "In Promptu" used by the Chief of the Name of Dunbar, Dunbar of Mochrum. The arms were registered to mark the Burgh's 450th anniversary.[11]

BURGH OF DARVEL

Azure, a distaff and a shuttle paleways in fess Or; on a chief Argent, a roundel Sable, charged with an estoile of the Second.

Below the Shield which is ensigned with the coronet proper to a Burgh is placed in an Escrol this *Motto* "Non Sibi Sed Cunctis".

(Lyon Register, xli, 50: 26 October 1956)

DARVEL stands on land which belonged at one time to the Knights Templar and was independent of tenure, not even holding of the Crown. It became a Police Burgh in 1873.

The arms are a heraldic version of the device on the 1893 Burgh seal. The livery colours appear to have no special significance, the distaff and shuttle represent the weaving industry (now mostly lace and madras manufacturing) and the black roundel with its golden estoile a local variety of lamp called a "crusie". The black and silver colours in the chief could also allude to the banner—"per fess sable and argent"—of the Knights Templar. The Latin motto—"Not for themselves but for all"—comes from the seal. The arms were registered in connection with the acquisition of a Chain-of-Office for the Provost.[12]

BURGH OF GALSTON

Per pale: dexter, Argent, a dexter hand in a steel gauntlet Proper fessways, holding up a heart Gules, and on a chief Gules three pallets Or; sinister, Azure, a cross moline Argent, on a chief Ermine two weavers' shuttles saltirewise Azure, threaded Or, between as many escallops Gules.

And in an Escrol below the Shield which is ensigned of a coronet befitting a Police Burgh (videlicet: Azure masoned Argent) is placed this *Motto* "Labore Et Fiducia".

(Lyon Register, xlv, 91: 27 February 1964)

GALSTON, which grew up around the cotton mills on the banks of the river Irvine, became a Police Burgh in 1864.

The arms, which were registered in honour of the Burgh's centenary, show on the dexter side the Keith family arms to recall Sir William Keith of Galston who brought back to Scotland the heart of King Robert I after Sir James Douglas, who was taking it to the Holy Land, had been killed fighting the Moors in Spain. The mailed hand with the heart were specially included to commemorate this famous deed and also to make a canting reference to the neighbouring family of Lockhart of Barr, one of whom, John Lockhart, was well known for his support of John Knox and the Reformers. On the sinister side are the arms of Bentinck, the Duke of Portland being the Superior of the Burgh. The red shells on the ermine field allude to Campbell of Cessnock; Cessnock Castle was the original Tower of Garliestoun from which the town derived its name. The crossed shuttles are shown as a crest on the Burgh seal (which also shows, *inter alia*, the Bentinck arms) and refer to the weaving industry for which the town was once well known. The Latin motto—"By work and by confidence" —comes from the seal and is said to have been adopted by Galston in its early days.

GIRVAN was created a Burgh of Barony in 1668 in favour of Thomas Boyd of Pinkhill.[13] It became a Police Burgh in 1889.

The arms are based on the device on the 1892 Burgh seal. The field has been made silver and the ship red since these are the colours of Carrick, in which district

BURGH OF GIRVAN

Argent, on the waves of the sea in base undy Vert and of the field, an ancient three-masted ship, half her sails furled, flying pennants and flagged at the stern with the banner of Scotland all Gules, cantoned Azure charged with a Saint Andrew's cross of the First, the foresail charged with the arms of Boyd of Pinkhill, viz.: Azure, a fess chequy Silver and Gules, in base a cross moline Or.

[Above the Shield is placed a Burghal coronet] and in an Escrol below the Shield this *Motto* "Weave Industry with Truth".

(Lyon Register, xxix, 28: 27 June 1930)

of Ayrshire Girvan lies. The ship denotes that the town is a seaport and on its foresail are the arms of its founder, Thomas Boyd of Pinkhill. The motto, also from the seal, refers to the handloom weaving industry which was formerly prominent in the town.

KILWINNING became a Police Burgh in 1889. The Burgh has not recorded arms: its seal shows a figure of St. Winning, an Irish missionary who is reputed to have come to the district about 715 and to have founded a church there. In 1140, a monastery was built by one of the architectural fraternities which had received Papal permission to call themselves Free Masons; thus Kilwinning became the cradle of Freemasonry in Scotland. The device on the seal is based on an old seal of the monastery and the Latin motto—"Sine Te Domine Cuncta Nil"—"Without Thee, Lord, all things are nought"—is part of an inscription which appeared on a house belonging to the monastery.

LARGS was created a Burgh of Barony (as Newton of Gogo) in favour of John Brisbane of Bishopton and his wife, Ann Blair, in 1595, and (as Largs) in favour of William Alexander of Menstrie, 1st Earl of Stirling, in 1629. There was, however, a *de novo* creation (as Gogo or Largs) in 1631 in favour of the same John Brisbane of Bishopton.[14] It became a Police Burgh in 1876.

The arms are really a heraldic version of the "picture" of the Battle of Largs (1263) which appeared on the seal adopted by the Burgh in 1892. The three thistles

BURGH OF LARGS

Barry wavy Argent and Azure, a dragon-headed galley Sable in full sail, the mainsail Gules, charged with a lion rampant imperially crowned Or, armed and langued Azure, supporting between the paws a battle-axe erect in pale Argent; on a chief Vert, three thistles slipped Or, flowered of the Fourth.

[Above the Shield is placed a Burghal Coronet].

(Lyon Register, xxix, 73: 4 May 1931)

are in the Scottish Royal colours and stand on a green field to denote the victorious army of King Alexander III which repelled from the land the Norwegian invaders from the sea; the latter are represented by the black Viking ship, which bears on its sail the Royal Arms of Norway.

BURGH OF MAYBOLE

Argent, a chevron Gules between three lions rampant Azure, armed and langued of the Second.

Above the Shield is placed a Burghal coronet and a Helmet befitting their degree, with a Mantling Gules doubled Argent, and on a Wreath of their Liveries is set for *Crest* a dolphin naiant Proper, and in an Escrol over the Shield this *Motto* "Ad Summa Virtus".

(Lyon Register, xxix, 61: 22 January 1931)

MAYBOLE was created a Burgh of Barony in 1516 in favour of Gilbert Kennedy, 2nd Earl of Cassilis.[15] It became a Police Burgh in 1857.

The arms follow pretty closely the device on the seal adopted by the Burgh in 1892. The silver field and red chevron of the old Earldom of Carrick denote that Maybole is the capital of that district of Ayrshire. The three blue lions are for King Robert I who was Earl of Carrick before he became King; the original arms of the Bruce family before they assumed the arms of the Lords of Annandale showed a blue lion rampant on a silver field. The dolphin crest is that of Kennedy, Marquis of Ailsa, the leading proprietor in the district, while the Latin motto—"Courage to the End"— is one of those used by the Bruce family.

BURGH OF NEWMILNS & GREENHOLM

Per chevron Gules and Ermine, a chevronel embattled on its upper edge of the First in base, and in chief a spinning rock and a shuttle Or.

Below the Shield which is surmounted of a coronet proper to a Burgh is placed on an Escrol this *Motto* "Weave Truth with Trust".

(Lyon Register, xxxviii, 47: 28 January 1951)

NEWMILNS & GREENHOLM became a Police Burgh in 1872, the former having become a Police Burgh in 1844. Newmilns was created a Burgh of Barony in favour of George Campbell of Loudoun in 1490–91 and was raised to a Burgh of Regality in favour of Hugh Campbell, 3rd Earl of Loudoun, in 1707.[16]

The arms have for their field the red and ermine colours of Campbell of Loudoun. The red embattled chevronel recalls the Old Tolbooth (erected 1739) and thus the Lordship of the Regality of Loudoun; a representation of this building appeared on the seal adopted by the Burgh in 1892, as did the spinning rock and shuttle which represent the weaving industry of the town. This is thought to have sprung from Dutch and Huguenot refugees, who settled in Ayrshire in the seventeenth century, and now consists mainly of lace and madras manufacturing. The motto is that of the First Guild of Weavers of Newmilns to whom President Abraham Lincoln presented an American flag in gratitude for their messages of support and sympathy during the American Civil War. This flag became a cherished possession of the town and was given a place of honour in ceremonial processions, its last appearance being recorded in 1884. In recognition of the special connection, the United States Government presented another American flag to the Burgh in 1949.

BURGH OF PRESTWICK

Gules, within a shrine Or, the figure of Saint Nicholas habited Proper, his dexter hand raised in benediction and his sinister hand holding a crosier, all between a castle triple-towered Argent, masoned Sable, in the dexter, and in the sinister a branch of laurel Silver.

[Above the Shield is placed a Burghal coronet] and in an Escrol below the same this *Motto* "Loyalty, Vigilance, Foresight".

(Lyon Register, xli, 26: 23 September 1955)
(Previously matriculated without motto, xxv, 4: 23 March 1921)

PRESTWICK is an ancient Burgh of Barony going back at least to 983 and is the oldest recorded Baronial Burgh in Scotland. It is mentioned as a Burgh of Walter Fitzalan, High Steward of Scotland, in a Charter granted by him to Paisley Abbey between 1165 and 1174. Prestwick's ancient liberties were confirmed in 1600 by King James VI on his own behalf and on behalf of his eldest son, Henry, Duke of Rothesay.[17] It became a Police Burgh in 1903.

The arms were originally recorded in 1921 so that they could be displayed on the Burgh War Memorial.[18] At the request of the Town Council, they were rematriculated with the addition of the motto in 1955. They are based on the seal adopted in 1893, which was in turn adapted from an old seal of the Burgh of Barony, of which an impression dated 1464–65 is on record.[19] The Fitzalan red and gold colours are used and St. Nicholas, patron saint of the Burgh, is shown standing in a shrine. The triple-towered castle on the dexter may be the nearby Castle of Ayr; the meaning of the laurel branch is also obscure, but a somewhat similar branch appears with the figure of the Saint on the medieval seal of St. Nicholas' Hospital, Glasgow.[20] The motto was a local suggestion—Loyalty (to the past), Vigilance (for the present), Foresight (for the future).

SALTCOATS was created a Burgh of Barony in favour of Hugh, 1st Earl of Eglinton, in 1528–29; this charter proved ineffective, but a Charter of confirmation

BURGH OF SALTCOATS

Quarterly: 1st, Argent, a galley, sail furled, oars in action Sable, flagged Gules; 2nd, Argent, on a rock a ruined salt-works Proper; 3rd, Azure, a salmon naiant Argent; 4th, Gules, three rings Or, gemmed Azure.

Above the Shield is placed a mural coronet suitable to a Burgh and in an Escrol under the same this *Motto* "Per Mare Per Terras".

(Lyon Register, xxx, 44: 12 December 1932)

was issued in 1576 in favour of his great-grandson, Hugh, 3rd Earl.[21] It became a Police Burgh in 1885.

The arms are based on the device on the Burgh seal adopted in 1902. The galley recalls the former shipbuilding and shipping interests of the town; the ruined saltworks are a reminder of the salt-making from sea water and ashes which was carried on there until early in the nineteenth century; the salmon is for the fishing industry; the gemmed ring on the red field is from the Eglinton arms. The Latin motto—"By sea and by land"—comes from the seal.

STEWARTON became a Police Burgh in 1868. The lands of Stewarton were granted in 1283 to James, 5th High Steward of Scotland. After the Stewarts had succeeded to the throne, the lands were granted in 1426 to James Douglas, Lord Balvenie, and later 7th Earl of Douglas, and in 1467 to Thomas Boyd, Earl of Arran. After a reversion to the Crown, they were conferred in 1545 on Neil Montgomerie of Lainshaw, 3rd son of Hugh, 1st Earl of Eglinton, and in 1672 they passed into the possession of Sir Alexander Cunningham of Corsehill.

The arms show the coats of Stewart on the dexter and Boyd on the sinister; the Eglinton and Douglas connections are shown by the gemmed ring and the silver star. The black shakefork is for Cunningham and has been put overall to denote that Stewarton is in that district of Ayrshire. The Scotch blue bonnets recall the manufacture of bonnets and woollen goods associated with the Burgh and the Bonnetmakers

BURGH OF STEWARTON

Per pale Or and Azure: a fess chequy per pale, dexter of the Second and Argent, sinister of the Third and Gules, surmounted of a shakefork Sable [overall], all between a bonnet of the Second, with a round tassel of the Fourth, and an annulet of the First, stoned of the Fourth, in chief, and another similar bonnet and a mullet of the Third in base.

And in an Escrol below the Shield, which is ensigned of a Burghal coronet, this Motto "Knit Weel".

(Lyon Register, xli, 8: 22 February 1955)

of Stewarton, a corporation prior to 1630, which was managed by the Bonnet Court of Corsehill, which itself dates from 1549. The appropriate motto—"Knit Weel"— also refers to this; it was chosen in the light of an anonymous suggestion made to the Town Council of "Long Lastin'—Weel Knittit".[22]

BURGH OF TROON

Argent, on a chevron Gules, between a lymphad, sails furled Vert, flagged Azure, and an anchor of the Third, roped of the Fourth, both in chief, and in base a wheel of the Fourth with a pile nebuly issuant therefrom barry wavy of eight, Sable, Argent, Azure and Argent, alternately, three otters' heads erased of the field, langued of the Fourth; on a chief of the Fourth, a cross moline between ten bees volant, five on either side, of the First.

Below the Shield which is ensigned of a coronet suitable to a Police Burgh (viz.: Azure masoned Argent) is placed in an Escrol this *Motto* "Industria Ditat".

(Lyon Register, xli, 148: 11 May 1960)

TROON developed as a port and a resort once the railway (originally horse-drawn) from Kilmarnock and Ayr was opened in 1812. It became a Police Burgh in 1896.

The arms show in a heraldic form many features of the device on the Burgh seal adopted in 1896, a seal which is said to have been designed by William, 6th Duke of Portland.[23] In the chief, the silver cross moline of Bentinck on its blue field refers to the Duke of Portland, the Superior of the Burgh, while the ten bees recall the beehive on the seal and denote industry. The silver field and red chevron in the lower part of the shield come from the arms of the Cochrane Earls of Dundonald (Troon is in Dundonald parish), and the otters' heads refer to the Fullartons who owned the lands of Troon up to 1805. The ship and anchor represent the shipping and shipbuilding interests of the town, while the wheel with its pile nebuly stands for the Rocket-type engine purchased by the 4th Duke of Portland to operate on the railway line between Troon and Kilmarnock, probably the first in Scotland, for transporting coal from the Central Ayrshire coalfields to Troon for export to other parts of Britain. The Latin motto—"Industry enriches"—comes from the seal.

BURGH OF STEVENSTON

Argent, a shakefork between a lozenge Sable in chief, a billet Or, enflamed Gules, in the dexter, and in the sinister a heart of the Last within a fetterlock Azure.

Below the Shield which is ensigned by a coronet appropriate to a Burgh is placed in an Escrol this *Motto* "To Spread Her Conquests Farther".

(Lyon Register, xxxix, 47: 23 December 1952)

STEVENSTON takes its name from Stephen de Loccard to whom the lands of Stevenston were granted about 1170. It became a Police Burgh in 1952.

The arms show the black shakefork of Cunningham on its silver field, since Stevenston is in that district of Ayrshire; the shakefork also denotes the agricultural interests of the area. The black lozenge is for coal-mining, the flaming billet for the I.C.I. (Nobel) works at Ardeer nearby, and the Lockhart padlocked heart recalls Stephen de Loccard. The motto comes from Robert Burns' song "Bonny Lesley", which he wrote in honour of Miss Lesley Baillie, daughter of Robert Baillie, of Mayville, Stevenston.

P

The County Council of THE COUNTY OF AYR bears arms which were designed to show the four main features of the County, the Royal Castle of Ayr, as administrative seat of the Sheriffdom, and the districts of Carrick, Cunningham and Kyle. The castle recalls the same feature in the arms of the Royal Burgh of Ayr, and the other quarters come respectively from the arms of the old Earldom of Carrick, the Cunningham family, and the Stewart family which owned Kyle. The motto is taken from the tomb in Kilbirnie Churchyard, in the north of the County, of Captain Thomas Crawford of Jordanhill, who captured Dumbarton Castle in 1571 for the

AYR COUNTY COUNCIL

Quarterly: 1st, Gules, issuant from the sea in base undy Azure and Argent, a castle triple-towered of the Last, masoned Sable, windows and port of the First, the towers capped by pointed turrets Vert, each having a ball Or; 2nd, Argent, a chevron Gules; 3rd, Argent, a shakefork Sable; 4th, Or, a fess chequy Azure and Argent.

In an Escrol under the Shield is this *Motto* "God Schaw the Richt".

(Lyon Register, xxx, 6: 23 June 1931)
(Different arms were matriculated Lyon Register, xii, 34: 8 July 1890)

King's Lords by a feat of considerable military skill. Prior to 1931, the County Council had used arms matriculated in 1890, but it was thought appropriate to re-matriculate in view of the important changes in County Council jurisdiction introduced by the Local Government (Scotland) Act, 1929, and obtain arms which were more representative of the County as a whole. The previous arms were: "Or, a saltire Gules, on a chief of the Second a Holy Lamb, cross, staff and banner of St. Andrew Proper, between two lyres of the First stringed Argent." These were the arms of Bruce, Lord of Annandale, to which had been added in the chief, the Holy Lamb from the Ayr Burgh arms and two lyres to denote the County's special connection with poetry and song through Robert Burns, its most famous son.

29

COUNTY OF WIGTOWN

The County of WIGTOWN has four Burghs, the Royal Burghs of Wigtown, Whithorn and Stranraer (the County town), and the Police Burgh of Newton-Stewart.

WIGTOWN, formerly the County town, was a Royal Burgh by 1292, and may date from slightly earlier in the reign of King Alexander III. In 1341, it was granted to the Flemings from whom it passed to the Douglas family. On their forfeiture in 1455 it reverted to the Crown, and in 1457 the Burgh received a new Royal Charter from King James II.[1] The Burgh has not recorded arms; its seal bears a device showing a three-masted sailing-ship on the sea with the sun shining down from the top right-hand corner. The surrounding legend is in Latin and means "The Common Seal of the Most Ancient Burgh of Wigtown".

ROYAL BURGH OF WHITHORN

Azure, the representation of the figure of Saint Ninian, seated upon a siege-dragonée, with his dexter hand raised in benediction and his sinister hand supporting his crosier all Proper, between two fetters paleways in chief Argent.

Above the Shield is placed a mural crown as befitting a Royal Burgh and in an Escrol below it this *Motto* "Resurgam".

(Lyon Register, i, 462: 2 October 1947)

WHITHORN, the cathedral town of the old diocese of Galloway, was granted as a Burgh by King Robert I to the Prior and Convent of Whithorn in 1325, was erected a Burgh in favour of the Prior of Whithorn in 1451, and a Burgh of Barony in 1459. In 1511, King James IV created it a Royal Burgh.[2]

The arms are a pretty faithful copy of the device on the Burgh seal, of which a fifteenth-century impression is on record.[3] Using the blue and silver colours of Galloway, they show St. Ninian, the first known apostle of Scotland, who was born on the shores of the Solway Firth in the fourth century. He visited Rome where he was made a Bishop and also St. Martin at Tours, returning to Whithorn about 400 to found his famous "Candida Casa" and dedicate it to St. Martin. He then evangelised the Southern Picts and died "perfect in life and years" at Whithorn in 432.   His shrine there was for many centuries one of the most celebrated Scottish places of pilgrimage. The saint is vested as a bishop seated on a throne; on either side are fetterlock chains which may represent the evils he overcame by his teaching or may refer to some special sanctuary afforded by Whithorn Priory. The Latin motto means "I shall rise again" and was chosen to indicate the Burgh's wish to relive its past glories. The arms were matriculated in connection with the presentation of a Chain-of-Office for the Provost by the Whithorn Unit of the National Fire Service.[4]

ROYAL BURGH OF STRANRAER

Argent, in the sea Proper, a ship with three masts riding at anchor Sable.

The *Motto* "Tutissima Statio".

(Lyon Register, i, 467: c. 1673)

STRANRAER was created a Burgh of Barony in favour of Ninian Adair of Kinhilt in 1595 and was made a Royal Burgh by King James VI in 1617.[5]

The arms are characteristic of a seaport; the Lyon Office was fond of black ships for quite a long period. The Latin motto—"The safest station"—obviously refers to the safe anchorage which Loch Ryan, on which the town stands, offered to sailing vessels. The Burghal coronet was added in 1948 on the suggestion of the Lyon Office and was included by the Herald Painter in a drawing specially commissioned in that year.

NEWTON-STEWART was created a Burgh of Barony in 1677 in favour of William Stewart of Castle Stewart, third son of James, 2nd Earl of Galloway.[6] About 1778, Sir William Douglas, founder of Castle Douglas (q.v.), purchased the estate of Castle Stewart, changed the name to Newtown Douglas, and under this name obtained a charter for it as a Burgh of Barony, but the name soon fell into disuse. Newton-Stewart became a Police Burgh in 1861. The Burgh has not recorded arms: its seal shows a representation of the McMillan Hall, which was erected in 1888 and was provided from a bequest from two local ladies, the Misses Marion and Jane McMillan.

WIGTOWN COUNTY COUNCIL

Per pale indented: dexter, Azure, a lion rampant Argent, armed and langued Gules, crowned of an antique crown Or, and gorged of an antique crown Vert; sinister, Gules, a chevron Argent, and issuing from the sinister chief a quadrant of the sun arrayed Or; on a chief Azure, having a fillet Ermine, a saltire Or, charged with nine lozenges also Azure.

Which Shield is ensigned with the proper coronet of a County Council, videlicet: Issuing from a circlet Vert, five paling piles also Vert, alternately with four garbs Or, banded Sable.

(Lyon Register, xli, 1: 13 February 1955)

The County Council of THE COUNTY OF WIGTOWN bears arms which symbolise much of the County's history. On the dexter appears the crowned lion of Galloway on its blue field; the lion wears an antique crown as a collar and thus recalls not only the Douglas Lords of Galloway but also the historic family of Macdouall; on the sinister there is the silver chevron on a red field of Fleming, Earl of Wigtown, with a sunburst from the seal of the Royal Burgh of Wigtown in the top sinister corner. In the chief, the nine blue lozenges on the gold saltire recall a similar device (with the colours reversed), which is a feature of the arms of Dalrymple, Earl of Stair. The saltire in the chief and the chevron below also recall the Agnews of Lochnaw in whose arms these ordinaries appear. Since the backgrounds of both sections of the lower part of the shield are colours as distinct from metals and since the background of the chief is one of these colours, the chief had to be separated by something distinctive from the rest of the shield; the choice of an ermine fillet for the purpose acknowledges that each of the three compartments of the arms is derived from the arms of a Peerage House. The seal adopted by the Council in 1890 showed a lion rampant on a shield with a sword and sceptre crossed in saltire behind it, a crown above and a thistle below; it was adapted from a device belonging to the old Galloway Militia.

30

STEWARTRY OF KIRKCUDBRIGHT

The Stewartry of **KIRKCUDBRIGHT** has five Burghs, the Royal Burghs of Kirkcudbright (the County town) and New Galloway, and the Police Burghs of Castle Douglas, Dalbeattie and Gatehouse-of-Fleet. Kirkcudbrightshire has been known as the Stewartry since the fourteenth century, when Archibald the Grim, the first Douglas to hold the Lordship of Galloway, appointed a Steward to administer his estates in Easter Galloway.

ROYAL BURGH OF KIRKCUDBRIGHT

Azure, a lymphad with sails furled Argent, in the stern Saint Cuthbert seated, holding on his knees the head of the martyr Saint Oswald, all Proper.

[Above the Shield is placed a Burghal coronet.]

(Lyon Register, xxv, 3: 11 March 1921)

KIRKCUDBRIGHT, probably a Royal Burgh by 1330, appears to have been granted by King David II in 1369 to Archibald, 3rd Earl of Douglas ("The Grim"), when he became Lord of this part of Galloway and to have remained a Douglas Burgh until their forfeiture in 1455. That same year, King James II created the town a Royal Burgh.[1]

The arms are based on the device on the oldest known seal of the Burgh of which a fifteenth-century impression is on record.[2] Using the blue and silver colours of

Galloway, they show St. Cuthbert, patron saint of the town and from whom it takes its name, seated in the stern of a ship, holding the head of the martyred King Oswald of Northumbria. Oswald, a champion of Christianity, was slain in battle in 642 by Penda, King of Mercia, who fixed his head to a stake. The head of King Oswald was later sent to Lindisfarne, where it was ultimately buried with St. Cuthbert's body and, with it, transferred to the Saint's final resting-place in Durham Cathedral. The arms were matriculated in 1921 so that they could be displayed on the front of the Town Council gallery in the parish church;[3] at the same time, the device of the Incorporated Trades of Kirkcudbright and the arms of Sir Charles Hope-Dunbar were placed on the Trades gallery and the St. Mary's Isle or Selkirk gallery in the church. In 1927, there was discussion with the Lyon Office about the addition of a motto, but nothing was ever settled.

ROYAL BURGH OF NEW GALLOWAY

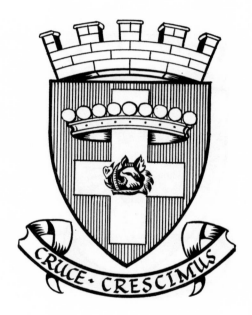

Gules, a [long] cross couped and reversed, charged with a boar's head erased, and encircled in chief with a viscount's coronet of sixteen pearls all Proper.

Above the Shield is placed a mural coronet and in an Escrol below the Shield this *Motto* "Cruce Crescimus".

(Lyon Register, xxxiii, 16: 26 April 1938)

NEW GALLOWAY was created a Royal Burgh by King Charles I in 1630, the Charter transferring to it the rights and privileges bestowed on the Old (St. John's) Clachan of Dalry by an inoperative charter of 1629.[4]

The arms are something of a mystery, though it is known that they are based on the device on the old Burgh seal, but without the crest and supporters, since the Town Council did not wish to have them. The boar's head and the Viscount's coronet evidently commemorate Sir John Gordon of Lochinvar, 1st Viscount Kenmure (cr. 1633), on whose lands the Burgh was established and who was himself involved in its foundation; the 6th Viscount Kenmure was executed in 1716 for his part in the 1715 Jacobite Rebellion. The explanation of the red field and silver cross can only be the subject of conjecture. There seems to be no local connection with St. Peter to explain the cross reversed, and it therefore appears reasonable to suggest that, as the original site for the Burgh was St. John's Clachan of Dalry, the cross may have some reference to the Knights of St. John who bore "Gules, a cross Argent". It may well be that the seal engraver (as in Barrhead's case) took some artistic licence: instead of depicting the cross surmounted by the coronet, he extended it through the coronet so that it would stand out better. This he did without appreciating the heraldic significance of his action. The use of the Latin motto—"By the Cross we prosper"— would seem to support the view that the cross is that of the Knights of St. John. The cost of the fees for registration of the arms was met from a fund collected in 1929–30 to enable the Burgh arms to be registered.

BURGH OF CASTLE DOUGLAS

Barry of six Argent and Azure, a heart Gules ensigned with an imperial crown between two wings Or.

[Above the Shield is placed a Burghal coronet] and in an Escrol beneath the Shield this *Motto* "Forward".

(Lyon Register, xxviii, 49: 10 September 1929)

CASTLE DOUGLAS was created a Burgh of Barony in 1791 in favour of Sir William Douglas[5] (see also Newton-Stewart), a local man who had prospered in the West Indies and had purchased the estate of Gelston in Kirkcudbrightshire and built a castle there. The lay-out of the town is an interesting example of late eighteenth-century town-planning. Castle Douglas became a Police Burgh in 1862.

Based on the device on the seal adopted by the Burgh in 1892, the arms have the silver and blue colours of Galloway for a field; the crowned and winged heart and the motto were the crest and motto of Douglas, Marquess of Queensberry, with whom Sir William Douglas claimed kinship.

BURGH OF DALBEATTIE

Argent, a double-headed eagle displayed Sable, beaked and membered Azure, bearing on its breast an escutcheon, viz.: Argent, between in chief a birch tree eradicated Proper and three mullets Gules in flanks and base, a saltire Sable charged with an urcheon Or.

Above the Shield is placed a mural crown masoned Sable, thereon a Helmet befitting their degree with a Mantling Sable doubled Argent, and on a Wreath of their Liveries is set for *Crest* a stag lodged Proper, attired Or, in front of a holly bush fructed Proper, and in an Escrol under the Shield this *Motto* "Respice Prospice".

(Lyon Register, xxviii, 79: 29 January 1930)

DALBEATTIE was founded about 1780 by Alexander Copland of King's Grange and George Maxwell of Munches, and quickly grew after the opening of the rich granite quarries there. It became a Police Burgh in 1858.

The arms follow closely the device on the seal adopted by the Burgh in 1892, which was designed locally by Mr. James Austin.[6] They use as a base the arms of the Maxwell Earls of Nithsdale (of the Herries branch) which form the 1st and 4th quarters of the arms of Maxwell of Munches. The eagle's beaks and claws have been coloured blue instead of red, and the small shield on the eagle's breast shows not only the golden hedgehog of Herries but also retains two features which Mr. Austin had added: a birch tree for Dalbeattie—"valley of the birch"—and three red mullets for Copland of Colliston, a family with many close connections with the Burgh. The crest of the stag sitting below the bush is that of Maxwell, Earl of Nithsdale and of Maxwell of Munches. The Latin motto—"Look Backward, Look Forward"—comes from the seal and evidently refers to the eagle looking both ways.

GATEHOUSE-OF-FLEET was created a Burgh of Barony in 1795 in favour of James Murray of Broughton and Cally.[7] It became a Police Burgh in 1852.

The arms are based on those of Murray of Broughton which have silver stars on a blue field (for Murray), a silver/blue fess chequy on a gold field (for Stewart of Dalwinton and Stewart of Girthon) and two red roses (for Lennox of Cally). The tower represents the Burgh Clock Tower, built partly by a bequest and partly by public subscription in 1871, a representation of which appeared on the seal adopted by the Burgh in 1894; its colour recalls the Stewarts of Garlies, ancestors of the present

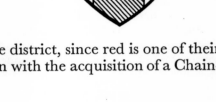

BURGH OF GATEHOUSE-OF-FLEET

Per fess Azure and Or, a fess chequy Argent and of the First between two mullets in chief of the Third, and as many roses Gules, barbed and seeded Vert, in base; over all a pale of the Third charged with a tower of the Fourth, windows and port of the Second, situated upon a mount of the Fifth.

The said Shield is ensigned of a coronet appropriate to a Burgh.

(Lyon Register, xxxviii, 92: 11 July 1951)

Earls of Galloway, another family associated with the district, since red is one of their livery colours. The arms were registered in connection with the acquisition of a Chain-of-Office for the Provost.[8]

KIRKCUDBRIGHT COUNTY COUNCIL

Azure, a lion rampant Argent, armed and langued Gules, crowned with an antique crown Or, surmounted of a bar chequy of the Second and Vert.

Which Shield is ensigned of a coronet appropriate to a County Council as the same is now defined and assigned by us, videlicet: Issuant from a circlet Vert, five paling piles also Vert, alternately with four garbs Or, banded Sable.

(Lyon Register, xxxviii, 76: 15 May 1951)

The County Council of THE STEWARTRY OF KIRKCUDBRIGHT bears arms which show the crowned silver lion of Galloway on its blue field. The silver/green chequy of the fess denotes the checked table cloth used by the Stewards when collecting taxes and other dues, thus recalling that this part of Galloway is still known as the Stewartry of Kirkcudbright. This is the first example of the granting of a County Council coronet. The seal adopted by the Council in 1890 showed the crowned lion of Galloway on a shield with an open crown above.

31

COUNTY OF DUMFRIES

The County of DUMFRIES has seven Burghs, the Royal Burghs of Dumfries (the County town), Annan, Lochmaben, and Sanquhar, and the Police Burghs of Langholm, Lockerbie and Moffat.

ROYAL BURGH OF DUMFRIES

Azure, semée of estoiles Or, standing on a cloud the figure of the Archangel Michael, wings expanded, brandishing in his dexter hand a sword over a dragon lying on its back in base with its tail nowed fessways all Proper, on his sinister arm an escutcheon Argent charged with a cross Gules; in dexter flank an increscent, in the sinister flank the sun in his splendour of the Second.

Above the Shield is placed a mural coronet suitable to a Royal Burgh and under the same this *Motto* "A Lore Burne".

(Lyon Register, xxx, 3: 20 August 1931)

DUMFRIES is a Royal Burgh of King William the Lion, dating from about 1186.[1] The Police Burgh of Maxwelltown was joined to Dumfries in 1931.

The arms are taken in almost complete detail from a Burgh seal, of which a fourteenth century impression is on record[2] and of which the matrix was discovered in 1910.[3] St. Michael is the patron saint of the Burgh and the scene on the shield recalls the Archangel's triumph over the great red dragon (Revelation 12:3–4) whose "tail drew the third part of the stars of heaven and did cast them to the earth". Thus we have the blue field spattered with stars and the dragon in red (but called "Proper" to avoid putting colour on colour), with the sun and moon above to complete the firmament. The Scots motto is the old mustering cry of the Burgh and means "To the Lower Burn".

ROYAL BURGH OF ANNAN

Or, a saltire and chief Gules, the latter charged with five barrulets wavy conjoined Argent and Azure.

Above the Shield is placed a mural crown and in an Escrol below the Shield this *Motto* "Ut Flumen Sic Oppidum".

(Lyon Register, xxiii, 63: 29 October 1918)

ANNAN seems to have been a Burgh of the Bruce Lords of Annandale in the twelfth century and, after several changes of overlord, presumably passed to the Crown when the main line of the Earls of Douglas became extinct in 1440. It is mentioned as a Royal Burgh in 1532 and received a Charter of Novodamus from King James V in 1538–39.[4]

The arms are those of Bruce, Lord of Annandale, differenced by five wavy barrulets in the chief to denote the river Annan, and thus, as Dr. George Neilson, the local historian, said, "bring in the Annan water to flow along the chief division of the shield".[5] The Latin motto—"Like river, like town"—is a happy one. The arms were matriculated so that the Burgh could have its own flag for use in the annual ceremony of riding of the marches.[6]

LOCHMABEN, by 1296 a Burgh of the Bruce Lords of Annandale, later went through some changes of overlord and reverted to the Crown when the main line of the Earls of Douglas died out in 1440. By 1447, it appears to have been recognised as a Royal Burgh, and would thus be a creation of King James II.[7] It received a Charter of Confirmation from King James VI in 1612.

The arms illustrate the very close connection of the Bruce Lords of Annandale and King Robert I with Lochmaben. This connection began in 1124 when King David I made a grant of all Annandale to Robert de Brus, a Norman Knight who already held lands in Yorkshire. The Bruces built a castle at Lochmaben on a hillock

ROYAL BURGH OF LOCHMABEN

Parted per pale Or and Argent: on the dexter a saltire and chief Gules, the latter charged with a ruined castle of the Second, masoned Sable; on the sinister, on a mount Vert, the figure of King Robert the Bruce Proper.

Above the Shield is placed a mural coronet and in an Escrol under the same this *Motto* "E Nobis Liberator Rex".

(Lyon Register, xxxiii, 55: 9 March 1939)

between Kirk Loch and Castle Loch and there is a tradition that King Robert I made Lochmaben a Royal Burgh. On the dexter side are shown the arms of the Bruce Lords of Annandale with their Castle of Lochmaben added in the chief; on the sinister is King Robert I in full armour, the details being copied from his statue at Lochmaben. Apparently the statue, which was described in 1939 as "the finest of Bruce there is", was originally destined for Bannockburn, but owing to the efforts of the Rev. W. Graham, author of *Lochmaben 500 Years Ago*, was secured for the Burgh. The Latin motto—"From us is sprung a liberator King"—is another proud reference to King Robert I; it was suggested by Mr. Robert Fraser who was Provost and Headmaster of Lochmaben School in 1939.[8] The cost of the fees payable for obtaining the Grant of arms was met from the Jeffrey Johnstone Trust.[9]

SANQUHAR was probably a Burgh of Barony dependent on the Crichton family by 1335 and was erected into a Burgh of Barony in favour of Robert Crichton of Sanquhar in 1484. It was made a Royal Burgh by King James VI in 1598.[10]

The arms are based on an old Burgh seal, of which a 1732 impression is on record.[11] Using the colours of Scotland and Crichton, they show the old Castle of Sanquhar, the Crichton Peel, first the seat of the Rosses and then of the Crichtons of Sanquhar. The five steps leading up to the gate recall the Five Incorporated Trades of Sanquhar (Hammermen, Squaremen, Weavers, Shoemakers and Tailors) and that it was only through the Five Trades that one could secure trading privileges in the Burgh. The thistle in the crest has a special association with the town. It encircled the Castle on the flag of the Five Incorporated Trades of Sanquhar which is dated 1819, and among the poems and songs of James Kennedy (Dumfries, 1823) is one

ROYAL BURGH OF SANQUHAR

Azure, on a rock in base Proper, a double-leaved gate Gules, triple-towered, on an ascent of five steps flanked by two towers all Argent, towers arch-roofed and masoned Sable, vanes of the Second.

Above the Shield is placed a coronet suitable to a Royal Burgh and thereon a Helmet befitting their degree with a Mantling Azure doubled Argent, and on a Wreath of their Liveries is set for *Crest* a thistle slipped Proper, and in an Escrol over the same this *Motto* "On Sanquhar On".

(Lyon Register, xxviii, 61: 11 November 1929)

called "The Auld Castle and Thistle of Sanquhar".[12] The war-cry of the Crichtons was "On Crichton On" and the choice of "On Sanquhar On", which was suggested by Mr. Tom Wilson, of Blawearie, Sanquhar, is a good echo, and since Sanquhar means "the old castle" is a good example of "armes parlantes".

BURGH OF LANGHOLM

Azure, a saltire Argent between in chief, a thistle slipped Proper, on the dexter, a spade in pale blade upwards wreathed with heather Proper, on the sinister, a wooden platter surmounted of a barley meal bannock charged with a salt herring paleways Proper, and in base a golden fleece Or.

[Above the Shield is placed a Burghal coronet].

(Lyon Register, xxix, 35: 1 August 1930)

LANGHOLM was created a Burgh of Barony in favour of Robert Maxwell, 2nd Earl of Nithsdale, in 1621 and was raised to a Burgh of Regality in favour of Anne, Duchess of Buccleuch in 1687.[13] It became a Police Burgh in 1845.

The arms are closely based on the device on the seal adopted by the Burgh in 1893. The Scottish saltire is used as a base, but this could also recall the Maxwell Earls of Nithsdale who have a saltire in their arms. The silver and blue colours are also those of the Armstrongs who once owned Langholm Castle and have a special association with the town. The thistle, the heather-wreathed spade, and the platter with the bannock and salt herring are emblems carried in the annual Common Riding Ceremony at Langholm. The thistle is also the Scottish emblem and the golden fleece represents woollen manufacturing, which is an important industry of the town. After much discussion, the Town Council decided against having a motto.[14]

BURGH OF LOCKERBIE

Quarterly: 1st and 4th, Argent, within an orle a man's heart Gules, imperially crowned Proper; on a chief Azure, three mullets of the field; 2nd, Argent, a saltire Sable, on a chief Gules three cushions Or; 3rd, Azure, a bend between six cross-crosslets fitchée Or.

[Above the Shield is placed a Burghal coronet] and in an Escrol below the Shield this *Motto* "Forward".

(Lyon Register, xxix, 21: 4 June 1930)

LOCKERBIE grew up around the square tower of the Johnstones of Lockerbie and became a Police Burgh in 1863.

The arms are taken very much from the device on the seal adopted by the Burgh in 1892. This showed the arms of Mr. Arthur Henry Johnstone-Douglas of Lockerbie, whose family had owned the estate of Lockerbie since the sixteenth century and who, himself, suggested that the Burgh should incorporate his arms in its seal.[15] The Johnstone-Douglasses of Lockerbie were descended from Sir William Douglas of Kelhead who married the daughter of the last Johnstone laird of Lockerbie and whose son Charles became 6th Marquess of Queensberry. In the arms a small difference has been made in the 1st and 4th quarters (Douglas, Marquess of Queensberry) where the Royal tressure has been replaced by a silver orle; the 2nd quarter is for Johnstone and the 3rd for Mar, this last also appears in the arms of the Marquess of Queensberry, whose motto is also used (cf. Castle Douglas).

BURGH OF MOFFAT

Azure, a winged spur Or, leathered Gules.

Above the Shield is set a Burghal crown, and in an Escrol under the same this *Motto* "Nunquam Non Paratus".

(Lyon Register, xxix, 27: 26 June 1930)

MOFFAT was created a Burgh of Regality in favour of James Johnstone of Corhead in 1648 and this was confirmed to James Johnstone, 3rd Earl of Annandale, in 1662.[16] It became a Police Burgh in 1864.

The arms repeat the device on the Burgh seal in use in 1892. The gold winged spur with red leathering is the crest of the Earls (later Marquesses) of Annandale, whose arms, surmounted by an Earl's coronet, were on a bell dated 1660 which hung in the turret of the Burgh Courthouse. The blue field seems to have no special significance, apart from being a favourite colour for a Scottish town, unless it has some reference to the river Annan on which the town stands. The Latin motto—"Never unprepared"—is that of the Marquesses of Annandale.

DUMFRIES COUNTY COUNCIL

Argent, a saltire Sable, in chief a man's heart Gules imperially crowned Or; on a chief of the Third, two mullets of the First.

(Lyon Register, xxvii, 71: 26 January 1928)

The County Council of THE COUNTY OF DUMFRIES bears a very simple coat of arms, which nevertheless recalls many of the distinguished families associated with the County. The saltire and chief feature in the arms of the Bruces of Annandale, the Johnstones of Annandale, the Jardines, the Griersons and the Kirkpatricks. The black saltire on the silver field also refers to the Maxwells of Nithsdale and Caerlaverock, while the silver field itself represents the Crichton Earls of Dumfries. The crowned heart and the stars are for the Douglasses, the latter also recalling the Scotts and the Murrays. The seal adopted by the Council in 1890 had a device which showed two escutcheons, one bearing arms attributed to John Balliol, and the other the arms of Robert Bruce, Lord of Annandale; above was the Scottish Crown, and below, the Bruce heart; this was intended to symbolise the close connections of Dumfries-shire with both branches of the ancient Scottish Royal family.

32

COUNTY OF PEEBLES

The County of PEEBLES has two Burghs, the Royal Burgh of Peebles (the County town) and the Police Burgh of Innerleithen.

ROYAL BURGH OF PEEBLES

Gules, three salmon counternaiant in pale Proper.

And in an Escrol this *Motto* "Contranando Incrementum".

(Lyon Register, xiii, 47: 18 December 1894)

PEEBLES seems to have been created a Royal Burgh about 1153 by King David I.[1]

The arms, which are sometimes used with a Burghal coronet added to them, are very old and appear on a seal of which an impression dated 1473 is on record.[2] The device of the three salmon appears on shields on the Town Cross, which is thought to date from 1320.[3] The red field is well authenticated, though the reason for the choice of colour is not known. The salmon recall the many salmon in the river Tweed, on which the Burgh stands; their arrangement on the shield refers to the habit of the fish travelling upstream from the sea to spawn and implies that for every salmon swimming up river, two return to the sea. The Latin motto means "Increase by swimming against (the stream)". The arms were matriculated by the Town Council following some correspondence in *The Peebleshire Advertiser*, which was started by a letter from

Mr. A. C. Fox-Davies, author of *The Book of Public Arms* and other notable works on heraldry, in which he questioned Peebles' right to use its ancient armorial bearings, a right which was stoutly defended by Mr. William Buchan, who was then the Town Clerk.[4]

BURGH OF INNERLEITHEN

Vert, issuant from a bar wavy Argent in base, charged with a barrulet also wavy Azure, a boat Or, therein standing the figure of Saint Ronan, vested and mitred, all Proper, holding in his dexter hand a crosier of the Fourth.

Above the Shield is placed a coronet suitable to a Burgh masoned Sable, and in an Escrol over the same this *Motto* "Live and Let Live"; and in a Compartment below with this *Motto* "Watch and Pray" are set for *Supporters*, on the dexter side, a bear Proper muzzled Gules and therefrom a leash reflexed over its back Or, on the sinister, a bay horse langued and bridled Gules.

(Lyon Register, xxviii, 75: 14 January 1930)

INNERLEITHEN has grown up in the last one hundred and fifty years or so through its woollen manufactures and because of its popularity as a spa—the medicinal properties of St. Ronan's Well were made famous by Sir Walter Scott. It became a Police Burgh in 1868.

The arms show the figure of St. Ronan, the patron saint of the town, coming up the Tweed in a boat. The field is green to denote the fertile farming lands around Innerleithen. The supporters recall two famous local families closely associated with the Burgh: the bear, the Stewart Earls of Traquair—Traquair House is just outside the town—and the horse, Horsbrugh of that Ilk; a bay horse was chosen because it is mentioned in a Roll of Horses dated 1298 that a bay horse, valued at twelve pounds, belonging to Sir Simon de Horsbrok, was killed in Selkirk Forest on 3 October in that year.[5] The two mottoes come from the seal adopted by the Burgh in 1892. Mr. Robert Mathieson, who was Provost of Innerleithen (1900–1941) took a leading part in obtaining the Grant of arms.

PEEBLES COUNTY COUNCIL

Quarterly: 1st, Sable, five fraises Argent; 2nd, Azure, a horse's head couped Argent; 3rd, Vert, a golden fleece; 4th, Or, fretty Gules, a chief embattled of the Last charged with two thunderbolts of the First.

Above the Shield is placed a Helmet befitting their degree with a Mantling Sable doubled Argent, and on a Wreath of their Liveries is set for *Crest* on a horse passant, a border horseman fully armed all Proper, and on a Compartment below the same with this *Motto* "Onward Tweeddale", are set for *Supporters* two salmon Proper.

(Lyon Register, xxix, 60: 16 January 1931)

The County Council of THE COUNTY OF PEEBLES bears quartered arms. The 1st quarter has five silver fraises (or cinquefoils) on a black field from the arms of Fraser of Oliver Castle, one of the most ancient and famous families of Tweeddale, the old name for Peebles-shire; from this family, whose arms are said to have been "Sable, six cinquefoils Argent, 3, 2 and 1", are descended by marriage the Hays of Yester, Marquesses of Tweeddale, who also bear fraises (on a blue field) in their arms. The 2nd quarter shows the arms of Horsbrugh, a family whose connection with Tweeddale is almost as old as that of the Frasers. The 3rd quarter shows a golden fleece on a green field to represent the County's staple industries: agriculture, sheep-farming and woollen manufacturing. In the 4th quarter are the arms of Mr. M. G. (later Sir Michael) Thorburn of Glenormiston, who was both Lord Lieutenant and Convener of the County in 1931, and had rendered many years of distinguished service to the County. The salmon supporters symbolise the river Tweed and the Royal Burgh of Peebles; the crest is a sixteenth-century Border knight and the motto looks forward to the future with confidence. Provost Robert Mathieson of Inner-leithen, who was a County Councillor at the time, played a prominent role in the discussions about the coat of arms.

33

COUNTY OF SELKIRK

The County of SELKIRK has two Burghs, the Royal Burgh of Selkirk (the County town) and the Parliamentary Burgh of Galashiels.

ROYAL BURGH OF SELKIRK

Or, on a mount before a grove of oak trees, the Blessed Virgin seated on a bench with the Holy Child in her arms, all Proper, against her feet an escutcheon of the Royal Arms of Scotland—Or, within a double tressure flory counterflory a lion rampant Gules, armed and langued Azure.

Above the Shield is placed a mural crown suitable to a Royal Burgh and in an Escrol under the Shield this *Motto* "Et Spreta Incolumem Vita Defendere Famam".

(Lyon Register, xxix, 24: 14 June 1930)

SELKIRK dates as a Royal Burgh certainly from 1328 in the reign of King Robert I and may be an earlier foundation. Its status was confirmed by King James V in 1535–36 and this and later Charters were confirmed by Parliament in 1633. Nevertheless, in 1602 it appears as a Burgh of Barony created in favour of William, 10th Earl of Angus, who was for a time Lieutenant over the whole Scottish Borders.[1]

The arms come from the Burgh seal which, according to Lord Bute and Thomas Craig-Brown, the historian of Selkirkshire, is based on the seal on the Abbey of St. Mary and St. John the Evangelist founded at Selkirk by King David I about 1120.[2]

Selkirk means "the church in the forest" and the Virgin and Child and the oak trees stand for the Church of St. Mary in the Royal Forest of Ettrick. The use of the Royal escutcheon was accepted by Lord Lyon Grant after it had been proved to have been in use on the Burgh seal prior to 1426; there is an impression of the seal of that date on record.[3] The Latin motto—"And to defend her sacred honour at the risk of life itself" —would seem most appropriate to the blazon; it is, however, just possible that it may have some reference to a local legend associated with Ladywoodedge near the town.

BURGH OF GALASHIELS

Argent, issuing from a mount in base a plum tree fructed between two foxes sejant, that on the dexter contournée, both looking upwards all Proper.

[Above the Shield is placed a Burghal coronet] and in an Escrol below the Shield this *Motto and Date* "Sour 1337 Plums".

(Lyon Register, xxix, 18: 15 May 1930)

GALASHIELS was created a Burgh of Barony in favour of James Hoppringill (or Pringle), of Galashiels, in 1599.[4] A Police Burgh from 1850, it became a Parliamentary Burgh under the 1867–68 Reform Act.

The arms come from the Burgh seal, though their origin is uncertain. Officially they commemorate a successful skirmish in 1337 against a band of Englishmen at a place called Englishman's Syke just outside the town. The English were gathering the wild plums of the district when they were surprised and overcome by a group of local men who, after their victory, called themselves "the sour plums in Galashiels"; a song with the same title, whose words have long been forgotten, was written about their exploits; its tune was a favourite of Sir Walter Scott's uncle, Thomas Scott, a noted piper in his day.[5] The motto also relates to the incident. But there have been other theories about the arms. Some authorities considered that it was wrong to have the foxes in the arms at all and that they should merely show the plum tree in fruit; others held the view that the device of "The Tod and the Plum Tree" referred to the fable of the fox and the grapes and was a classical theme used by the engraver of the seal (cf. Haddington). In passing, it may be noted that the silver field is the same as that used by Pringle of Galashiels.

SELKIRK COUNTY COUNCIL

Argent, on a mount in base a stag lodged reguardant, in front of an oak tree, all Proper.

And in an Escrol under the Shield this *Motto* "Leal to the Border".

(Lyon Register, xxvii, 46: 8 July 1927)

The County Council of THE COUNTY OF SELKIRK bears arms which are very appropriate to "the Shire of the Forest". They show a stag at rest in Ettrick Forest, a favourite Royal hunting ground. This device has a long association with the County, and was used by the Selkirkshire Volunteers; there is an example on a regimental medal dated 1807. It is also said to be connected with Sir Walter Scott, who refers to it and to the motto in a letter of 1827 addressed to the Friendly Society of Selkirk, whose flag he had been asked to design; the stag and forest motif also appears, in a somewhat different form, in the 1799 colour of the Selkirkshire Yeomanry Cavalry.[6] The motto, which appears on the 1807 medal, typifies the Borderer's love of his country and is reminiscent of that used by Lord Polwarth—"True to the End"; the Polwarth family has a long connection with the County.

34

COUNTY OF ROXBURGH

The County of ROXBURGH has four Burghs, the Royal Burgh of Jedburgh, the Parliamentary Burgh of Hawick, and the Police Burghs of Kelso and Melrose. The County town, Newtown St. Boswells, is not a Burgh.

ROYAL BURGH OF JEDBURGH

Gules, on a horse saliant Argent, furnished Azure, a chevalier armed at all points, grasping in his right hand a kind of lance (called the Jedburgh Staff) Proper.

The *Motto* in an Escrol is "Strenue et Prospere".

(Lyon Register, i, 459: 1680)
(Coronet added in Extract of Matriculation dated 15 March 1956)

JEDBURGH has certainly been a Royal Burgh from between 1159 and 1165, and thus probably a creation of King Malcolm IV or King William the Lion. In 1320, King Robert I granted it to his famous commander, Sir James Douglas, but by 1424 it was again a Royal Burgh.[1]

The arms were the subject of dispute between the Town Council and Lord Lyon Erskine. From about 1650, the Burgh had used a seal which showed "a unicorn trippant or passant",[2] but Lord Lyon Erskine apparently regarded this as an improper use of part of the Royal arms and declined to register it;[3] nevertheless in 1798 a similar feature was allowed in the achievement granted to the County of Roxburgh. The arms of Jedburgh show one of the famous Border riders armed with a Jedburgh or Jethart staff; the reason for the red field is not clear. It is the only Burgh coat which includes a horse; Innerleithen has one as a supporter only. The Latin motto, the choice of which was left to the Lord Lyon, means "Stoutly and Well". The Burghal coronet was added on 15 March 1956 when an Extract of Matriculation was obtained: the coronet was coloured reddish-brown as the "Proper" colour to represent the sandstone of Jedburgh Abbey and the surrounding district.

BURGH OF HAWICK

Argent, an altar, thereon an open Bible, both Proper, between on the dexter, a flag Azure charged with a saltire Or (for Hexham Priory) and inscribed with the date 1514 Gold, waving towards the dexter from a staff of the Last, and on the sinister a man's heart Gules ensigned with an imperial crown Gold; on a chief Sable, a lamp with two branches also Gold, enflamed and irradiated Proper.

Under the Shield which is ensigned of a Burghal coronet is placed in an Escrol this *Motto* "Tyr-ibus Ye Tyr Ye Odin".

(Lyon Register, xli, 74: 20 August 1957)
(Previously matriculated without motto) Lyon Register, xxviii, 39: 14 June 1929

HAWICK was created a Burgh of Barony in 1511 in favour of Sir James Douglas of Drumlanrig and was raised to a Burgh of Regality in 1669 in favour of William, Viscount Drumlanrig, who later became 3rd Earl, 1st Marquess, and 1st Duke of Queensberry.[4] A Police Burgh from 1845, it became a Parliamentary Burgh under the 1867–68 Reform Act.

The arms reflect the device on the Burgh seal in use in 1892. The altar and the Bible stand for the parish church, dedicated in 1214, and the Douglas crowned heart is for Sir James Douglas of Drumlanrig. The blue flag with its golden saltire and date of 1514 recalls the defeat, at nearby Hornshole, of a body of English soldiers connected with Hexham Abbey, some time after the Battle of Flodden (1513).[5] This English standard, or a replica of it—a gold saltire on a blue field (for Hexham Abbey)—is said to have been carried in every subsequent Common Riding Ceremony at Hawick. The lamp in the chief is a reminder of the condition in the first Charter that a lamp should be kept burning before the great altar in the parish church "in time of High Mass and evening prayers on all Holy Days throughout the year, in honour of our Blessed Lord and Saviour Jesus Christ, for the souls of the Barons of Hawick, founders of the said lamp and their successors".[6] The placing of the lamp on the black field is thus very fitting. The motto, which is said to have been an invocation to Thor and Odin, comes from the refrain to the Hawick Common Riding Song written by James Hogg, the Ettrick Shepherd, "to commemorate the laurels gained by the men and youth of Hawick at and after Flodden". When the arms were matriculated in 1929, the motto, which had been long in use, was for some reason overlooked, but the omission was put right in 1957. At the same time, an error was discovered and corrected in the drawing in the Lyon Register where the Hawick banner had been given a silver saltire instead of a gold one.

BURGH OF KELSO

Azure, springing from a meadow in base a rose-tree in full flower, and pendant therefrom, between an eagle and a dove addorsed Argent, an escutcheon charged with the Royal Arms of Scotland—Or, within a double tressure flory counterflory, a lion rampant Gules, armed and langued Azure.

Above the Shield is placed a mural coronet suitable to a Burgh and in an Escrol under the same this *Motto* "Dae Richt Fear Nocht".

(Lyon Register, xxxii, 21 : 30 June 1936)

KELSO is mentioned in 1237 as a Burgh dependent on the Abbey and Convent of Kelso (founded by King David I in 1128); it was created a Burgh of Barony in favour of Robert Kerr, 1st Earl of Roxburghe, in 1614.[7] The present town became a Police Burgh in 1838 and includes part of Old Roxburgh, which was created a Royal Burgh by King David I probably about 1124[8] and was one of the original members of the Curia Quattuor Burgorum (Berwick, Edinburgh, Stirling and Roxburgh); by 1460 it consisted only of its Castle, which was destroyed in that year on its recapture from the English.

The arms follow closely the device on the Burgh seal in use in 1892. The rose tree, with the Royal arms and the two birds, appears on a seal of the Royal Burgh of Roxburgh, of which an impression of 1296 is on record;[9] in effect, Kelso has been allowed to inherit the arms of the ancient Royal Burgh. The birds have been made an eagle (for St. John) and a dove (for the Virgin Mary), since Kelso Abbey was dedicated to them. In an old seal of the Abbey the Virgin is shown holding a branch on top of which a dove is perched and so, on this occasion, the dove has been used to symbolise her.[10] The Scots motto was chosen in 1936 at the suggestion of Mr. John Pennie, then Town Clerk, and has a brave ring about it.[11]

BURGH OF MELROSE

Azure, issuant from a representation of the wall of the Abbey of Melrose in base Proper, door Gules, between two pinnacles a gothic canopy Or, therein seated the Virgin Mary and Holy Child also Proper; in dexter chief a mell and in sinister chief a rose Argent.

Above the Shield is placed a mural coronet suitable to a Burgh and in an Escrol under the same this *Motto* "Truth and Loyalty".

(Lyon Register, xxx, 11: 3 November 1931)

MELROSE is said to have been a Burgh of Regality under Melrose Abbey (founded by King David I in 1136). It is mentioned as a Burgh of Barony in 1605 and was so created *de novo* in favour of John Ramsay, Viscount Haddington, in 1609; it was raised to a Burgh of Regality in 1621 in favour of Sir Thomas Hamilton, Earl of Melrose, who with Royal consent changed his title to Earl of Haddington in 1627.[12] Melrose became a Police Burgh in 1895.

The arms show part of the Abbey wall with a shrine above containing the Virgin and Child; the Cistercian Abbey of Melrose was dedicated to the Virgin Mary and the latter detail comes from an Abbey seal dated 1422.[13] The mell (a small wooden mallet) and the white rose (symbolic of the Virgin) constitute a rebus on the town's name. Examples of these are carved at various places in Melrose and the monks of the Abbey seem to have used a badge of a mason's mell surmounted by the Cistercian rose. The motto "Truth and Loyalty" was suggested by the parish minister, the Rev. R. J. Thompson; it comes from the words "Trouthe and Laute" which appear in the inscription around the arms of Master Mason John Morow in the south transept of the Abbey. A great deal of thought was given locally to the design of the arms and Sir Robert Lorimer, the celebrated architect, was consulted about them.[14]

The County Council of THE COUNTY OF ROXBURGH bears arms which were granted to the County in 1798. Very little appears to have been recorded about them, though they seem to have had associations with local Defence Forces, as an

ROXBURGH COUNTY COUNCIL

Azure, a unicorn saliant Argent, horned, maned, and unguled Or, the tail tufted of the Last; on a chief of the Second a hunting horn Sable, stringed and viroled Gules, between two esquires' helmets of the field.

With *Crest* a dexter arm from the shoulder vambraced and brandishing a scimitar aloft Proper, the last hilted and pommelled Or, with *Motto* in an Escrol below the Shield "Ne Cede Malis Sed Contra Audentior Ito", which arms are ensigned with a coronet suitable to a County, videlicet: Issuant from a circlet Vert, eight paling piles also Vert alternately with as many garbs Or, banded Sable.

(Lyon Register, i, 485: 9 July 1798)
(Coronet added in Extract of Matriculation dated 8 May 1962)

example of them appears on a fragment of an 1804 Colour of the Kelso Volunteers which is preserved in Kelso Old Parish Church. Any attempt at explanation must, however, be largely conjectural.

The unicorn appears in the arms of Kerr, Duke of Roxburghe, and Kerr, Marquess of Lothian, and seems to have been a symbol long associated with the County. About 1650, it was adopted by the Royal Burgh of Jedburgh as the device on its seal, but in 1680 Lord Lyon Erskine would not allow the Burgh to have arms containing it, as it seems that he regarded the use of a Royal supporter, without special authority from the Crown, to be improper. It is possible, however, that the unicorn may have appeared in some badge or seal connected with the Sheriffdom and may have been granted to the County to mark a special Royal connection. The helmets and the hunting-horn almost certainly represent the famous Border riders, one of whom appears in the arms of Jedburgh, and their rallying-cry "A-Henwoody, A-Henwoody" which, "when once raised, made every heart burn with ardour, and every hand grasp a weapon, and every foot hasten to the Henwood",[15] an old forest which probably extended from Oxnam to the river Jed. The crest is very like that of the old Earls of Marchmont, now represented by Lord Polwarth, who had a naked arm brandishing a scimitar, and to that of Eliott of Stobs who use a mailed arm brandishing a cutlass. Both these families are closely associated with the history of Roxburghshire. The Latin motto—"Yield not to evil things but rather go on more boldly"—is a quotation from Virgil, *Aeneid*, vi, 95; its sentiments are similar to those expressed in the mottoes of other well-known Border families, but its choice may well have been inspired by the words "Nec Aspera Terrent" (the motto of the Hanoverian Order of Guelph), which have a long connection with the famous Scottish regiment, the King's Own Scottish Borderers (formed in 1782).

In 1890, the Lyon Office offered to add a helmet and mantling, but this was not taken up by the County Council. When an Extract of Matriculation was issued on 8 May 1962, only a County Council coronet was added.

It may also be noted that in the official drawing in 1798 the hunting horn was shown with the horn to the dexter and the mouthpiece to the sinister, but in later drawings issued by the Lyon Office it has been shown the other way round, in accordance with Scottish practice.

The original Grant was found among the family papers of the Rutherfurds of Edgerston and was presented to the Burgh of Jedburgh in 1932 by Captain Alexander Oliver Rutherfurd, whose great-great-grandfather, William Oliver, had been Sheriff of Roxburgh in 1798. After a long dispute between the Town Council and the County Council, it was agreed that the document belonged to the County Council but could remain in Jedburgh in the Sheriff Court Room there. It has recently been transferred to Queen Mary's House in Jedburgh.

35

COUNTY OF BERWICK

The County of BERWICK has four Burghs, the Royal Burgh of Lauder, and the Police Burghs of Coldstream, Duns (the County town) and Eyemouth.

ROYAL BURGH OF LAUDER

Or, the Blessed Virgin standing and holding the Holy Child all Proper.

Above the Shield is placed a mural crown suitable to a Royal Burgh and in an Escrol below the Shield is this *Motto* "Avito Jure".

(Lyon Register, xxxiii, 10: 21 March 1938)

LAUDER is an ancient Burgh which may have been a Royal Burgh in the reign of King Robert I (1306–1329) or else a Burgh of Barony granted by the same King to his famous commander, Sir James Douglas. But it fell to the Crown on the forfeiture of the Douglases in 1455 and its privileges as a Royal Burgh were confirmed by King James IV in 1502.[1]

The arms are based on the Burgh seal, which bore a representation of the Virgin and Child; there is a 1725 impression on record but the seal is obviously much older.[2] The gold field is the obvious choice if the Virgin and Child are to have their proper colours. The connection of the Virgin Mary with Lauder is not clear, as she does not seem to have been the patron saint of the town. It may, however, come from

Dryburgh Abbey whose monks had the advowson of Lauder parish church until the Reformation and the Virgin and Child appear on several Abbey seals. Alternatively, the connection may have something to do with the Hospital of Lauder (founded c. 1170), which appears to have been dedicated to the Virgin and to St. Leonard.[3] The Latin motto—"By ancestral right"—was adopted in 1938 and denotes that the arms have been used by Lauder for many centuries. The cost of the Grant of arms was met by donations from Lauder "exiles" resident in Edinburgh.[4]

BURGH OF COLDSTREAM

Per pale Azure and Vert: a salmon hauriant Proper, issuing from its mouth a cross flory fitchée Or, between two mullets in chief Argent, the sun in his splendour of the Third and a rose Gules, barbed and seeded also of the Third, in the flanks, and in base two crescents of the Fourth.

Above the Shield is placed a coronet appropriate to a Burgh and in an Escrol below the Shield this *Motto* "Nulli Secundus".

(Lyon Register, xxxix, 12: 30 May 1952)

COLDSTREAM was created a Burgh of Barony in 1621 in favour of Sir John Hamilton of Trabroun, 3rd son of Sir Thomas Hamilton, Earl of Melrose, later Earl of Haddington.[5] It became a Police Burgh in 1833.

The arms are based on the device on the Burgh seal in use in 1892 which had been adapted from the seal of the Cistercian Abbey of Coldstream, founded by Cospatrick, Earl of Dunbar, in 1143. The shield is parted blue, probably for the Abbey, which was dedicated to the Virgin Mary, and green for the Earls of Home, Superiors of the Burgh. The stars and the crescent come from the Abbey seal as does the salmon with the cross in its mouth. The rose (an example of colour on colour) recalls the connection of the Dunbar family with the Burgh: the wheel-like device at this point on the monastic seal was thought by Lord Lyon Innes to be possibly a primitive version of the Dunbar rose. The salmon also recalls the river Tweed, which passes through Coldstream, and its fine fish; the cross in its mouth is of the same pattern as that on the Crown of Scotland. The Latin motto—"Second to None"—is that of the Coldstream Guards, which were originally embodied in the town; the Town Council, with the full agreement of the regiment, specially asked for it to be granted with the arms.

BURGH OF DUNS

Parted per pale Argent and Vert: a castle triple-towered per pale Gules and of the First, windows port and turret caps Sable, a bordure parted per pale of the Third and First, charged with four roses, barbed and seeded of the Second, alternately with as many escutcheons, all counterchanged; on a canton Or, a cushion of the Third.

Below the Shield, which is ensigned with a Burghal coronet, on a Compartment along with this *Motto* "Duns Dings A'", are set for *Supporters* dexter, a lion guardant barry Argent and Vert, sinister, a goat barry Ermine and Gules, attired and unguled Or.

(Lyon Register, xxxix, 23: 21 July 1952)

DUNS was created a Burgh of Barony in favour of George Home of Ayton in 1489–90[6] and became a Police Burgh in 1842. In 1314, King Robert I had given the lands of Duns to his nephew, Thomas Randolph, Earl of Moray, from whom they passed to his daughter, Agnes, Countess of March and Dunbar. Since 1698, Duns Castle has been in the possession of the family of Hay of Drumelzier.

The arms recall in a pleasing and colourful way the various eminent families associated with the Burgh as well as bearing some resemblance to the device on the Burgh seal in use up to 1929. The field is divided into silver and green halves, these being the Home livery colours, and the castle, which represents Duns Castle, is parted red and silver, the livery colours of both Hay and Dunbar. The bordure is similarly parted and bears the Dunbar roses and the Hay escutcheons, while the red cushion in the gold canton recalls Randolph, Earl of Moray. The supporters, which were granted because Duns is a County town, are the lion of Home and a goat from the crest of Hay of Drumelzier; the lion wears the Home silver and green and the goat the ermine and red of Gifford of Yester to indicate that the Hays of Drumelzier are descended from that ancient family through John, 1st Earl of Tweeddale (d. 1653). The motto "Duns Dings A'" is a local saying which originated from an incident in 1377 when a group of Duns townsmen frightened off a band of Englishmen by making loud noises on home-made drums.

EYEMOUTH was created a Burgh of Barony in favour of Sir George Home of Wedderburn in 1597–98.[7] It became a Police Burgh in 1866.

The arms show a silver lion on a green field for Home of Wedderburn, and a silver lion on a black field for John Churchill, 1st Duke of Marlborough, who was

BURGH OF EYEMOUTH

Tierced in pairle reversed: 1st, Vert, a lion rampant Argent, armed and langued Gules; 2nd, Sable, a lion rampant Argent, armed and langued Gules; 3rd, Argent, a fish hauriant Vert between two roses Gules, barbed and seeded Vert.

Below the Shield, which is ensigned of a coronet befitting a Burgh of Barony (videlicet: Gules masoned Argent) is placed in an Escrol this *Motto* "Remis Velisque".

(Lyon Register, xlv, 157: 4 April 1966)

created Lord Churchill of Eyemouth in 1682. The red roses on the silver field recall Wedderburn of that Ilk, the heiress of which house married Sir David Home of Thurston, later Wedderburn. The fish, coloured green by choice of the Town Council, represents Eyemouth's staple industry and also recalls its long history as a port, since it is known to have had a harbourmaster as early as 1214. The Latin motto— "By oars and by sails"—is the same as that used by Eyemouth Secondary School.

BERWICK COUNTY COUNCIL

Argent, on a mount Vert, a bear Sable, collared and chained Or, standing in front of a tree Proper.

(Lyon Register, xii, 39: 10 October 1890)

The County Council of THE COUNTY OF BERWICK bears arms which show a bear chained to a wych-elm, this being a punning reference to the name Berwick (Bear wyck). Legends tell that in olden times Berwickshire was covered by forest and that many bears inhabited it. The coat of arms symbolises how the bears were brought under subjection after the building of the Castle of Berwick. It closely resembles the ancient arms of Berwick-upon-Tweed (q.v.) and has obviously had a long association with the County.

36

POSTSCRIPT

It would not be typically Scottish unless there was a postscript; we start it with the unusually interesting case of the Borough of Berwick-upon-Tweed.

BOROUGH OF BERWICK-UPON-TWEED

Per pale Azure and Gules, upon a mount in base Vert, a wych-elm Proper and in front of the same a bear passant Proper, muzzled and chained to the base of the tree with a chain Or.

Below the Shield, which is ensigned of the coronet proper to a Royal Burgh, upon a Compartment suitable to a Burgh Royal, along with this *Motto* "Victoria Gloria Merces", are set for *Supporters* two bears Proper, muzzled and chained with chains reflexed over their backs Or.

(Lyon Register, xli, 103: 14 November 1958)

BERWICK-UPON-TWEED, though now in England, was once a Royal Burgh of Scotland dating probably from about 1124 in the reign of King David I.[1] It was one of the original members of the Curia Quattuor Burgorum (Berwick, Edinburgh, Stirling and Roxburgh) and was at one time the principal Burgh of the Kingdom of Scotland. It finally passed from Scottish hands in 1482.

The arms of the Borough were granted by Lord Lyon Innes in 1958 under the "ancient user" privilege allowed under the Act of 1672. There is evidence from old seals that Berwick-upon-Tweed used a form of arms while a Scottish Royal Burgh; this evidence was accepted by Lord Lyon Innes, and since, under Scots law, arms are incorporeal heritable property, he held that the Borough of Berwick-upon-Tweed was entitled "to decree for matriculation and, consequently by that, to investiture in the said armorial property". Similarly, as a former Royal Burgh of Scotland, he had no hesitation in granting supporters and the Royal Burgh compartment. The action of the Lord Lyon caused a good deal of publicity and much controversy with the College of Arms in London, but there is little doubt that he was on sound ground under Scots law.

The arms are based on those which the town had used for many years. The bear and the wych-elm are a punning reference to the name Berwick, and they appear on municipal seals of which thirteenth- and fourteenth-century impressions are on record.[2] The field is parted blue (for France) and red (for England) to recall the two shields, showing the arms of England as used between 1405 and 1603 (France quartered England), which appear on either side of the bear and the tree on the present Burgh seal. The Latin motto—"Victory, Glory, Reward"—is the traditional one associated with the town and recalls that of North Berwick.

We now turn to the three armigerous Burghs which have become part of adjacent Cities, the Parliamentary Burghs of Leith (merged with Edinburgh, 1920) and Portobello (merged with Edinburgh, 1896), and the Police Burgh of Govan (merged with Glasgow, 1912).

BURGH OF LEITH

Argent, in the sea Proper, an ancient galley with two masts sails furled Sable, flagged Gules, seated therein the Virgin Mary with the infant Saviour in her arms and a cloud resting over their heads all also Proper.

In an Escrol below the Shield is placed this *Motto* "Persevere".

(Lyon Register, xii, 12: 27 February 1889)

LEITH, the port of Edinburgh, had an early burghal history, which is a little confused. In 1636, however, it was created a Burgh of Barony *de novo* in favour of the City of Edinburgh,[3] and it became a Parliamentary Burgh under the 1832 Reform Act.

The arms, which are certainly very old, show the Virgin and Child seated in a ship with a cloud above. The parish church of South Leith is dedicated to St. Mary, and the ship is for the port and its sea-going trade. The significance of the cloud is not clear: it appears that, during the discussions about the Grant of arms, the Town Clerk's suggestion that what appeared above the Virgin's head (and the ship) in an impression of an old Burgh seal[4] was a protecting cloud, was accepted by Lord Lyon Burnett. Lord Bute, however, takes issue with this decision and says that, as shown on a later seal, the Virgin should be seated within a Gothic shrine.[5] The motto was apparently introduced in 1833. The arms were registered so that they could be displayed in the British Section of the 1889 Paris Exhibition: at the time, Leith was the sixth largest town in Scotland.[6]

BURGH OF PORTOBELLO

Quarterly: 1st and 4th, Azure, a three-masted vessel under sail Or; 2nd and 3rd, Argent, a cannon mounted on a carriage Sable.

Above the Shield is placed a suitable Helmet with a Mantling Gules doubled Argent, and on a Wreath of the proper Liveries is set for *Crest* a tower Argent masoned Sable, and in an Escrol over the same this *Motto* "Ope Et Consilio".

(Lyon Register, xi, 80: 18 March 1886)

PORTOBELLO was created a Parliamentary Burgh under the 1832 Reform Act. According to tradition, the town was started about 1750 by a Scottish sailor who had served under Admiral Vernon in the capture of the Central American fortress of Puerto Bello from the Spanish in 1739; hence the name Portobello.

The arms, which are said to have been based on the design of a medal brought home by the sailor, are an example of canting heraldry: the ships representing the port (Porto) and the cannons, war (Bello), but as Lord Bute observed, the Spanish "bello" means "beautiful" and not "war". The castle in the crest is thought to stand for one of the castles by which Puerto Bello was defended, and the Latin motto—"With help and counsel"—to the skilful manner in which Admiral Vernon and his colleagues captured it. The arms were registered in connection with the Edinburgh International Exhibition of 1886.[7]

GOVAN, which became a Police Burgh in 1864, has a long ecclesiastical history going back to 565 when Constantine, King of Cornwall, is reported to have founded a monastery there. Up to 1856, it remained "a quiet village with old-fashioned thatched houses", but thereafter the arrival of shipbuilding and related engineering

BURGH OF GOVAN

Argent, [on land in base] the hull of a ship on the stocks Proper; on a chief Azure, two mullets pierced of the field.

Above the Shield is placed a suitable Helmet with a Mantling Gules doubled Argent, and on a Wreath of the proper Liveries is set for *Crest* a garb surmounted of a salmon on its back Proper, and in an Escrol over the Shield this *Motto* "Nihil Sine Labore", and on a Compartment below the Shield are placed for *Supporters* on the dexter side, an engineer holding in his exterior hand a plan, and on the sinister a ship carpenter resting his exterior hand on a mallet, both habited Proper.

(Lyon Register, xi, 42: 7 June 1884)

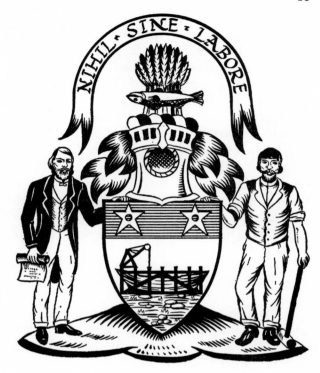

trades transformed it into a busy and important industrial centre whose population had reached about 60,000 by 1889.

The arms, which were matriculated on local initiative, are based on the device on the Burgh seal in use at the time; this was designed by Mr. John Brown, a local lithographer.[8] They make reference to several industries which have been important to the life of the town. Ship-building, from modern times, is represented by the ship on the stocks and by the engineer and ship carpenter who support the shield. Agriculture and salmon fishing, from olden times, are recalled by the garb and salmon in the crest, the salmon also referring to Govan's close links with Glasgow. The chief with its two pierced mullets and the garb in the crest come from the arms of William Rowand of Bellahouston and denote the close connection with Govan of his descendants, the Rowans of Homefauldhead. The Latin motto—"Nothing without hard work"—is very fitting to the rest of the blazon. The supporters were granted after some discussion, because of the Burgh's size, importance and historical antiquity.

*   *   *

Next, a brief note about the other Burghs which have disappeared since Porteous' book on *The Town Council Seals of Scotland* was published in 1906. He lists two hundred and three Burghs, omitting three (Armadale, Eyemouth and Penicuik) which were in being in 1905, apparently because they did not, to his knowledge, possess seals. Of these two hundred and six Burghs, unions have taken six, Wishaw (united with Motherwell in 1920), and the five affected by the Local Government (Scotland) Act, 1929, Anstruther Easter and Anstruther Wester (united with Kilrenny), Earlsferry (united with Elie), Lasswade (united with Bonnyrigg) and Rattray (united with Blairgowrie); mergers with large adjacent Cities or Burghs have taken eight, Leith being taken over by Edinburgh in 1920, Broughty Ferry by Dundee in 1913, Kinning Park (1905) and Govan, Partick and Pollokshaws (1912) by Glasgow in the years shown, Dysart by Kirkcaldy in 1930 and Maxwelltown by Dumfries in 1931. This reduction of fourteen in the number of Burghs has been largely made good as the creation of nine new ones, Findochty, Portknockie, St. Monance, Pitlochry, Stevenston, Bearsden, East Kilbride, Bishopbriggs and Cumbernauld, has brought the total back to the present figure of two hundred and one.

Except for Leith and Govan, none of the Burghs which have disappeared had recorded arms; details of their seals are given in the works of both Porteous and Lord Bute.

*   *   *

Finally, a forward look to the Reform of Local Government in Scotland, which will come into effect in 1975 and for which these are the present proposals.

The country will be divided into nine Regions, viz.: Highlands, Grampian, Tayside, Fife, Lothian, Borders, Central, Strathclyde, and Dumfries & Galloway, and three Island Authorities, viz.: Shetland, Orkney and Western Isles. Under the nine Regions there will be forty-nine Districts, four of which will be centred on the four large Cities and many of the others based on the present Counties, but in most cases with some boundary changes. The Burghs will cease to perform any Local Government function, and Town Councils, County Councils and existing District Councils will be abolished.

This comprehensive reorganisation might well result in much of the heraldry described above being allowed to pass into history. It is hoped that this will not be so. The Burghs should be enabled and encouraged to retain and use their present armorial bearings. The coats of arms of the four large Cities and of many of the County Councils could, if desired, very appropriately pass, by re-matriculation, to the relevant new District Authorities, as could those of Zetland and Orkney to the two new Island Authorities. For the other Districts and Island Authority, and for the Regions, I am sure that the Court of the Lord Lyon can be relied upon to devise ensigns armorial which are appropriate and imaginative and in the best traditions of Scottish Heraldry.

CHRONOLOGICAL TABLE OF MATRICULATIONS OF ARMS OF BURGHS AND COUNTIES

Year	Burgh
c. 1673	Perth; Kirkcaldy; Dumbarton; Tain; Queensferry; Stranraer
1673	Linlithgow; Dundee; Pittenweem; Ayr; Banff
1674	Aberdeen
1676	Renfrew
1678	Elgin
1680	Jedburgh
1694	Montrose
1732	Edinburgh
1771	Musselburgh
1849	Stirling
1866	Glasgow
1882	Lerwick
1884	Govan
1886	Portobello; Hamilton; Kirkwall
1889	Leith; Rutherglen
1894	Peebles
1897	Dingwall
1900	Arbroath; Inverness
1901	Oban
1902	Alloa
1906	Falkirk
1909	Dunfermline
1912	Paisley; St. Andrews
1918	Armadale; Annan
1921	Kirkcudbright; Prestwick
1923	Greenock
1925	Rothesay
1927	Inveraray; Irvine; Haddington

Year	*Burgh*
1929	Lanark; Inverbervie; Hawick; Dornoch; Kinghorn; Campbeltown; Castle Douglas; Cupar; Kilmarnock; Brechin; Stonehaven; Rosehearty; Sanquhar; Port Glasgow; Peterhead; Helensburgh
1930	Bo'ness; Innerleithen; Dalbeattie; Clydebank; Dalkeith; Fraserburgh; Kirriemuir; Portsoy; Galashiels; Lockerbie; Airdrie; Selkirk; Fort William; Grantown-on-Spey; Moffat; Girvan; Leslie; Kilrenny, Anstruther Easter & Anstruther Wester; Elie & Earlsferry; Grangemouth; Langholm; Motherwell & Wishaw; Biggar; Inverurie; Coatbridge; Inverkeithing
1931	Maybole; Rothes; Forres; Largs; Macduff; Dumfries; Melrose; Dunoon
1932	Dundee (re-matriculation); Saltcoats
1934	Kinross
1935	Ellon
1936	Huntly; Kelso
1938	Lauder; Penicuik; Burntisland; New Galloway; Falkland; Bathgate; Culross; Kirkintilloch; Crail; Whitburn; Milngavie
1939	Cromarty; Lochmaben; Banchory; Nairn
1942	Dunbar
1943	Cockenzie & Port Seton; Keith
1947	Ardrossan; Whithorn; North Berwick
1948	Tobermory; Forfar; Lochgelly; Barrhead; Alyth
1949	Lochgilphead
1950	Auchterarder
1951	Newmilns & Greenholm; Blairgowrie & Rattray; Gatehouse-of-Fleet; Buckie; Coupar Angus
1952	Loanhead; Coldstream; Bonnyrigg & Lasswade; Duns; Cowdenbeath; Thurso; Stevenston
1953	Carnoustie; Montrose (re-matriculation); Newburgh; Pitlochry; Dunblane; Tayport
1954	Fortrose; Wick; Old Meldrum; Gourock
1955	Stewarton; Johnstone; Prestwick (re-matriculation); Leven
1956	Denny & Dunipace; Cullen; Newport-on-Tay; Darvel; Monifieth
1957	Burghead; Hawick (re-matriculation); Cove & Kilcreggan
1958	Stornoway; Berwick-upon-Tweed
1959	Kintore; Bearsden; Cumnock & Holmhead
1960	Troon
1961	Crieff
1962	Ballater; Stirling (re-matriculation); Alyth (re-matriculation); St. Monance
1963	East Kilbride
1964	Galston; Invergordon; Portknockie; Bishopbriggs.
1965	Callander
1966	Eyemouth; Dufftown; Auchtermuchty
1969	Cumbernauld
1972	Markinch; Kilsyth

Year	County
1798	Roxburgh
1800	Perth
1886	Lanark
1889	Renfrew
1890	Ayr; Aberdeen; Stirling; Berwick
1927	Clackmannan; Angus (as Forfar); Kinross; Fife; East Lothian; Kincardine; Inverness; Selkirk; Bute; Moray; Dunbarton; Nairn
1928	Dumfries
1931	Peebles; Orkney; Ayr (re-matriculation)
1935	Caithness
1951	Kirkcudbright; Midlothian
1952	West Lothian
1953	Banff; Argyll
1955	Wigtown
1956	Zetland
1957	Ross & Cromarty; Sutherland
1971	Banff (re-matriculation)

Note: Roxburgh and Perth were granted to the County; Lanark and Renfrew to the Commissioners of Supply; all others were granted to the County Councils.

BIBLIOGRAPHY

In the Notes set out below the following bibliographical abbreviations have been used:

Barron, *Regalia*   *In Defence of the Regalia.* Edited by the Rev. Douglas G. Barron. London, 1910.

Bain   *Calendar of Documents relating to Scotland, 1108–1509.* Edited by Joseph Bain. 4 vols. Edinburgh, 1881–88.

Bentinck, *Dornoch*   Bentinck, Rev. Charles D., *Dornoch Cathedral and Parish.* Inverness, 1926.

Birch   Birch, Walter de Gray, *History of Scottish Seals.* 2 vols. Stirling, 1907.

Buchanan, *Scotland*   Buchanan, George, *History of Scotland.* A translation and new edition. Edinburgh, 1821.

Burke, *General Armory*   Burke, Sir Bernard, *The General Armory of England, Scotland, Ireland and Wales.* London, 1884.

Burgoyne   Burgoyne, Gerald, *The Fife and Forfar Imperial Yeomanry and its Predecessors.* Cupar-Fife, 1904.

Bute, *RPB*   Bute, John, Marquess of, Macphail, J. R. N., Lonsdale, H. W., *The Arms of the Royal and Parliamentary Burghs of Scotland.* Edinburgh, 1897.

Bute, *BPB*   Bute, John, Marquess of, Stevenson, J. H., Lonsdale, H. W., *The Arms of the Baronial and Police Burghs of Scotland.* Edinburgh, 1903.

Craig-Brown, *Selkirkshire*   Brown, Thomas Craig-, *The History of Selkirkshire.* 2 vols. Edinburgh, 1886.

CRB, *Extracts*   *Extracts from the Records of the Convention of Royal Burghs of Scotland, 1615–1676.* Edited by J. D. Marwick. Edinburgh, 1888.

CRB, *Minutes*   *Minutes* of the Convention of Royal Burghs of Scotland.

CRB, *1905 Report*   *Report of the Sub-Committee on "The Matriculation of Burgh Arms",* presented to the Convention of Royal Burghs in 1905 (Convention Minutes 1905, page 16, No. 32, refer).

Cruickshank   Cruickshank, John, *The Armorial Ensigns of the Royal Burgh of Aberdeen.* Aberdeen, 1888.

Dickinson, *Scotland*   Dickinson, William Croft, *Scotland from the Earliest Times to 1603.* A New History of Scotland, Vol. 1. Edinburgh, 1961.

Fittis, *Perthshire*   Fittis, R. S., *Illustrations of the History & Antiquities of Perthshire.* Perth, 1874.

Forbes, *Scottish Saints*   Forbes, Alexander P. (Bishop of Brechin), *Kalendars of Scottish Saints.* Edinburgh, 1872.

Fox-Davies, *Heraldry* Fox-Davies, A. C., *A Complete Guide to Heraldry*. Revised and annotated by J. P. Brooke-Little. London, 1969.

Fox-Davies, *Public Arms* Fox-Davies, A. C., *The Book of Public Arms*. 2nd edition. London 1915.

Hay, *Arbroath* Hay, George, *History of Arbroath to the Present Time*. Arbroath, 1876.

Imperial Gazetteer *Imperial Gazetteer of Scotland*. Edited by the Rev. John M. Wilson. 4 vols. Edinburgh, 1854.

Innes Innes of Learney, Sir Thomas, *Scots Heraldry*. 2nd edition. Edinburgh, 1956.

Jeffrey, *Roxburghshire* Jeffrey, Alexander, *The History and Antiquities of Roxburghshire and Adjacent Districts*. 4 vols. Edinburgh, 1855–64.

Laing, *i* Laing, Henry, *Descriptive Catalogue of Impressions from Ancient Scottish Seals*. Edinburgh, 1850.

Macarthur, *Port Glasgow* Macarthur, W. F., *History of Port Glasgow*. Glasgow, 1932.

MacDonald, *Kingussie* MacDonald, J. A., *The Burgh of Kingussie, 1867–1967*. Kingussie, 1966.

Mackintosh, *Elgin* Mackintosh, H. B., *Elgin Past and Present*. Elgin, 1914.

Macgeorge Macgeorge, Andrew, *An Inquiry as to the Armorial Insignia of the City of Glasgow*. Glasgow, 1866.

Murray, *Early Burgh Organisation* Murray, D., *Early Burgh Organisation in Scotland*. 3 vols. Glasgow, 1924.

New Statistical Account *The New Statistical Account of Scotland*. Collected edition. 15 vols. Edinburgh, 1845.

Nisbet Nisbet, Alexander, *A System of Heraldry*. New Edition. 2 vols. Edinburgh, 1816.

Ordnance Gazetteer *Ordnance Gazetteer of Scotland*. Edited by Francis H. Groome. 6 vols. Edinburgh, 1882–85.

Paisley Handbook *Paisley Official Industrial Handbook*. Cheltenham, 1964.

Paul, *Scots Peerage* Paul, Sir James Balfour (editor), *The Scots Peerage*. 9 vols. Edinburgh, 1904–14.

Porteous Porteous, Alexander, *The Town Council Seals of Scotland*. Edinburgh, 1906.

Pryde Pryde, George Smith, *The Burghs of Scotland*, Oxford, 1965.

Pryde, *Government* Pryde, George S., *Central and Local Government in Scotland since 1707*. London, 1960. Historical Association Pamphlet G.45.

Pryde, *Scotland* Pryde, George S., *Scotland from 1603 to the Present Day*. A New History of Scotland, vol II. Edinburgh, 1962.

PSAS *Proceedings of the Society of Antiquaries of Scotland*. Edinburgh, 1851–52.

RMS *Registrum Magni Sigilli Regum Scotorum, 1308–1668*. Edited by J. Maitland Thomson and others. 11 vols. Edinburgh, 1882–1914.

Ronald, *Seals of Stirling* Ronald, J., *The Seals of the Royal Burgh of Stirling*. A paper read to the Stirling Natural History and Archaeological Society, October, 1895.

Ross, *Hawick Flag*   Ross, Andrew (Ross Herald), *Report on the Flag of the Burgh of Hawick*. Prepared for Hawick Town Council, Edinburgh, 1903.

Seton   Seton, George, *The Law and Practice of Heraldry in Scotland*. Edinburgh, 1863.

SHR   *Scottish Historical Review*. Edinburgh, 1903–28, 1947–.

Small, *Scottish Market Crosses*   Small, J. W., *Scottish Market Crosses*. Stirling, 1901.

SNQ(1)   *Scottish Notes and Queries*. 1st Series. Aberdeen, 1887–99.

Spalding Club Miscellany   *The Miscellany of the Spalding Club*. Edited by J. Stuart. Aberdeen, 1851–52.

Storer Clouston, *Orkney*   Clouston, J. Storer, *A History of Orkney*. Kirkwall, 1932.

SW   Stevenson, J. H., Wood, Marguerite, *Scottish Heraldic Seals*. Glasgow, 1940.

Suter, *Memorabilia*   Suter, J., *Memorabilia of Inverness*. Inverness 1887 (reprinted from *Inverness Courier*, 1822).

TDGS(3)   *Transactions and Journal of Proceedings of the Dumfries-shire and Galloway Natural History & Antiquarian Society*. 3rd Series. Dumfries, 1913–.

Thomson, *Lauder & Lauderdale*   Thomson, Andrew, *Lauder and Lauderdale*. Galashiels, 1913.

Tullibardine   *A Military History of Perthshire, 1660–1902*. Edited by Katharine, Marchioness of Tullibardine (later Duchess of Atholl). Perth, 1908.

Watt, *Banchory*   Watt, V. J. R., *The Book of Banchory*. Edinburgh, 1947.

Wilkie, *Musselburgh*   Wilkie, James, *History of Musselburgh*. Edinburgh, 1919.

Wood, *Lanarkshire Yeomanry*   Wood, Russell E., *Records of the Lanarkshire Yeomanry*, Edinburgh, 1910.

REFERENCE NOTES

I BURGH HERALDRY IN SCOTLAND

1a Dickinson, *Scotland*, 112
1b Pryde, *Scotland*, 196
2 *Spalding Club Miscellany*, v, 151
3 Macgeorge, 6–8
4 Bain, ii, 813–15, 819–20; SW, i, 68–80
5 Bain, iii, 1652
6 SW, i, 56, 66, 79
7 ibid., i, 54, 58
8 ibid., i, 52–80
9 Seton, 16; Macgeorge, 2–3
10 CRB, *Extracts*, 635
11 ibid., 665
12 *Jedburgh Burgh Records*, 30 March 1680
13 CRB, *1905 Report*
14 Sutor *Memorabilia*, 49; *SNQ(1)*, v, 97–9: Anderson, P. J., *The Armorial Ensigns of Inverness*
15 Much of the information in this chapter comes from CRB, *1905 Report*
16 Seton, 72
17 Innes, 78, footnote 3
18 Bute, *RPB*, 7
19 *PSAS*, xxx, 252–6
20 *Heraldic Exhibition (1891) Catalogue*, Edinburgh, 1892
21 *Scotsman*, 5 April 1899
22 See under articles on individual Burghs for references
23 Much of the information in this chapter comes from CRB, *1905 Report*
24 CRB, *Minutes*, 1905, p. 16, No. 32
25 See under articles on individual Burghs for references
26 Banchory, Ballater, and Old Meldrum Town Council *Minutes*, 1929
27 Inverbervie Town Council *Minutes*, 8 May 1929
28 See articles under individual Burghs for references
29 CRB, *Minutes*, 1930, p. 29
30 *Border Telegraph*, 11 February 1930
31 Lyon Office File, 33/27
32 *Scotsman*, 6 April and 24 May 1938
33 See articles under individual Burghs for references
34 *Banffshire Journal*, 6 June 1964
35 Fox-Davies, *Heraldry*, 282, 276
36 Fox-Davies, *Public Arms*, xiii

II COUNTY HERALDRY IN SCOTLAND

1 *Ordnance Gazetteer*, vi, General Survey, 100
2 Pryde, *Government*, 23
3 Inscription formerly in County Hall, Perth; *Dundee Courier & Advertiser*, 16 April 1927
4 Craig-Brown, *Selkirkshire*, i, 1
5 Burgoyne, 6 et seq.
6 Wood, *Lanarkshire Yeomanry*, 18–19
7 *Scotsman*, 12 May 1927
8 Innes, 82
9 *House of Lords Debates*, 67, col. 1095
10 *Scotsman*, 5 June 1954

III THE ARMS OF THE BURGHS AND COUNTY COUNCILS

In addition to the references listed below, much useful information has been obtained in the majority of instances from the Lyon Office Case Files and in many instances from the Town/County Council Minutes of the time. There are, however, one or two cases of special interest where direct references to these sources are cited.

2 THE COUNTIES OF CITIES

Edinburgh
1 Pryde, 4
2 SW, i, 61
3 CRB, *1905 Report*, 5–9

Dundee
4 Pryde, 29, 94
5 SW, i, 59
6 Bute, *RPB*, 108
7 *Dundee Courier & Advertiser*, 30 March 1932

Aberdeen
8 Pryde, 7
9 ibid., 162
10 SW, i, 52
11 *Spalding Club Miscellany*, v, 151
12 Cruickshank, 29, 41
13 Seton, 511

Glasgow
14 Pryde, 70, 90, 243; *RMS*, v. 1406
15 SW, i, 64
16 Nisbet, i, 358

3 ZETLAND

Lerwick
1 Pryde, 478
2 *Shetland Times*, 1 April 1882

County Council
3 *Shetland News*, 24 May 1890

4 ORKNEY

Kirkwall
1 Pryde, 52
2a SW, i, 70

Stromness
2b Pryde, 476

County Council
3 Storer Clouston, *Orkney*, 375
4 *Orkney Herald*, 13 May 1931
5 ibid., 28 May 1890

5 CAITHNESS

Wick
1 Pryde, 63, 129
2 *John o' Groat Journal*, 4 June 1954

Thurso
  3 Pryde, 326; *RMS*, viii, 2207
  4 SW, i, 81
  5 *Caithness Courier*, 10 December 1952

6 SUTHERLAND

Dornoch
  1 Pryde, 73
  2 SW, i, 58
  3 Bentinck, *Dornoch*, 72

County Council
  4 *Northern Times*, 5 July 1957

7 ROSS & CROMARTY

Tain
  1 Pryde, 48
  2 Bute, *RPB*, 377
  3 SW, i, 81

Dingwall
  4 Pryde, 34, 117
  5 SW, i, 57
  6 *Ross-shire Journal*, 18 June 1897

Fortrose
  7 Pryde, 98
  8 ibid., 64, 142, 232
  9 Laing, *i*, 930

Cromarty
  10 Pryde, 36, 111, 423
  11 *Northern Chronicle*, 28 September 1938

Stornoway
  12 Pryde, 280
  13 *Stornoway Gazette*, 4 October 1957

8 INVERNESS

Inverness
  1 Pryde, 20
  2 SW, i, 66
  3 *SNQ(1)*, v, 97–9: Anderson, P. J., *The Armorial Ensigns of Inverness*
  4 Suter, *Memorabilia*, 49
  5 *Inverness Courier*, 11 January 1898 and 9 March 1900

Fort William
  6 Pryde, 303
  7 Bute, *BPB*, 218

  8 *Oban Times*, 15 February 1930
  9 One of these badges is preserved in the Scottish United Services Museum in Edinburgh Castle
  10 *People's Journal (Inverness & N. Counties Edition)*, 13 April 1929

Kingussie
  11 Pryde, 148
  12 MacDonald, *Kingussie*, 21

County Council
  13 *Highland News*, 24 May 1890

9 NAIRN

Nairn
  1 Pryde, 25, 109
  2 SW, i, 74
  3 *Nairnshire Telegraph*, 17 October 1939

10 MORAY

Elgin
  1 Pryde, 13, 108
  2 SW, i, 63
  3 Mackintosh, *Elgin*, 239; a copy of the Discharge is printed on pp. 9–11 of *Documents relating to the Province of Moray*, edited by E. Dunbar Dunbar, Edinburgh, 1895

Forres
  4 Pryde, 8, 107
  5 SW, i, 64
  6 Bute, *RPB*, 146–7

Grantown-on-Spey
  7 Pryde, 284, 432
  8 Bute, *BPB*, 246

Lossiemouth & Branderburgh
  9 Porteous, 207

Rothes
  10 *Elgin Courant*, 16 January 1931

County Council
  11 *Elgin Courant*, 6 May 1927

11 BANFF

Banff
  1 Pryde, 27
  2 SW, i, 54

3 Bute, *RPB*, 32
4 *Banffshire Journal*, 23 June 1897

Cullen
5 Pryde, 28
6 SW, i, 56
7 *Banffshire Journal*, 18 September 1956

Aberlour
8 Pryde, 475

Buckie
9 Information given in letter from Town Clerk
10 *Banffshire Journal*, 17 April 1951

Keith
11 *Banffshire Herald*, 16 October 1943

Macduff
12 Pryde, 211, 468
13 Laing, *i*, 334
14 Nisbet, *i*, 276
15 *Banffshire Journal*, 7 January 1930

Portsoy
16 Pryde, 229

County Council
17 Information given in letter from County Clerk

12   ABERDEEN

Kintore
1 Pryde, 26

Inverurie
2 Pryde, 30, 93
3 SW, i, 67

Peterhead
4 Pryde, 240

Ballater
5 Forbes, *Scottish Saints*, 417–18

Ellon
6 Pryde, 457

Fraserburgh
7 Pryde, 227, *RMS* vi, 1167
8 Burke, *General Armory*, 376
9 SW, i, 64

Huntly
10 Pryde, 155
11 *Huntly Express*, 1 May 1936

Old Meldrum
12 Pryde, 385
13 Information given in letter from Town Clerk

Rosehearty
14 Pryde, 414

Turriff
15 Pryde, 203

13   KINCARDINE

Inverbervie
1 Pryde, 44
2 *Town Council Minutes*, 8 May 1929

Banchory
3 Bute, *BPB*, 49
4 Watt, *Banchory*, 4
5 *Town Council Minutes*, 11 April 1938

Laurencekirk
6 Pryde, 467

Stonehaven
7 Pryde, 241

County Council
8 Barron, *Regalia*, 21; the traditional version which accords a leading part to Mrs. Grainger does not seem to be well founded

14   ANGUS

Montrose
1 Pryde, 15
2 *Montrose Review*, 13 November 1952
3 SW, i, 73
4 Porteous, 220
5 SW, i, 73
6 Bute, *RPB*, 271

Brechin
7 Pryde, 77, 87
8 SW, i, 55

Arbroath
9 Pryde, 69, 91
10 Hay, *Arbroath*, 37
11 SW, i, 53
12 *Arbroath Herald*, 4 January 1900

Forfar
13 Pryde, 23

Carnoustie
14 *Broughty Ferry Guide & Carnoustie Gazette*,
7 June and 12 July 1952
15 ibid., 6 September 1952

Kirriemuir
16 Pryde, 145

County Council
17 Paul, *Scots Peerage*, i, 161, 167
18 *Brechin Advertiser*, 3 May 1927

15 PERTH

Perth
1 Pryde, 5
2 SW, i, 76; the date of 1378 is subject to
qualification
3 Fittis, *Perthshire*, 280–1

Auchterarder
4 Pryde, 35
5 SW, i, 53

Abernethy
6 Pryde, 146

Alyth
7 *Abbreviationis Inquisitionum Specialium*, ii,
(Perth), 313. Edinburgh, 1809
8 *Gazette & Guardian for East Perthshire*, 10
November 1961

Blairgowrie & Rattray
9 Pryde, 331

Coupar Angus
10 Pryde, 281
11 Laing, i, 999

Crieff
12 Pryde, 393

Doune
13 Pryde, 287

Dunblane
14 Pryde, 96
15 *RMS*, ii, 270
16 SW, i, 59

Pitlochry
17 Information given in letter from Town
Clerk

County Council
18 *Dundee Courier & Advertiser*, 16 April 1927

19 Tullibardine, 200, 223, plate facing p. 136
20 ibid., 131 (footnote 4), 205 (footnote 1)
21 ibid., Plate facing p. 109
22 ibid., 129, 181, 187
23 Nisbet, i, 61; Fox-Davies, *Heraldry*, 339

16 ARGYLL

Inveraray
1 Pryde, 79, 151
2 SW, i, 66
3 Porteous, 152
4 *Argyllshire Advertiser*, 23 March 1927

Campbeltown
5 Pryde, 80, 375

Oban
6 Pryde, 479; *Registrum Magni Sigilli Regum
Scotorum*, Lib. 161, No. 40

Dunoon
7 Bute, *BPB*, 189
8 Pryde, 165

Lochgilphead
9 *Argyllshire Advertiser*, 6 April 1949

Tobermory
10 *People's Journal (Inverness & N. Counties
Edition)*, 13 April 1929

17 BUTE

Rothesay
1 Pryde, 46
2 *Buteman & West Coast Chronicle*, 18 July
1924
3 SW, i, 78
4 Bute, *RPB*, 345
5 ibid., 346

18 DUNBARTON

Dumbarton
1 Pryde, 33
2 SW, i, 58

Helensburgh
3 Pryde, 472

Kirkintilloch
4 Pryde, 97, 207
5 Porteous, 180

Milngavie
  6 Bute, *BPB*, 390
  7 *Milngavie Herald*, 15 October 1938

Bearsden
  8 *Glasgow Herald*, 5 March 1959
  9 Information given in letter from Town Clerk

Cumbernauld
  10 *Ordnance Gazetteer*, ii, 325

County Council
  11 *Lennox Herald*, 5 April 1890

19   STIRLING
Stirling
  1 Pryde, 6
  2
  3 } SW, i, 80–1
  4 Bute, *RPB*, 367–8
  5 Ronald, *Seals of Stirling*

Falkirk
  6 Pryde, 266
  7 Small, *Scottish Market Crosses*, Plate 67

Denny & Dunipace
  8 Buchanan, *Scotland*, i, 23–4
  9 Bute, *BPB*, 164

Kilsyth
  10 Pryde, 308
  11 Bute, *BPB*, 293

20   CLACKMANNAN
Alloa
  1 Pryde, 173
  2 *Alloa Journal*, 17 May 1902

Dollar
  3 Pryde, 446

Tillicoultry
  4 Pryde, 330

County Council
  5 *Alloa Journal*, 2 April 1927

21   KINROSS
Kinross
  1 Pryde, 218

County Council
  2 Information given in letter from County Clerk

22   FIFE
St. Andrews
  1 Pryde, 72, 83, 294
  2 Bain, iii, 1652
  3 *Town Council Minutes*, 1 April 1912

Kirkcaldy
  4 Pryde, 78, 113
  5 Porteous, 177
  6 *Fife Advertiser*, 7 May 1927
  7 Bute, *RPB*, 222

Cupar
  8 Pryde, 40
  9 SW, i, 57
  10 *Fife News*, 20 July 1929

Kilrenny & Anstruther
  11 Pryde, 66, 237; *RMS*, iv, 2831
  12 Pryde, 60, 235; *RMS*, iv, 2032
  13 Pryde, 61, 219
  14 SW, i, 53, 68

Burntisland
  15 Pryde, 57
  16 *Fife Free Press*, 23 April 1938

Inverkeithing
  17 Pryde, 19, 92
  18 Bain, ii, 819; SW, i, 66
  19 *Dunfermline Journal*, 3 May 1930

Kinghorn
  20 Pryde, 21
  21 SW, i, 69
  22 Bute, *RPB*, 217

Pittenweem
  23 Pryde, 56, 206
  24 SW, i, 76

Dunfermline
  25 Pryde, 3, 106, 157
  26 SW, i, 60
  27 Porteous, 102
  28 *Dunfermline Press*, 9 November 1907

Crail
  29 Pryde, 16, 88

30 Bute, *RPB*, 57
31 SW, i, 56
32 *PSAS*, xxxvii, 160: Millar, A. H., *Notes on Ancient Burgh Seal of Crail*
33 *St. Andrews Citizen*, 16 April 1938
34 ibid., 10 June 1937

Culross
35 Pryde, 65, 164

Auchtermuchty
36 Pryde, 54

Elie & Earlsferry
37 Pryde, 262
38 ibid., 62, 136
39 *SHR*, ii, 20: Law, G., *The Earl's Ferry*

Falkland
40 Pryde, 51
41 SW, i, 64

Newburgh
42a Pryde, 75, 104, 158

Buckhaven & Melthil
42b Pryde, 357

Cowdenbeath
43 *Cowdenbeath Advertiser & Kelty News*, 18 July 1952

Leslie
44 Pryde, 144

Leven
45 Pryde, 285
46 Bute, *BPB*, 344

Markinch
47 Pryde, 398
48 *Ordnance Gazetteer*, v, 8

St. Monance
49 Pryde, 255
50 SW, i, 80; Bute *BPB*, 473
51 *Leven Mail*, 27 June 1962

Tayport
52 Pryde, 260

County Council
53 Laing, *i*, 334
54 Burgoyne, 6 et seq.
55 *Fife Herald & Journal*, 11 May 1927

23 EAST LOTHIAN
Haddington
1 Pryde, 9, 85
2 Bain, ii, 815; iii, 1652
3 *Haddingtonshire Courier*, 15 April 1927

Dunbar
4 Pryde, 50, 95
5 SW, i, 59
6 *Haddingtonshire Courier*, 20 March 1942

North Berwick
7 Pryde, 47, 128
8 SW, i, 75
9 *SHR*, ii, 20: Law, G., *The Earl's Ferry*

Cockenzie & Port Seton
10 Pryde, 118, 247

East Linton
11 Porteous, 109

Prestonpans
12 Pryde, 231

Tranent
13 Pryde, 225

24 MIDLOTHIAN
Musselburgh
1 Pryde, 112, 234; *RMS*, viii, 2100
2 Wilkie, *Musselburgh*, 35

Dalkeith
3 Pryde, 133, 216
4 Porteous, 82

Loanhead
5 Pryde, 383

County Council
6 Nisbet, i, 372
7 ibid., i, 163

25 WEST LOTHIAN
Linlithgow
1 Pryde, 14
2 SW, i, 72

Queensferry
3 Pryde, 76, 114, 236; *RMS*, viii, 1097
4
5 } SW, i, 77

Armadale
6 Bute, *BPB*, 30
7 *West Lothian Courier*, 9 November 1917 and 8 March 1918

Bathgate
8 Pryde, 361
9 *West Lothian Courier*, 13 May 1938

Bo'ness
10 Pryde, 380
11 *New Statistical Account*, ii, 129–30

Whitburn
12 *Imperial Gazetteer*, iv, 845; *Ordnance Gazetteer*, vi, 483
13 *West Lothian Courier*, 15 April 1938

26   LANARK

Lanark
1 Pryde, 18
2 *PSAS*, v, 153–9: Reid, Thomas, *The Seven Seals of Lanark*; Bain, iii, 1652
3 Bute, *RPB*, 238

Rutherglen
4 Pryde, 12
5 Bain, iii, 1652; SW, i, 79

Airdrie
6 Pryde, 480

Hamilton
7 Pryde, 58, 152
8 *Hamilton Advertiser*, 9 October 1886

Biggar
9 Pryde, 138

Motherwell & Wishaw
10 *Motherwell Times*, 8 August 1930

Bishopbriggs
11 Information given in letter from Town Clerk

County Council
12 Wood, *Lanarkshire Yeomanry*, 18–19

27   RENFREW

Renfrew
1 Pryde, 11, 86
2 *Renfrew Press*, 16 December 1932
3 Bute, *RPB*, 338–41

4 SW, i, 77
5 Porteous, 257
6 Macarthur, *Port Glasgow*, 4–5

Greenock
7 Pryde, 332

Paisley
8 Pryde, 156
9 *Paisley Handbook*, 19
10 *Glasgow Herald*, 10 April 1912

Port Glasgow
11 Pryde, 381

Barrhead
12 Porteous, 29–30

Gourock
13 Pryde, 433

28   AYR

Ayr
1 Pryde, 31
2 SW, i, 53

Irvine
3 Pryde, 45, 99
4 SW, i, 67

Kilmarnock
5 Pryde, 249
6 Fox-Davies, *Heraldry*, 326–7

Ardrossan
7 Pryde, 482
8 Bute, *BPB*, 27

Cumnock & Holmhead
9 Pryde, 185
10 *Registrum Magni Sigilli Regum Scotorum*, Lib. 69, No. 202
11 *Cumnock Chronicle*, 2 October 1959

Darvel
12 *Irvine Valley News & Galston Supplement*, 8 June 1956

Girvan
13 Pryde, 382

Largs
14 Pryde, 254, 319

Maybole
15 Pryde, 205

Newmilns & Greenholm
16 Pryde, 166

Prestwick
17 Pryde, 89, 267
18 *Troon & Prestwick Times*, 11 February and 4 March 1921
19 SW, i, 77
20 Birch, ii, 90, 225, Plate on p. 107; Murray, *Early Burgh Organisation*, ii, 76

Saltcoats
21 Pryde, 212

Stewarton
22 *Kilmarnock Standard*, 16 October 1954

Troon
23 Information given in letter from Town Clerk

29   WIGTOWN

Wigtown
1 Pryde, 38, 123

Whithorn
2 Pryde, 53, 120, 140
3 SW, i, 81
4 *Galloway Gazette*, 13 September and 25 October 1947

Stranraer
5 Pryde, 71, 253

Newton-Stewart
6 Pryde, 406

30   KIRKCUDBRIGHT

Kirkcudbright
1 Pryde, 43, 127
2 SW, i, 69
3 *Kirkcudbrightshire Advertiser & Galloway News*, 1 October and 31 December 1920

New Galloway
4 Pryde, 74

Castle Douglas
5 Pryde, 469

Dalbeattie
6 *Stewartry Observer*, 28 November, 1929

Gatehouse-of-Fleet
7 Pryde, 471
8 *Galloway News*, 17 December 1949

31   DUMFRIES

Dumfries
1 Pryde, 24
2 SW, i, 58
3 *TDGS(3)*, xi, 163–5; Shirley, G. W., *Notes on Arms of Burgh of Dumfries*

Annan
4 Pryde, 55, 82
5 *Annandale Observer*, 6 December 1918
6 ibid., 6 September 1918

Lochmaben
7 Pryde, 49, 105
8 Information given in letter from Town Clerk
9 *Annandale Herald & Record*, 8 December 1938

Sanquhar
10 Pryde, 68, 122, 154
11 SW, i, 80
12 *TDGS(3)*, iii, 88–90: M'Millan, Rev. W., *Arms of the Ancient and Royal Burgh of Sanquhar*

Langholm
13 Pryde, 310
14 *Eskdale & Liddesdale Observer*, 18 June 1930

Lockerbie
15 *Annandale Herald & Record*, 23 January 1930

Moffat
16 Pryde, 347

32   PEEBLES

Peebles
1 Pryde, 10
2 SW, i, 75
3 *Peebles-shire Advertiser*, 9 June 1894: Buchan, William, *Armorial Bearings of Burgh of Peebles*
4 *Peebles-shire Advertiser*, 2 June, 9 June and 14 July 1894

Innerleithen
5 Bain, ii, 1011

33 SELKIRK

Selkirk
1 Pryde, 41, 272
2 Bute, *RPB*, 360
3 SW, i, 80

Galashiels
4 Pryde, 264
5 Jeffrey, *Roxburghshire*, iii, 123; Craig-Brown, *Selkirkshire*, i, 481

County Council
6 Craig-Brown, *Selkirkshire*, ii, 150, i, 236, 240

34 ROXBURGH

Jedburgh
1 Pryde, 17, 115
2 SW, i, 68
3 *Jedburgh Burgh Records*, 30 March 1680

Hawick
4 Pryde, 193
5 Ross, *Hawick Flag*
6 Bute, *RPB*, 182

Kelso
7 Pryde, 100, 293
8 ibid., 2
9 SW, i, 78
10 Laing, *i*, 1057
11 Information given in letter from Town Clerk

Melrose
12 Pryde, 276
13 Laing, *i*, 1076

14 Information given in letter from Town Clerk

County Council
15 Jeffrey, *Roxburghshire*, *i*, 44

35 BERWICK

Lauder
1 Pryde, 39, 110
2 SW, i, 71
3 Thomson, *Lauder & Lauderdale*, 66
4 *Berwickshire Advertiser*, 26 July 1938

Coldstream
5 *RMS*, viii, 229

Duns
6 Pryde, 163

Eyemouth
7 Pryde, 258

36 POSTSCRIPT

Berwick-upon-Tweed
1 Pryde, 1
2 SW, i, 54, 55

Leith
3 Pryde, 337
4 SW, i, 71, 72
5 Bute, *RPB*, 250–3
6 *Leith Herald*, 9 February 1889

Portobello
7 *Midlothian Journal*, 13 February 1886

Govan
8 Bute, *BPB*, 238

Map of Scotland

Showing The Burghs and The Counties

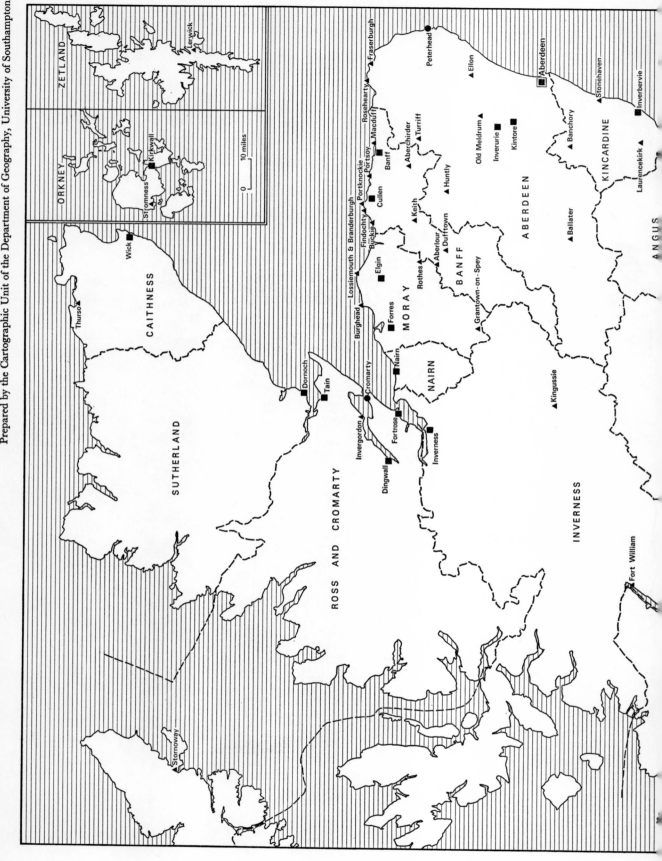

Prepared by the Cartographic Unit of the Department of Geography, University of Southampton

ZETLAND

Lerwick

ORKNEY

Kirkwall

Stromness

10 miles

0

CAITHNESS

Wick

Thurso

SUTHERLAND

Dornoch

Tain

ROSS AND CROMARTY

Invergordon

Cromarty

Dingwall

Fortrose

Inverness

Stornoway

Fort William

INVERNESS

Kingussie

NAIRN

Nairn

MORAY

Forres

Burghead

Elgin

Lossiemouth & Branderburgh

Rothes

Aberlour

Grantown-on-Spey

Findochty

Portknockie

Portsoy

Buckie

Cullen

Keith

Dufftown

BANFF

Rosehearty

Macduff

Banff

Aberchirder

Turriff

Huntly

Fraserburgh

Peterhead

Ellon

Old Meldrum

Inverurie

Kintore

ABERDEEN

Aberdeen

Banchory

Ballater

KINCARDINE

Stonehaven

Inverbervie

Laurencekirk

ANGUS

INDEX

This index contains only direct references to Burgh and County names. The entries relating to the main article about each Burgh and County Council are shown in bold type.